COMMON, DELINQUENT, AND SPECIAL

STUDIES IN THE HISTORY OF EDUCATION
VOLUME 9
GARLAND REFERENCE LIBRARY OF THE HUMANITIES
VOLUME 1446

STUDIES IN THE HISTORY OF EDUCATION

EDWARD R. BEAUCHAMP, *Series Editor*

COMMON, DELINQUENT, AND SPECIAL
THE INSTITUTIONAL SHAPE OF SPECIAL EDUCATION

JOHN G. RICHARDSON

FALMER PRESS
A MEMBER OF THE TAYLOR & FRANCIS GROUP
NEW YORK AND LONDON
1999

For Jane Mercer
Teacher, colleague and friend

Library of Congress Cataloging-in-Publication Data

Richardson, John G.
    Common, delinquent, and special : the institutional shape of special
education / John G. Richardson.
      ISBN 0-8153-3077-4 (alk. paper)
        p. cm. — (Studies in the history of education ; v. 9)
      Includes bibliographical references and index.
      1. Special education—United States—History—19th century.
    2. Special education—United States—History—20th century.
    I. Title. II. Series: Studies in the history of education (Falmer Press) ; v. 9.
    LC3981.R525   1999
    371.0'0973—dc21   99–13736
                                              CIP

Printed on acid-free, 250-year-life paper
Manufactured in the United States of America

Series Preface

Garland's Studies in the History of Education series includes not only volumes on the history of American and Western education, but also on the history of the development of education in non-Western societies. A major goal of this series is to provide new interpretations of educational history that are based on the best recent scholarship; each volume will provide an original analysis and interpretation of the topic under consideration. A wide variety of methodological approaches from the traditional to the innovative are used. In addition, this series especially welcomes studies that focus not only on schools but also on education as defined by Harvard historian Bernard Bailyn: "the transmission of culture across generations."

The major criteria for inclusion are (a) a manscript of the highest quality, and (b) a topic of importance to understanding the field. The editor is open to readers' suggestions and looks forward to a long-term dialogue with them on the future direction of the series.

Edward R. Beauchamp

Contents

Tables

Acknowledgments

This book represents many years of thinking about special education. From a doctoral dissertation on the volatile issue of minority misclassification in California schools, I have wandered away from special education on countless occasions, only to then see that I had never really gone far. I would always be reminded, by the accumulation of research and by collegial discussions, that the study of special education is not a separate specialty, but a path that leads to so many other topics. From accumulated research and collegial discussions, I was able to see how special education was so intricately linked to delinquency and to the history and treatment of disabilities.

My research on these linkages has been assisted by grants from the Spencer Foundation and from the National Science Foundation. As written work emerged from this assistance, I profited greatly from exchanges with colleagues at professional meetings. As I began to collect this work into the form it takes here, I would rely upon the careful readings and penetrating comments offered by colleagues who complained that much was out of their expertise. This, of course, was not true. Most of all I want to thank my colleagues Carl Simpson and Karen Bradley, Carl for the detail, the accuracy and pointed honesty of his comments, and Karen for sharing her uncanny ability to see the larger picture, and to question when it is unnecessarily obscured. While both know I could not incorporate all of their comments, without them I simply would have missed more than I wish to admit. I want also to thank Heath Hoffman for his willingness to read the manuscript and offer comments and encouragement. And special thanks to Laura Heenan for invaluable and timely technical assistance.

Finally, I want to express my deep and sincere thanks to Jane Mercer, to whom this book is dedicated. Her own work, so genuinely inter-disciplinary, made an immediate impact and lasting imprint on me. Although the paths I explored about the topic of special education have been different, I know that so much of my curiosity and thinking about special education is traceable to what she gave to me, both directly and indirectly.

Some of the chapters have drawn on articles previously published in professional journals. Much of Chapter 2 is taken from "Common, Delinquent, and Special: On the Formalization of Common Schooling in the American States," *American Educational Research Journal* 31 (1994): 695-723, adapted by permission of the publisher. Portions of Chapter 3 were published in "The Institutional Genesis of Special Education: The American Case," *American Journal of Education* 101 (1993): 359-392, The University of Chicago Press.

Introduction

"Those children are exceptional who, on account of psychological and social considerations, ought not, or in spite of supplementary assistance cannot, be educated along with the typical group." John Louis Horn, The Education of Exceptional Children (1923).

"Each exceptional child is primarily a child with the same rights to acceptance, understanding, and education as other children." Lloyd M. Dunn (Ed.), *Exceptional Children in the Schools,* (1963).

THE UPRISING OF SPECIAL EDUCATION

Special education has come of age in the past few decades. The federal mandate entitled *The Education for All Handicapped Children Act* [EAHC] of 1975 is the legal watershed that acknowledged and authorized the educational rights of exceptional children. It has been renamed the *Individuals with Disabilities Education Act* [IDEA]. Prior to this legislation the numbers of school-age children receiving special education was barely keeping pace with the growth of public school enrollment generally. Figures for 1938–1940 reported 313,722 children in special classes in urban public schools accounting for only 1% of the total school-age population. By 1958 this number had risen to 889,600, yet was still only 2.7% of the school-age population. By 1978, however, 3,751,000 children were in special education classes amounting to 7.5% of the school-age population. In 1995, the figure reached 5,440,000, representing nearly 12% of the school-age population. The combination of federal authority and financial support has gone far to expand the provisions for exceptional children and to remove special education from the margins of full-time, public instruction.

Much of the achievement of educational provisions for exceptional children certainly is owed to parental struggles that secured the simple admission of their children against formal statutes that long excluded them from public instruction. It is, as well, the history of professional educators who often wrote outside and against what was considered mainstream American education. Much like the status of the exceptional child, their works were often marginalized, reaching only those confined to the field of special education, itself viewed as distinct from the real matters of public instruction.

The history of special education involves the stories of the deaf and blind communities, the mentally retarded, the socially maladjusted, and the range of physical disabilities. These groups have at times endured prejudice as "deviant," with their conditions often viewed as the subject of experimentation and treatment. Their conditions have been seen as alien, dangerous, and mysterious, and interpersonally they may be treated with fear, pathos, or scorn. Much like oppressed ethnic or racial minorities, each of these groups has historically been subject to formal and informal segregation.

A long-term direction of the "special classes" has been toward an increased inclusion into the essential spheres of social life. When we view the recent dramatic expansion of special education, these gains in access to public schooling can obscure the many barriers that confronted attempts to secure simple admission into public schools, the extension of provisions for instruction, and the recognition of educational rights long available to nonhandicapped children.

The price of this recognition has been high. Both parental organizations and minority groups have authored a myriad of court challenges against the resistance of an entrenched regular education. Most exemplary was the turmoil of the 1960s when evidence of "racial overrepresentation" in classes for the mildly retarded burst special education into a storm of legal controversy it neither anticipated nor wanted. This evidence was incontrovertible, for it was given in statistics gathered by city and state school authorities. Many consequences of this turmoil persist as a legacy of legal anxiety and professional vulnerability.

Stimulated by the evidence of overrepresentation, a flurry of court cases filed as class action suits aimed largely, but not wholly, at the procedures which inaccurately diagnosed and classified minority students into special education. Most celebrated was *Larry P. v. Riles*, filed in 1970 by civil rights groups who sought an injunction against the use of IQ tests on black students in San Francisco. While the preliminary injunction issued in 1972 did not explicitly prohibit the use of IQ tests, *Larry P.* had established the judicial relevance of cultural bias in intelligence testing. This relevance was made concrete with the mandate that an alternative means of assessment be developed that would minimize the cultural bias of the IQ test.

Paralleling *Larry P.* were two significant cases that established the educational rights of exceptional children as a national issue. The cases of *Mills* (1972) and *Pennsylvania Association for Retarded Children [PARC]* (1972) extended to all retarded school children the right to a publicly supported education, as well as a host of procedural due process rights. As affirmed in *Brown v. Board of Education* (1954), both cases argued that the exclusion of students because of their mental handicap was a violation of the constitutional right of access to a publicly supported educational system. The thrust of these challenges centered on due process violations, for the policy of exclusion, *de jure* and *de facto,* denied the right to a hearing. In both decisions, the school system was enjoined to find those not in school, and to provide special education provisions within the public schools. The scope of these challenges was considerable, for the conclusion was that all children must have access to a public education regardless of their handicapping condition. The impact of *Mills* and *PARC* led to the legislative watershed in the education of exceptional children. When Congress enacted the *EAHC* affirming the right to instruction regardless of handicapping condition special education was tied to the federal level, elevating its financial base above local districts and states.

THE HISTORIES OF SPECIAL AND REGULAR EDUCATION

There can be no disputing that the history of special education is inseparable from the history of regular education. Yet the nature of this relation is complex. A common, if not prevailing interpretation sees special education as the dependent "stepchild" of regular education. From this view, the origins of special education may be neatly defined: when popular schooling ceased to be voluntary the special class arose as a means to handle those students who could not move easily through the graded curriculum. As participation in public education grew, so did the numbers of *atypical* or *exceptional* students. Accordingly, so did the organization of special education.

There is much evidence for this account, and such evidence is explored in subsequent chapters. Nonetheless, this account runs a risk of being overly one sided, precisely because it assigns special education to a dependent status. An alternative account is one that accords special education more autonomy; it is not so much a stepchild as a cousin to regular education. Its origins are not so neatly located, nor is its own growth a simple function of the expansion of public education. Its origins predate the cessation of voluntary common schooling, and its expansion became intertwined with the formalization of public education. Their relationship thereby becomes more complicated. The very growth of public education has relied and built upon this parallel system of instruction. It is difficult to conceive of a history of American public education without significant reference to special education. What American public education *would have been like* without special education would be an imaginative exercise in historical reconstruction.

Whether stepchild or cousin, the relation of special education to public education was forged early and has deepened with the enlargement of educational participation in the twentieth century. The root source of this early link was the historical arrangement of *apprenticeship* and the legally enforced practice of *binding out*. The practice of *binding out* children through *covenants* of apprenticeship was in name and in fact an arrangement for the acquisition of an education, to gain the skills of a trade, to learn the capital laws of the community and the rudiments of book learning.

The *binding out* of children as apprentices was much more than a means to transmit the skills of various trades. It was the social mechanism for the control and care of the poor and infirm. It was, as such, a principle means whereby communities could fulfill broader social obligations toward those less able. It was, in short, an early form of special education.

The dual mechanisms of *binding out* and *covenants of apprenticeship* set the social and legal precedents for the subsequent institutional connection between special education and common schooling. The mutual expansion of both is founded, in part, on the 'rationalization' of the principle of *binding out*. The authority to *bind out* children was the legal rationale for the commitment of poor and infirm children to state institutions. In turn, the legal rationale for the placement of children into special education classes is traceable to these historical precedents. The thread that joins special and regular education is the authority to supersede the traditional rights of parents for the promotion of a broader welfare.

PART 1: FORMALIZING THE *RULES OF ACCESS*

Part 1 examines these institutional origins of special education and reveals its central role in defining the *rules of access* to public education. With the passage of compulsory attendance legislation, three broad sectors defined the institutional composition of a state's school-age population: the world of common pupils, those whose normal ability or acceptable status permitted admission to the common school; the world of delinquency, those whose criminal act or socially offensive conduct led to their exclusion from common schooling; and the world of special children, those whose physical or mental condition prompted their exemption from attendance. These worlds of common, delinquent, and special youth were organizationally separate, but institutionally connected by way of the language that defined the *rules of access* to public education.

The chapters that comprise Part 1 explore how these three worlds became institutionally bound to each other. Chapter 1 focuses on the crucial decades prior to the rise of the "institutional society." I begin with the 1840s and 1850s, for these decades were intellectually volatile: the course that this "new nation" would take was a topic of intense debate. During these decades, the economic forces that undermined the traditional arrangement of apprenticeship and exposed the problem of hereditary pauperism and the "infirmities" of the body and mind were felt as keenly as they were in Europe. Yet while the European response was to build the almshouse, prison, and state asylum, the American response would be different. The answer to the haunting specter of the large institution would be arrangements of smaller scale and ones informed by the spirit of religion and the values of democracy. The American vision was a perpetuation of a universal education by the formation of a "chain of common schools," a configuration linking common schools, reformatories, and residential institutions.

With the formalization of compulsory attendance legislation, states erected this chain of schools. A central thesis of this volume, given in Chapter 2, is that enactment of compulsory attendance marks the institutional "birth" of a state school system. The date of passage marks the *institutional age* of this chain of schools, a fact that I argue holds considerable explanatory information about the development of special education in this century. The variation in *institutional age* predicts much of the subsequent expansion of special education categories and, in turn, the timing of a state's participation in the substantive reforms that have elaborated rights for handicapped children in recent years.

PART 2: STRUCTURING THE *RULES OF PASSAGE*

The chapters that comprise Part 2 are united by the theme that has defined the latter half of this century: the formulation of *rules of passage*. As state school systems grew "older" by distance from the beginnings of compulsory attendance, one mark of their organizational maturity was the expansion of the non-normative categories of special education. The line of continuity from the early category for Backward children, to the elaboration of categories for the mildly retarded, to the current expansion of learning disabled has been shaped by institutionally older state school systems. As these states (principally Massachusetts, New York, California, Pennsylvania, and Illinois) expanded across these categories, they became embroiled in the tempest of racial overrepresentation and were central figures in the series of court challenges that elevated special education into the judicial spotlight. In Chapter 4 the statistical expansion of these non-normative categories is examined against the twin forces of school tracking in public education and the changes in the demographic composition of school populations. The non-normative continuity of special education categories cannot be separated from the structuring of school tracks in public education; indeed the former is a critical foundation for the latter. I argue, in essence, that the predictable expansion of these categories has provided much of the rationale for the rules that define who passes through the "tracked" curriculum of public education.

In Chapter 5, a theoretical framework is outlined as a means to summarize the transition from the *rules of access* to the *rules of passage*. In this chapter, I propose that the transition has been structured by means of a sequential evolution in "pedagogical frames," that is, what constitutes the dominant referent for the explanation of school failure at a given time. Over the last century, the referent has shifted from culture to character to health. As the shift from one frame to another occurred, there is a corresponding shift in the "grammar" of educational explanations for school failure generally, and in the theories that prevail for the instruction of exceptional children in particular. I argue that the tropological sequence of metaphor, metonymy, synecdoche, and irony provides an especially useful model for this grammar of school failure. Moreover, this *grammar of motives* offers not only a means to reflect on long historical changes, but a means to explore in more detail the sequential structure of the more compact events that have shaped special education. Chapter 5 seeks to do just this by way of a closer scrutiny of the "long shadow" of racial overrepresentation, an event with defining consequences spilling over into public education.

In Chapter 6, the topic of educational rights for handicapped children is a fitting end to a focus on *rules of passage*. In this chapter, the significant court decisions, both state and supreme court, that have helped to shape the core "right to appropriate education" are examined. The elaboration of this core right is viewed as a part of the due process revolution that arose during the late 1960s. I see the "release" of substantive due process from earlier procedural rights and safeguards as having the most meaningful and pragmatic impact on special education. The substantive right to treatment is argued to be the forebear of the right to appropriate education. With the substantive right to treatment, the educational functions of reformatories and residential institutions could be defended on constitutional grounds. With these synchronic ties across delinquency and exceptionality, the meaning of an appropriate education for handicapped children within general education is strengthened institutionally. While many of the procedural rights for handicapped children have been defined by institutionally older state school systems, participation in the more contemporary fulfillment of substantive rights is now more "externally" impelled. That is, states with school-age populations that are more culturally and demographically similar engage in the debates and court challenges that define the content of substantive educational rights for handicapped children

The scope of this book is as broad as its goals may be ambitious. Although I begin with the claim that special education has come of age during the last few decades, the preconditions for this maturation must be located in the mid nineteenth century. I view this 150–year scope of time as necessary to gain a deeper comprehension of contemporary special education. The dawning of special education during the 1840s and 1850s reminds us that the institutional arrangements that have been in place for so long were not embraced as inevitable or especially beneficent. It was the passage of compulsory attendance laws that ended debate. These laws, so misnamed because they had nothing to do with compelling attendance, can be read as foundation documents that formalized the basis for a special education.

The cessation of voluntary attendance unintentionally carved out a space for special education within common schooling. Yet the timing of this cessation varied significantly across the American states. This variation is the heart of the theoretical perspective that guides this volume. Just as there is no uniform "origins" of special education, there is no uniform, national development of it either. On the contrary, the historical origins are implicated in regional contrasts, and the pace of institutional growth has been shaped by the time states and territories formally ended voluntary schooling. The *institutional age* of state school systems guides much of what is presented and interpreted in this volume.

But when we arrive at contemporary special education, the ninetheenth century scaffolding of *institutional age* loses much of its explanatory power. We must let go, as it were, of historical antecedents and look to forces that are not so neatly defining as a date of legislative passage. Contemporary regions are cultural and indeed legal entities, formed not by geographic proximity, but by economic and political status. States are made proximate by common social and demographic circumstances. These circumstances, in turn, define common educational issues.

The evidence presented in this volume is varied; accordingly, I do not limit interpretation to one disciplinary view. But it will become clear to readers that while my scope suggests a broad historical inquiry, the combined chapters do not constitute a history of American special education. I endeavor, throughout, to identify the main structural forms that have given special education its shape and that offer some account of its patterned growth over time.

PART I

Formalizing the *Rules of Access*

CHAPTER 1

Common Schooling in the New Nation

European Roots on American Soil

INTRODUCTION

It is well established that the American states achieved high levels of voluntary school attendance early and before it was formalized as compulsory. Save for frequent references to a southern difference, more unfounded than real, popular schooling was a uniform mark of early colonies, young territories and states. Despite substantial differences in starting points, popular education was universally acknowledged as ßboth necessary and valuable.

In certain respects this American *exceptionalism,* the avoidance of state centralization, church establishment, or aristocratic and class distinctions inherited from a feudal past, can limit what needs to be explained. That is, study of the origins of American education more often than not commences with the colonies. The historical records begin here, and it makes intuitively good sense. Colonial societies serve that anthropological function: they were "original" settlements, facing a new and threatening environment, constructing and revising institutions as they grew in size and political ambition.

Nevertheless, the starting point of American education must be pushed back to European sources. The colonists were immigrants whose values and institutions were not constructed afresh. Much of their early commitment to education was owed to an English heritage. Identifying the specific elements of that debt emerges as the essential starting point for the study of American education generally, and for the institutional character of special education in particular (Lipset 1996, pp. 32–35, passim; see also Hamilton and Sutton 1989, pp. 2–5).

With an eye to this European heritage, I begin by identifying two roots of influence that shaped common schooling by way of their particular combination on American soil. The first is institutional: the traditional arrangement of apprenticeship and its central principle of binding out children into "enrollments of indenture" to learn a trade and the rudiments of book learning. By the mid seventeenth century apprenticeship was transplanted to the amenable climate of a first new nation and stamped onto American education a popular and exceptional character. Yet, by the early nineteenth century, the specter of an "institutional society" was widely felt. With the advance of economic changes that weakened local communities, the management of pauperism and its associated infirmities could not be contained by the voluntary arrangement of apprenticeship. The erosion of traditional and voluntary arrangements for community welfare and education was marked by the rise of the poorhouse as apprenticeship declined. The traditional practice of binding out indigent children was transferred to an agency of state authority and the path toward delimiting a common education was thus begun.

The second influence is intellectual: general ideas about a popular education in a democratic republic, and more pragmatic ideas about the education of deaf, blind, and "idiotic" children. The former were forcefully and eloquently articulated by Horace Mann, whose reports and lectures as the first Secretary of the Massachusetts Board of Education in 1838 helped to shape the subsequent organization and character of many state systems of common schooling. And far from esoteric or peripheral, theories about the education of deaf, blind, and idiotic children were particularly relevant at a time when reformers sought the best methods of instruction and debated the form of a common school curriculum. Here the ideas of Edward Seguin, the influential French pedagogue on the treatment of idiocy, and Samuel Gridley Howe, first head of the Massachusetts Asylum for the Deaf and Blind, are most representative.

The threads that joined Mann, Seguin, and Howe conceived an embryonic "special education" that marks a critical moment (compressed into the two decades of the 1840s and 1850s) in the transition from voluntary to compulsory schooling. As states were on the eve of mandating compulsory school attendance, lectures and reports sounded a cautionary voice toward large-scale institutions. This voice was urged on by the advance of economic changes that weakened apprenticeship as a model of community welfare and education and by fears and critiques of institutions for the poor and dependent classes.

The two influences formed an arch, as it were, that framed the early beginnings of special education. The decades of the 1840s and 1850s were crucial, for during these years the social problems that came with the decline of apprenticeship were most keenly felt. America experienced many of the same economic changes that led to the rise of the poorhouse and prison in European cities. Yet such custodial places were not seen as a proper or efficient answer to the problems of poverty and dependency. American soil was different. The custodial response to the decline of apprenticeship could be avoided. The almshouse and prison could be supplanted by a "chain of common schools," a vision of a universal education not restricted to those of sound mind and body.

The American resistance to the prospect of large and custodial institutions drew much of its intellectual content from what was known and being taught about the education of deaf, blind, and idiotic children. A main theme of this chapter is how the American resistance to large institutions was nourished by a religious motivation that would guide the imposing task of building a free and republican nation. What Alexis de Tocqueville saw as particularly distinctive of "democracy in America" (1945) was the intimate union of the spirit of religion and the spirit of liberty. This union, what Rousseau had termed a "civil religion," infused social and political ideas and their reform outlets with a religious impulse that complemented a deeply felt suspicion toward any concentration of power. To European observers America was youthful precocity, a nation that revered symbols and ceremonies, but not leaders and officials, and where citizenship in a democratic republic was analogous to citizenship in the Kingdom of God (Woodward 1991, p. 74; also Lipset 1963, p. 94).

By the early nineteenth century, when the economic forces that had been so visible in Europe became evident in America, the response to poverty and its associated infirmities reflected this union of a religious and political spirit. On the eve of formalizing a system of common schooling the American debate was more of a "revival" than a legislative act. Central to this revival was the promise that a universal education could be established that drew upon the pedagogical methods learned from teaching the "special classes."

THE INSTITUTIONAL HERITAGE: BINDING OUT AND COVENANTS OF APPRENTICESHIP

Apprenticeship was the most concrete reminder of the European heritage transplanted to the colonies. By any standard, it was an old institution, deeply embedded in family relations and the demographics of community life, and infused with religious meanings. It is the key to the European roots of colonial education and to the irreversible transformation of American education generally (cf. Bailyn 1960, p. 117; Cremin 1970, p. 133). It was in practice well before it was codified into law. In time, colonies, territories, and states formalized this traditional practice into a single law "concerning masters, servants and apprentices."

Early American apprenticeship was constituted by two essential elements. At the core of apprenticeship was the principle of binding out. Authority to bind out a minor was vested primarily in the father, or in case of his death, absence or incompetence, the mother or legal guardian. Parents could bind out a child as a means of economic relief. With parental consent, a young boy or girl could voluntarily bind out to learn a trade or occupation. Outside of this voluntary initiation of apprenticeship, authority was typically vested in county or probate courts, or Trustees of the Poor, to bind out pauper children who were at risk of becoming an economic burden on the community (cf. Morgan 1966, p. 78; Demos 1970, pp. 70–72) or orphan children as an early form of adoption (Presser 1972, pp. 456–461). In addition to pauper or orphan children, the authority to bind out anticipated "delinquent" children. The Laws of the Massachusetts Colony of 1648 allowed for the removal of "rude, stubborn, and unruly" children by state authority and to bind them out as apprentices. Under both voluntary and compulsory apprenticeship, terms specified the length of indenture and the duties to be performed by each young apprentice. Most common was a period of indenture to age 21 for boys and to age 18 for girls. For girls marriage could legally interrupt their apprenticeship.

The second element identified the educational obligations of the master toward the apprentice. Most important was the obligation to prepare the boy or girl in the trade or occupation (or "mystery") to which he or she was indentured. The master was also obligated to instruct the apprentice in the capital laws of the community and to impart a minimal level of book learning in reading, writing, and ciphering. Upon completion of the indenture the master was obligated to release the apprentice with some money and clothing. In addition to these expectations, masters were subject to restraints on their treatment of apprentices. If they were found to be excessively harsh or cruel, they were liable for strict penalties or punishments. These constraints on masters extended a modicum of due process rights to apprentices, who could appeal instances of contractual violation or disciplinary misconduct.

The laws pertaining to indenture defined apprenticeship as primarily an educational arrangement. The bilateral exchange between master and apprentice was set down in a written covenant that was in turn sealed by a representative of the community. All covenants, or "enrollments" of apprenticeship, were to be witnessed by a Justice of the Peace and maintained as public records until the indenture was fulfilled. In essence, the system of apprenticeship bound three parties, not two, into an exchange that was fundamentally educational in purpose, content, and consequence (cf. Jernegan 1931; Seybolt 1969; Douglas 1921; Davies 1956; Unwin 1966).

When we look at early American education, apprenticeship emerges as the base of its expansionary potential. In spite of the purposes to which apprenticeship was put, the elements of its legal codification were established long before;[1] and ensuring this principle with a social durability was always the recognition of an external community or public interest that stood prior to the interests of either master or apprentice. The authority to bind out a child as apprentice was an original expression of community interests. The elements of apprenticeship comprised an organized and coherent whole that met economic and political interests, and yet resolved the "educational" implications of their mutual dependency.

Nonetheless, the purposes to which binding out were put is the relevant issue here, for it is a source of comparative differences in the origins of special education. Precisely as apprenticeship declined, the principle of binding out was utilized as the authoritative means to commit the poor and dependent to almshouses and the idiotic to asylums. With apprenticeship's decline, the strategies for educating poor and dependent youth, and the physically and mentally defective as well, may be interpreted as the particular manner of continuing this voluntary, traditional arrangement for a common schooling.

The accelerated decline of apprenticeship during the early nineteenth century brought the question of how to continue the education of poor and dependent youth to a heightened visibility. The path taken did not avoid large institutions but delayed how entrenched and autonomous they would be. The American compromise for the education of poor and dependent youth was the spread of small-scale foundling homes intermediate in size and purpose between the Christian family and the secular state.

The American Compromise: Christian Obligation, Binding Out and Child Welfare

By the early nineteenth century, the capacity of apprenticeship to regulate the problems of poverty and to give a rudimentary education to dependent young had diminished significantly. With the spread in the northeast of factory production and a wage-labor form of capitalism, the problems of poverty and dependency were no longer confined within the boundaries of local communities. The decline of apprenticeship signaled more than local troubles, for it exposed broader and more unmanageable consequences of "hereditary pauperism." The language of "dependent and dangerous classes" was a way to describe pauperism and crime and the infirmities of the body and mind. These groups were without reliable statistical counts that gave them a concrete presence. These changes went unchecked by the traditional mechanism of apprenticeship, and the prospect that such populations would rise in number became a focus of debate and discussion. The center point of these discussions and debates was poverty, or more exactly, hereditary pauperism.

If Europe is taken as a model, as forces of economic change penetrated local communities and weakened apprenticeship we would expect legislation permitting the founding of poorhouses for the compulsory care of the indigent and infirm. As such, the rise of the poorhouse reflects a critical juncture: as industrialization undermines traditional apprenticeship, the authority to bind out is transferred "upward" to the state. The "education" of pauper, orphan, stubborn and infirm children is likewise transferred "outward" from family and community.

Yet this European model assumed a different character on American soil. The transfer of authority to bind out the poor and infirm to workhouses was not simply a response to advancing economic changes. In her analysis of New York state, Hannon (1985) shows that the use of the poorhouse "did not follow an acceleration in urbanization" (pp. 239–240) nor "an extended period of exceptionally rapid growth in pauperism" (p. 240). Contrary to social control explanations, the rise of the poorhouse was promoted more by rural than by urban reformers. To rural communities, pauperism was symptomatic of the European conditions immigrants feared and abhorred most. In contrast to European origins, the rise of poverty was more than a reminder of conditions left; it symbolized a threat to the promise of a new, Puritan republic. As Hannon succinctly put it (p. 251): "Yet, if conditions in America were sufficiently different from those in Europe to hold out the promise of the eventual elimination of pauperism, poverty on the frontier must have seemed totally enigmatic."

The enigmatic character of poverty on the frontier contributed to the equally instructive fact that the use of the poorhouse declined between 1845 and 1859. As the nature of poverty changed so did prevailing opinion. From an initial opinion of personal culpability, pauperism was later seen as a temporary condition into which a respectable person could fall. This contributed to a critique of the poorhouse as ill conceived and uneconomic. Moreover, critiques were specific, noting that "educational facilities for children were found to be virtually nonexistent" (Hannon 1985, p. 251).

By mid century, the rise of the poorhouse may have been a "logical" extension of traditional arrangements for the welfare and education of indigent and dependent members of local communities. Yet the American experiment in almshouses soon appeared as a step toward an institutional society that foreshadowed the loss of personal liberty and the enclosure of local communities. The plight of indigent children confined and languishing in an almshouse was much more than economic inefficiency; it was an offense against Christian principles, and especially the obligation to save souls. During the 1840s and 1850s, the reactions against the almshouse were motivated and informed by an intense religious spirit that sought to save the souls of dependent and wayward children who otherwise would be lost in the confines of large and impersonal almshouses.

No example of charitable reform better represents this reaction than the "placing out" of poor and vagrant urban children into homes in western states by the Children's Aid Society of New York. Established in 1853 by Charles Loring Brace, the Society was the personification of Brace's philosophy of youthful poverty and crime and his own best method of "disposing" of dependent children.

For Brace, there was much to learn from the asylum and reformatory systems of England. Yet, a direct replication of their methods would have opposite consequences, compounding the intentions of reform and education. The decisive difference between England and America was in the condition of labor: in England there was an oversupply, in America there was an undersupply and a vast open territory. For both, the large institution that congregated a few hundred prisoners or dependent children was evil in design and outcome. Where England had less choice but to utilize the large asylums and reformatories, America had an opportunity to avoid this evil. The opportunity was unique to America, for its vast rural West allowed for the feasible "putting out" of poor and vagrant children to farm, and Christian families. This open land was indeed a blessing, for urban children could be put out to families and thereby avoid both confinement and indenture.

Brace's Children's Aid Society was remarkably successful, placing nearly 20,000 dependent children in western states until legislation essentially ended the practice. Yet Brace's influence may have derived more from his opposition to the houses of refuge and juvenile asylums. Both of these agencies sought to divide up the spoils of child-saving reform by distinguishing a quadripartite scheme of criminal, wayward, neglected, and destitute children (Garlock 1979, p. 374). To Brace, such distinctions mattered little; the only real category was children who had committed crimes. All others were essentially the same whether they be called wayward, neglected, or stubborn.

The content of Brace's philosophy led him to oppose classification. Differences in economic background played no real causal role in development, for the children of the poor "are not essentially different from the children of the rich;" both are "individuals" (Brace 1859, p. 4).

The same principles which shape development operate across rich and poor, as these principles are the natural laws which Providence has established in human nature. To confine poor and vagrant children in institutions is to congregate bad habits and diminish the great natural impulses that can only be found in a Christian home. The uniquely American alternative to institutions and indenture was the farm family of western states. In contrast to the evils of city life, the farm family was "God's reformatory," and the best possible place for individual reformation (Brace 1859, p. 12).

Despite Brace's opposition to institutions and classification, both were tendencies that would accelerate during the latter decades of the nineteenth century. Nonetheless, Brace's "putting out" system was one part of an indigenous movement of child saving that only really delayed the founding and spread of the larger asylum and reformatory. Over the first half of the nineteenth century, some seventy-seven privately controlled "foundling homes" for the care and education of dependent children were established; fifty-six of these arose between 1830 and 1850. At least forty-seven such agencies were founded during the 1850s alone, and another seventy-nine during the 1860s. The spread of these "homes" attests to the continued popular support for small, private and voluntary means to control problems of childhood poverty and dependency.

Brace articulated the "enigmatic" fear of institutions and offered a strategic alternative that seemed to resolve the plight of urban economic dependency by linking eastern cities to their western rural neighbors. Moreover, Brace offered a practical action that offset the debates over classifying dependent children. For the decade of the 1850s, the Children's Aid Society appeared to be one answer to the erosion of apprenticeship and the specter of institutions. The institutional path taken by England appeared to be unnecessary. Bad and dangerous habits were not the inherent ways of poor and vagrant children; nor were they better understood by devising classifications that appeared to fit these habits.

What Brace articulated for poor and neglected children had its complement in debates over the care and education of deaf, blind, and idiotic children. For both, the theme of a universal human nature dispelled the notion of natural divisions and their politically motivated classifications.

THE INTELLECTUAL LINK: THE EDUCATION OF DEAF, BLIND AND IDIOTIC CHILDREN AND THE COMMON SCHOOL REVIVAL

Edward Seguin and The Education Of Idiots: The Dawn of Special Education

Throughout the nineteenth century, the intellectual links to European educational reformers were certainly many. No prominent American reformer could ignore the allure of Pestalozzian pedagogy, or the practical strategies of Joseph Lancaster or the utopian schemes of a Robert Owen. But at the same time these and other European reformers were commanding attention, work with the deaf and blind and the idiotic enjoyed a particular attraction. With the publication of Abbe Sicard's first textbook for educating deaf children in 1800 and Jean-Marc Itard's report on the education of the "Wild Boy" of Aveyron in 1807, the beginning of the nineteenth century may be seen as a dawning of "special education."

Yet this was an auspicious beginning, for the prevailing metaphor of the deaf, blind idiotic was that of a savage. Savages, like animals in the wild, live in moral isolation. If methods could be devised for their "education," the pedagogical implications would be immense. It would indeed be revolutionary, not only for conditions long believed incurable, but for the education of the majority in common schools. One important link between this European dawning of special education and the American "common school revival" of the early nineteenth century was the work of Edward Seguin (1812–1880).

As a student of Itard (albeit briefly), Seguin inherited both the optimism and pessimism that intellectual powers could be enhanced in idiots. Itard had declared his efforts with the "Savage of the Aveyron" to have been in vain because he was indeed an idiot and not simply untaught. For Seguin, however, the error was not in the diagnosis but in the method. After reaching the limits of his "philosophical programme," Itard's efforts began to resemble the physiological methods reported by teachers of the deaf. The work of Jacob Rodrigues Pereire was especially impressive to Seguin, for he taught the deaf to speak by distinguishing between sound and vibration. By sensing the vibration, the deaf could "hear through the skin." Thus, for Seguin, Itard's pessimism was premature; he had not gone far enough with the discoveries of the physiological methods then developing with the education of the deaf.

To Seguin, Pereire's work with the deaf offered pedagogical formulas for a universal, common education. Seguin pointed to the contribution a special education may have for a universal education when he noted the comparative merits of Pereire and Rousseau: "But, in looking closely at their literary relics, we may more easily find ideas of Pereire in the *Discours sur l'Inegalite des Conditions*, than ideas of Jean Jacques in the memoirs on the restoration of the speech to congenital deaf mutes" (Seguin 1907, pp. 20–21). This tie was only a nascent idea at best; even Itard never so much as hinted at the possibility of systematizing his views for the treatment of idiots at large, nor at organizing schools for the same purpose" (p. 22). Thus, Seguin was a beneficiary of the contrast between ostensible failure and empirical discoveries. More importantly, Seguin exploited this contrast at a time when reform programs for a common schooling were in need of pedagogical theories.

Seguin exploited this opportunity by extending the physiological discoveries in the treatment of deaf mutes to the treatment and education of idiots. While a firm believer in the central role played by the senses, and especially that of touch, Seguin did not believe that intellectual growth resulted from the direct experience of the senses. Departing from the materialism of Locke and Condillac, Seguin argued that the role of the senses was mediated by notions, names, or categories for objects and experiences. Notions were not ideas, for they were given to or impressed upon the student by the teacher. Ideas, not mere notions, were the true source of intellectual growth and knowledge. They were different from externally imposed notions; they were the products of reflection, a process stimulated by "natural curiosity," or, more precisely, by will.

Seguin's insertion of will gave him an optimistic conception of idiocy. To Seguin: "That which most essentially constitutes idiocy, is the absence of 'moral volition,' superseded by a 'negative will'; that in which the treatment of an idiot essentially consists is, in changing his 'negative will' into an affirmative one, his *will of loneliness into a will of sociability* and usefulness; such is the object of the 'moral training'" (Seguin 1856, p. 151, my emphasis; see also Seguin 1907, p. 71). Seguin's addition to Pereire and others was attributing a prior and dynamic role to volition. In so doing, "the behavior of idiots was not the 'natural' outcome of idiocy but rather the outcome of an unnatural flaw—a flawed interaction between of the will and the nervous system that affected the mind" (Trent 1994, p. 46).

At the core of Seguin's physiological methods was the conception of the idiot as locked in a state of loneliness. To combat this, moral training was an incessant pressure by the physician to impel the idiot to enter into the "sphere of activity, of thinking, of labor, of duty and of affectionate feeling" (Seguin 1856, p. 151). The principles of physiology provided Seguin with the scientific evidence to affirm that such growth does happen, for such is "the great natural law of activity and repose." Such principles and natural laws were evidence as well to dispel the metaphor of the idiot as savage and to bridge the distance between idiocy and normalcy.

Nonetheless, Seguin was not free of the metaphor. Comparisons to animals appear throughout his physiological education and reduce to a heuristic distinction: "The motor of life in animals is mostly centripetal; the motor of life in man is mostly centrifugal" (1907, p. 141). The centripetal life is an individual life; centrifugal existence is a social, active movement that "progresses to God." Because animals lack education they have only instincts, whereas man has soul "when engrafted by education and revelation." Yet this distinction is not so qualitative as to excuse man from these "animal" traits. On the contrary, the distinction is a means for Seguin to draw evolutionary comparisons across human groups when he includes idiots among "women, Jews, peasants, Indians and Negroes" who "are not now," but were "once denied a soul by religious or civil ordinances" (p. 141). Such ordinances overeducate the few to the neglect of the many; a practice that has been fatal to whole nations. Contrary as it is to the natural laws of God, the practice denies universal education and renders the human will immobile, thereby depriving individuals and whole groups of their fundamental rights to liberty. Thus, Seguin's physiological education was more than a method of procedures for the instruction of idiots; it was a coherent set of principles that resonated with early nineteenth century debates over the political viability of common schooling.

In 1850, Seguin emigrated to the United States with established credentials as a leader in the education of idiots. But these credentials were tainted by his being fired in 1843 from his post at the Bicetre and being forced to end his medical studies. Despite this disgrace, between 1844 and his emigration he published his most significant works on the physiological education of idiots. As these works gained notoriety outside of France, his reputation as a successful practitioner and theoretician became mentioned in reports to state legislatures on the demographic status and educational treatment of idiots.

After some years at Hervey Wilber's school in Albany, Seguin took up permanent residency in New York City from which he would visit and report on both private and public institutions. Seguin's impact on changing professional beliefs about idiocy is hardly disputable; yet his influence on American thought is equally significant. He represents, as Trent aptly notes (1994, p. 41), "the intellectual mentor to the first generation of superintendents." Yet his ideas and beliefs could not be directly replicated on American soil. As the debates over the "common school revival" intensified during the 1840s and 1850s, the intellectual momentum that Seguin initiated would be reinterpreted and reshaped.

THE AMERICAN COMPROMISE: A COMMON SCHOOL REVIVAL IN A DEMOCRATIC REPUBLIC

The Messianic Vision of Horace Mann

The influence of Horace Mann on the definition and organization of American common schooling is well documented (see Hinsdale 1900; Kaestle 1983). As the first Secretary of the Massachusetts Board of Education, appointed in 1837, Mann found a position from which he could compose and deliver his ideas about a common education. His most prominent interest, if not preoccupation, was the role of a common education in a democratic republic. For Mann, this role was messianic, for education held the key to the proper growth of individuals and, by extension, of the larger whole. Within a republic this connection was essential.

Mann's definition of education extended well beyond the ability to read and write. He conceived of education in religious terms, as a "culture of our moral affections" that "lead to a subjection and conformity of all our appetites, propensities and sentiments to the will of Heaven" (Mann 1969, p. 118). For Mann, education was a gift of the Law of God, an instrument of the Deity that was both cause and effect of the development and decline of human potential. In a democratic republic, popular education produces moral and productive citizens, while reducing "mobs and riots" and other violations of the natural order. As he put it, "Such an event as the French Revolution never would have happened with free schools; any more than the American Revolution would have happened without them" (p. 13).

While Mann was eloquent about the essential role of a common schooling in a democratic republic, this eloquence betrayed a haunting theme of human depravity and calamity. Underneath the natural order of a republic, natural when aligned with the laws of God, there is an ever-present potential for evil and decline. Mobs and riots erupt predictably as eventual outcomes of a vicious or defective education. Whole societies may be arrested in states of degradations, as Mann portrayed "Oriental and African despotisms." When "caverned in despotism" the "mind of the millions grows without strength, or beauty or healing balm" (p. 145). For Mann, it was "the mighty stimulus of Christianity" that propelled [some] societies away from despotism, for it inserted the conviction that the future existence is more important than the present.

This dualism between the order of Providence and the latent forces of degradation is replicated at the level of man's individual nature. Herein lies the core of Mann's pedagogical theory. Human nature is composed of faculties, organized as a vertical layer of propensities. The superior layer is conscience, a faculty that establishes a moral relation to God. Beneath this is a set of faculties that are social and sympathetic, enabling relations of compassion and kindred association. Lastly, at the base of human faculties is "a horde of bandit propensities," each one of which "is deaf to the voice of God" (pp. 126–127). These propensities are likened to animal appetites for survival; they are merely self-propelling, lacking social perception and moral conscience.

In this portrait of human nature Mann is careful to note that faculties and propensities are universal; all individuals have the capacity for a moral conscience and social associations, as well as the potential for animal appetites. As Mann claimed, the animal propensities "have no affinity with reason or conscience" (p. 139), for the appetites and indulgences, habits and depravities are temptations that an individual may risk if not restrained by reason, conscience, or religion. Like riots and mobs, individuals can fall into depravity if their latent propensities become unbalanced in relation to the whole.

It was indeed the whole that was key. Whether it be the republic or an individual, the persistent emphasis was on relations that bind and preserve, restrain and enable. At the very center of the multitude of relations was the critical tie between parents and children, a relation that defined the historical transmission of one generation's legacy onto another. The behavior of parents, as progenitors, has decisive consequences; indeed the "sins" of the parents are visited onto the children. If not restrained by education, the propensities of one generation pass onto the next, which is to say that individuals inherit an absence of the relations that nourish and solidify. Individuals fall outside the order of Providence.

The theme of latent forces that haunts Mann's commitment to a common education becomes, in essence, a fear of isolation. To be detached from relations that bring out a moral conscience and social association is to be solitary, attached only to one's self. Just as "diffusion is the duty of government" (p. 55), education impels us outward, away from our inner self. A common schooling diffuses individuals, reducing the social and political violations of crime and rioting. To these Mann would add the "calamities" of the mind and body. To suffer the infirmity of deafness or blindness, or of idiocy, is to be isolated from one's fellow man. To teach the deaf to speak or the idiotic to exercise and play music is to impel each outward and away from the confines and isolation of their physical infirmity. Thus, in his influential seventh report to the Massachusetts Board of Education, Mann expressed his admiration for the Prussian schools for the deaf and blind. To Mann, what was learned from educating the deaf and blind set forth the universal principles for a common schooling. Here, the pedagogical mission of Horace Mann met the pragmatic debates of Samuel Gridley Howe.

The Pragmatic Vision of Samuel Gridley Howe

If Horace Mann was a national spokesman for a system of common schooling, Samuel Gridley Howe was his complement for the education of deaf, blind and idiotic children. Mann and Howe were indeed complementary. Each was intellectually prolific, politically engaged, and passionately committed to his own objectives. When we come to

Howe, after a discussion of Seguin and Mann, we arrive at the pragmatics of the common school revival. Since he was a foreigner, the scope of Seguin's impact was delimited; yet it was limited also by Howe's prideful resistance to what he called the French inclination toward "charlatanism." While Seguin and Howe clashed as personalities, intellectually they shared much common ground. Yet between Mann and Howe there was only personal admiration; and they were both intellectual and political collaborators.

Howe's career was as full as it was diverse. He was head of the Massachusetts Asylum for the Blind. From this post he successfully persuaded the legislature to admit a limited number of idiotic children as an experiment for their treatment and education. He wrote prolifically, ranging over topics including the education of deaf-mutes, the causes of idiocy, slavery, and prison discipline. The last is particularly instructive, for it is a prelude to his ideas on the education of deaf, blind, and idiotic children and to his organizational conception of common schooling generally.

Early in the nineteenth century American penitentiaries had gained an international notoriety for their progressive designs and innovative practices. Which design was best became a contentious issue, pairing two rival systems against each other for the favorable commentary of professional and lay reviews. These were the solitary system practiced at the Eastern State Penitentiary in Philadelphia, and the congregate system followed at the Auburn State Prison in New York. In the former system, inmates lived virtually alone in their cells, rarely if ever relating to other inmates in group tasks or settings. Their only associations were with guards, teachers and visitors. In the latter system, inmates worked in groups but were forbidden to speak. As the rivalry between these two systems intensified, the Boston Prison Discipline Society sought views and opinions as to the respective merits and deficiencies of each system. Early in the 1840s, Howe had joined the Society, as did Horace Mann. Howe and Mann (along with Charles Sumner) favored the Pennsylvania system, while the remainder of the Society favored the Auburn system. As a sort of minority statement, Howe composed, with the concurrence of Mann and Sumner, his *Essay on Separate and Congregate Systems of Prison Discipline*, submitting it to the Society in 1846. The dispute between the factions had reached such a level that Howe's *Essay* had to be published privately.

Howe's support of the solitary system rested largely on one central claim: the isolation of prisoners removed them from the temptations of fellow inmates, diminishing further evil influences and degradations. The Pennsylvania system "is solitary with respect to the vicious, social with respect to the virtuous" (Howe 1846, p. 19). The aim of solitary living is not an extension of punishment; rather, its aim is moral reformation. The congregation of prisoners aggravates punishment to an unethical point, for it adds to the degradation that the individual prisoner brought upon himself by his "vices and crimes." When isolated from other prisoners, the vices and crimes are dispersed and the object of prison discipline becomes morally clear, to elevate and purify, not to shame and degrade.

To Howe the actual, pragmatic results of each system of discipline had been demonstrated. A more abstract argument, however, lay behind his scrutiny of these results. This was the issue, or consequence, of constructing prisoners into a qualitative category. As he stated, "It is a great mistake to regard convicts as forming a class apart; it is a worse one to treat them as such. . . . The convict class is a conventional, and not a natural division, and it has no precise boundaries" (p. 40). The congregate system affirms the vices and crimes of prisoners and forms them into a distinct class. In contrast, the solitary system allows for the individual prisoner's reflection upon his vices and crimes and resists, thereby, the formation of convicts as a "natural division."

The position taken in the *Essay* foretells much about Howe's beliefs regarding the education of deaf, blind and idiotic children. In *Remarks on the Education of Deaf-mutes* (1866) we encounter the same causal argument about the "evils of congregation." The concentration of deaf and blind children in residential asylums "intensifies the peculiarities growing out of their infirmity" (p. 25). The practice of isolation in prison discipline has its complement in the care of defective children; the guiding principle should be "separation and diffusion." Deaf and blind children "should be associated together as "little" as possible; and with ordinary persons "as much" as is possible; otherwise "morbid growth in certain directions" results (p. 14).

The form of prison discipline and the scale of institutional care for defective children are complementary. To Howe, they share the mutual premise that neither prisoners nor defective children are "natural divisions." The evil of congregating deaf-mutes, as with convicts, is that it "encourages a spirit of caste" (p. 25). For Howe, the infirmities of deafness or blindness "are not inherent or essential ones"; rather, with wider diffusion and education "the classes themselves gradually diminish and finally disappear" (p. 28). The belief that physical and mental infirmities are not essential conditions led Howe to express caution toward the residential asylum. The care and education of defective children should remain as close as possible to "ordinary family and social influences, not of a great deaf mute family, but of common life" (p. 14). As he summarized: "the plan of the Massachusetts Board of charities did not contemplate an asylum, but simply one or more schools, to which mutes could go for instruction, *as other children go to common schools*" (p. 14, my emphasis). In fact, the establishment of the Hartford school was conceived as an "experiment" that could be abandoned if it failed.

Howe's resistance to concentration was a timely complement to Mann's messianic vision of a common schooling and to Brace's experiments in child welfare. Their affinities were more than intellectual; their social ideas and educational strategies were argued as deductions from Christian principles. Empirical evidence was taken to be confirmation of these principles: the rejection of the congregate prison system and the residential asylum was theoretically consistent with the laws of Providence and confirmed by empirical evidence at hand. But importantly, these laws of God were not just strict and demanding; they were universal. They were applicable across convict and citizen, defective and ordinary children; they did not imply caste-like classifications. The depravity of convicts and the suffering of the deaf and blind were not confined within the fixed boundaries of "natural divisions." The universality of vice and crime, blindness and deafness implied a common susceptibility; not to the laws of "genetic heritability" but to sinful temptations and their due consequences.

To Howe it was a certainty that for all cases where children are born deaf, blind, or idiotic, the "fault lies with the progenitors," for "whether they sinned in ignorance or in wilfulness, matters not as to the effect of the sin upon the offspring" (1848, p. 5). Idiocy was not an evil forever inherent in society, nor was it an accident, or much less a "special dispensation of Providence"; it was the result of violating natural laws which are "simple, clear and beautiful." If these laws were observed correctly, over two or three generations idiocy would be removed completely.

That God's natural laws are neither mysterious nor inaccessible, but are simple, clear, and beautiful, placed a special ethical demand on individuals, families, and generations. The province of this demand was the body; the laws of physiology define the ethical constraints. With his emphasis on the health and vigor of the body as the core of [P]hysiology, Howe is in full agreement with Seguin. Yet Howe takes this emphasis beyond the boundaries of medicine, conceiving of the health of the body as "a trust fund given by the Creator" where "every debauch, every excess, every undue indulgence, is at the expense of this capital" (p. 5).[2] Where Seguin stops at the boundaries of nerve endings and muscle tissue, Howe's "causes of idiocy" are likened to the ethical constraints of Puritans, which were akin to the rules of business accounting.

CONCLUSIONS

The dawning of special education appeared as a rejection of the belief that dependent and wayward behavior and the infirmities of the body and mind marked an essential separation between distinct groups. Moreover, this rejection was joined to a reform-minded opposition against large institutions. The context of this attention to the dangerous and dependent classes was the advance of economic changes that weakened the traditional means to contain matters of pauperism and dependency within local communities. The traditional arrangement of apprenticeship and its authoritative principle of binding out were increasingly at odds with a growing impersonal market system. As the mid nineteenth century approached, there was both an institutional and intellectual "crisis." Debates over the disposition and education of dependent, delinquent and physically defective children gained an especial relevance as the vision of a common school system was spreading.

The mid-century "common school revival" was an expression of this crisis. What we see in the works of such figures such as Charles Loring Brace, Horace Mann, and Samuel Gridley Howe is a common theme, a similar and retelling opposition toward the concentration of social problems, or of bodily and mental infirmities. While the subject was different for each figure, their common thread was an advocacy for an American exceptionalism, a messianic reformism that opposed concentration as a reminder of Europe's course. Each was sustained by a time and place that tied his respective subjects to larger issues. For Brace it was the jurisdictional dispute over who would define and control the population of delinquent and wayward youth (Brace 1857); for Mann it was the challenge to authority by an organized body of headmasters and teachers (Association of Masters 1844); for Howe it was the raging struggle over slavery (Schwartz 1956, chs. 11–15). For all three, their books, lectures, and reports bore concrete results. Likely the most consequential was the spread of small and largely privately controlled schools for the care and education of neglected, delinquent, and physically and mentally defective youth.

This appearance of these small, private schools and boarding homes represents a compromise to the decline of apprenticeship and the failures of the almshouse. But more importantly, it was a loosely assorted foundation to the "tutelary complex" of reform and charitable organizations that would become more formalized during the latter decades of the nineteenth century. Joining this complex would be educational institutions, forming by centuries end a tripartite institutional arrangement. The structure of this arrangement would seem to mirror, if not fulfill, what Howe imagined as the role of the temporary boarding schools for the feebleminded. Describing in 1851 what is now the Fernald State School, Howe expressed that the institution was "a link in the chain of common schools- the last indeed, but still one necessary in order to make the chain embrace all the children in the state" (Wolfensberger 1976, p. 49). One year later Howe's own state of Massachusetts enacted the first compulsory school attendance law, formalizing a system of common schooling that was indeed a "chain" of sorts.

NOTES

1. It is in the *Twelve Tables* (circa 45–450) that we first encounter the meaning of *binding*. In the language of the *Twelve Tables* binding refers to an economic transaction, or nexum, wherein a person becomes implicated in a debt-contract to another. When the contract is exacted, a person's debt to a creditor is weighed out to him in the presence of witnesses. Nexum was an original point in a "legal chain" conceptualizing degrees of indenture. If Coulanges (1962) provides the best account of the sociological background of

Roman law, Henry Maine gives the superior interpretation of its sociological development in *Ancient Law* (1954). In this work Maine outlines the historical sequence of contractual law. At the root of this sequence is *nexum*, and out of this primitive, ceremonial binding is derived the forms of contract. Maine's treatment of Roman "institutional" law is a sociological inquiry into the inertial forces inhibiting the emergence of contractual obligation as known in modern terms. He captured this inertia succinctly: "The notion that persons under a contractual engagement are connected together by a strong bond or chain continued until the last to influence the Roman jurisprudence of contract; and flowing thence it has mixed itself with modern ideas" (p. 185). The Roman idea of *nexum* fused analytically separable rights and conditions of obligation, ones that were to be freed of this symbolic bond in later centuries. Its "freedom" from this symbolic meaning is a thread that weaves through the development of secular law in the western legal tradition (Berman 1983), explaining much of the authoritative basis for the development of public institutions. And with the rise of public institutions, this thread offers much to explain the authoritative basis for participation in these institutions, be it through "commitment" to a benevolent institution, or through "enrollment" to an educational institution.

2. Such references as these reflect the well-known influence that phrenology had upon both Mann and Howe (cf. Hinsdale 1900, pp. 94–104; Cremin 1957, pp. 13–14). It is clear that much of the religious motivation behind the pedagogical theories of Mann and Howe was given an added emphasis by their commitment to the principles of phrenology. Both men read and were persuaded by the writing of George Combe, principally his *The Constitution of Man* and *Lectures on Popular Education*. The attractiveness of phrenology lay in its depiction of the human mind as composed of thirty-seven universal faculties that were the endowment of Providence as natural laws. Adding to this religious interpretation of human psychology was the later discredited claim that these faculties could be measured by certain perturbations of the human skull. In spite of this notion, phrenology provided an imagery of order and purpose. It provided a seemingly empirical rationale for the educational reforms to which both Mann and Howe were committed. A universal, common schooling was deduced from the laws of Providence and was a sociological good.

CHAPTER 2

Compulsory Attendance and Special Exemptions

Formalizing the Rules of Access

INTRODUCTION

In the introductory chapter some European influences on American common schooling were explored. Of particular interest was how these influences were accommodated to the exceptional circumstances of this first new nation. This accommodation was especially intense during the decades of the 1840s and 1850s, during which local communities felt the strains of economic changes that eroded traditional arrangements for the care and education of indigent and infirm members. These decades were a critical juncture in this economic and social transformation. These years were witness to the "common school revival," an apt term for the religious motivation that informed and carried so many of the reform efforts seeking a broadened, universal public education. An important element of this motivation was an informed hesitancy toward institutions that would congregate the "dangerous and dependent" classes. An American compromise in the face of inexorable economic changes was the development of numerous intermediate arrangements that replicated the design and purpose of apprenticeship and avoided the large, impersonal institution. This network of foundling homes, children's asylums, and other forms of semipublic "schools" for indigent and infirm youth established the initial foundations of a "tutelary complex."

Historical works have recognized the educational intent and function of institutions outside the common school, whether they be state reformatories, vocational or industrial schools (Katz 1968, pp. 186–187; Lazerson 1971, pp. 85–92; Brenzel 1983; Schlossman 1977, p. 22), orphan houses for dependent and destitute children (Kaestle 1973, pp. 126–137; Clement 1985b, pp. 252–253), or other residential arrangements for the physically and mentally "special classes" (Rothman 1971, pp. 228–229; Lane 1984; Van Cleve and Crouch 1989, ch. 5). Yet, what is crucial to an understanding of the transition from voluntary arrangements to formal institutions are the *links* that joined this "dazzling array of tutelary complexes" (Finkelstein 1985, p. 112; also Donzelot 1979, ch. 4) into a coordinated system of common schooling. This chapter examines the coordination of these tutelary complexes into formal systems of common schooling by way of the passage of compulsory attendance legislation. With these laws, the *rules of access* to a public education were legally defined.

In this chapter, the formal structuring of American education into "three worlds" is explored: the worlds of the common, the delinquent, and the special. The common school was the model upon which states built systems of public education during the latter half of the nineteenth century. As distinct from the earlier independent pay or charity schools, the common school denoted "an elementary school intended to serve all the children in an area" (Kaestle 1983, p. xi). With the transition from charity schools to common schools, financial support became the charge of towns, and admission to the common-public schools was broadened beyond indigent status or the capacity of parents to pay.

On the margins of the common school was the world of "juvenile disorderly youth," a population of school-age children from poor and laboring classes. Excluded or expelled from the common school, delinquent children were incorporated into a separate educational system that paralleled public day schools: the state primary, reform, or industrial schools prevalent from the middle to the end of the nineteenth century. Reform and industrial schools constituted a true educational system that foreshadowed the terms and conditions of common school admission, length of attendance, and curricular instruction.

The special world was constructed around the population of mentally and physically handicapped children. These children were exempted ("excused") from attending the common schools on grounds that they were uneducable. Yet they were entitled or required to attend state institutions or asylums for their care, protection, and instruction. In vocabularies that recalled the rhetoric of Horace Mann and Samuel

Gridley Howe, states during the early decades of the nineteenth century promoted the education of the deaf, dumb, blind, and feebleminded children of schoolage. Along with the growth of reform schools, the sequential formation of these state institutions set the stage for legislating compulsory attendance at the common school.

The nineteenth century formalization of common schooling was above all a new discourse about education, refining the language of who was a pupil and what constituted a school. When we broaden the boundary of American education to include the delinquent and the special we see three sites of instruction which were interrelated by the late nineteenth century. While separate, these three were linked through the language of compulsory attendance laws which outlined the criteria regulating admission into common schooling. Whether enrolled in the common school, committed to the reformatory, or entitled to instruction in the state hospital, the children within each world were indeed pupils who received in ways more similar than different the "branches of knowledge" of that time. Further, and of critical importance, with the combination of these three worlds came truly universal education for *all* children.

Two lines of empirical inquiry are explored here. One is the series of legislative events occurring in the arenas of benevolent, correctional, and educational institutions. The succession of events that form the rise of institutions exhibits empirical features that are internal to each arena and relational to others. Thus, the founding of benevolent institutions, specifically the lunatic asylum and residential facility for the deaf, dumb, and blind, displays an internal property of "duration" across time. This temporal duration is similarly measurable for the establishment of state reformatories, and the dates that states enacted compulsory school attendance. Additionally, the succession of these events reveals a relational pattern, as when the founding dates for reformatories are paired against the dates of enacting compulsory attendance.

The second line of inquiry uses evidence from primary historical documents for the state of Massachusetts. The case of Massachusetts provides documentary evidence that resolves the empirical mismatch between school enrollment and compulsory attendance. Enactment of compulsory attendance was itself a series of acts and amendments to acts. The documentary evidence that relates enrollment to compulsory attendance is an "internal sequence" of a discourse that grew progressively conscious of authority jurisdictions and of the purposes charged to institutions. Particular attention is given to the procedural ties between the state reformatory and the common school. This relation framed the rules that bound the delinquent and special worlds to common schooling, thereby enabling the formal enactment of compulsory school attendance.

UNTYING THE CONCEPTUAL KNOT: SCHOOL ENROLLMENT AND SCHOOL ATTENDANCE

Levels of voluntary school enrollment have always been high from the colonial era forward, a fact that has much to do with the comparatively late implementation of compulsory attendance. There is, however, an important distinction between compulsory instruction and compulsory attendance. Colonies, young states, and territories alike mandated that children be instructed. Beyond stipulations of parental obligation, they did not, however, mandate attendance at school.

Prior to passage of compulsory school attendance, much of the form of common school systems was outlined in state and territorial constitutions (Tyack and James, 1986). The "infrastructure" of these systems was strikingly common to all political units. The necessary elements were typically those of finance, duties of school officers, expectations of parents, courses of study, and procedures of district formation, consolidation and dissolution. Beyond these constitutional ideals, a historical root of the "systematization" of common schools was the consolidation of independent pay or charity schools. As Kaestle details (1983, p. 57) the charity school movement "was the innovative sector of urban education." The growing contrast between this sector and rural community schooling, fueled by the Lancasterian system, "paved the way for rule making, standardization, and supervision" (p. 58). As frameworks that codified relations among persons and social units, such elements parallel the criteria that define the modern state as summarized by Strayer: "[units] stable in time and space, having permanent and impersonal institutions, achieving agreement on final authority, and loyalty to this authority" (Strayer 1970, p. 10). With these initial laws and standardized rules, states and territories affirmed a compulsory education by requiring the construction of schools and by obligating parents to send their children to the nearest available schoolhouse. By doing so, these early laws grounded the site of the common school in time and space.

With the passage of compulsory attendance laws a more definitive point was reached. All compulsory attendance laws were composed of three interrelated parts. First, all laws drew upon the mutual responsibilities of parents and schools, defining the "in loco parentis" authority of schools. Second, all laws specified physical and mental disability as conditions which exempted or excused children from attendance. Finally, all laws confirmed the authority to expel students from attendance whose behavioral conduct threatened the host function of schools.

Occurring as it did during the latter decades of the nineteenth century, the passage of compulsory attendance laws appears as capping the long history of voluntary school attendance, formalizing already high enrollment levels (Tyack 1976). Yet levels of enrollment do not explain the variation in dates of enacting compulsory attendance legislation (Richardson 1980), nor do these laws offer any ability to predict later increases in enrollment (Landes and Solmon 1972). Moreover, for northern and western states enrollment levels were negatively, not positively, related to features of bureaucratization, namely, pupil expenditures and length of the school year (Meyer et al. 1979, p. 596). While voluntary school enrollment enjoyed a long history, the passage of compulsory attendance was a relatively condensed series of events. In short, school enrollment and formalization were not similar phenomena.

This empirical mismatch between voluntary enrollment and compulsory attendance underlines the conceptual problem of school formalization. The scope and significance of formalizing schooling reached far beyond organizational properties of developing state school systems. If formalization is viewed as a new discourse, the real impact of compulsory attendance becomes visible outside the common school, for such laws had more to do with specifying the conditions for exclusion and exemption than with compelling attendance.

The conception of school formalization as a new discourse alters the focus of empirical attention. The shift is certainly one of scale, but is one of research strategy as well. In the terms of Foucault, attention must be given to the configuration of objects "that are otherwise highly dispersed" (Foucault 1972, p. 42).[1] Empirically, the task is to reveal the patterns that confer an overall unity to disparate events and practices, and that define the boundaries and content of discourse.

THE SEQUENTIAL PATTERNS OF INSTITUTIONAL FORMATION: FROM THE ASYLUM TO COMPULSORY ATTENDANCE

The nineteenth-century turn to state asylums was prompted by the breakdown of traditional community mechanisms for the regulation of the poor. The impulse to confine the physically and mentally defective was, in Rothman's evocative term, a "discovery" symbolizing a means to reconstitute the ordered community of eighteenth-century America (Rothman 1971). The expectation that the community would care for its own defective members in noninstitutional settings was reinforced by the regulative mechanism of expelling or "warning out" strangers. Rothman's thesis has been refined by locating the roots of asylum reform in earlier English practices, and by focusing much of the motivation in the middle class fears and disdain toward nonlaboring poor. Nonetheless, the decline of Jacksonian localism exposed the differences between community life and urban expansion (Scull 1977, pp. 337–351; Lasch 1973, pp. 3–17; Katz 1978; Bellingham 1986, pp. 533–537), a discrepancy filled by a turn to large-scale institutions "capable of meeting the challenge of the city while still preserving, even enhancing community" (Bender 1975, p. 132). The legitimization of this innovation in organizational structure required an alternative discourse and explanation for what should be done with the poor.

This alternative explanation was secular in tone and medical in practice. The physical design of the asylum was shaped by the portrayal of lunacy as inconvenient at best, and contagious at worst (Scull 1981, p. 154). The removal of defective and dependent populations to the asylum and state institution was founded on medical and psychiatric premises that saw such defects as curable if properly confined and treated. The impetus for the founding of a state asylum or hospital was as much intellectual as economic, drawing upon the groundbreaking ideas of Itard and Seguin and the vehement reform efforts of Samuel Gridley Howe. The Commissioners arguing for the founding of the state lunatic hospital at Worcester, Massachusetts, in 1832 reflected this heritage when they stated: "Gratuitous education, universally diffused; laws repressing licentiousness, and encouraging industry by securing to every man his honest gains, may be primary duties in the order of performance" (Mann, Taft, and Calhoun 1832, p. 27).

Notwithstanding the social control motives of states and localities, the founding of asylums and hospitals was not wholly a state-inspired movement to confine and reform. Rather, the insane and feebleminded, the deaf, dumb, and blind, were not simply removed to be confined, but were differentiated as entitled to medical care and moral instruction. Moreover, when the "clients" are the units of analysis, the practices of these large-scale organizations "appear [sic] to have been merely colonizing the infirmity of families," with individuals often electing institutional commitment for care and instruction (Bellingham 1986, p. 552; also Clement 1985a, p. 143). The founding of the asylum and state hospital was a mutual accommodation of state and domestic needs, the former meeting the "challenge of the city" and the latter the strategic adjustment of the poor to the infirmity of the local community. The asylum for the mentally defective and the state institution for the deaf, dumb and blind constituted initial forms of state-sponsored public instruction.

The early appearance of the asylum and state hospital may be graphically portrayed when paired to the establishment of the state reformatory. In Figure 2.1, the date of establishment of state reformatories (indicated by a square) is plotted against the timing of provisions for the insane (darkened triangle) and for the deaf (circle). The anchor for the plot is the date that states opened their first asylum for the institutional care of the insane. Thus, states are arrayed in ascending order from Virginia in 1768 to Oklahoma in 1895.[2] For the deaf, the provision is the founding date of the first state hospital.[3] The figure portrays the distance in years between the events, namely, how long after the date states established the asylum they established state hospital for the deaf and the first reformatory for delinquency. The figure demonstrates the sequential order of institutional formation. The correlation between dates establishing the insane asylum and the state hospital for the deaf is .82, with a mean difference in years between the two foundings of 9.9 years and a standard deviation of 12.7. If Virginia is removed, having begun distinctively early, the standard deviation is reduced to 9.1 years. More importantly, all states except for two (Delaware and Wyoming) established the asylum prior to the reformatory, and all but five opened the hospital for the deaf prior to the reformatory. Of the seven deviant cases, four are far-western territories or young states (California, Utah, Idaho, and Wyoming). Moreover, all of these nonconforming states except for Wyoming established either the asylum or

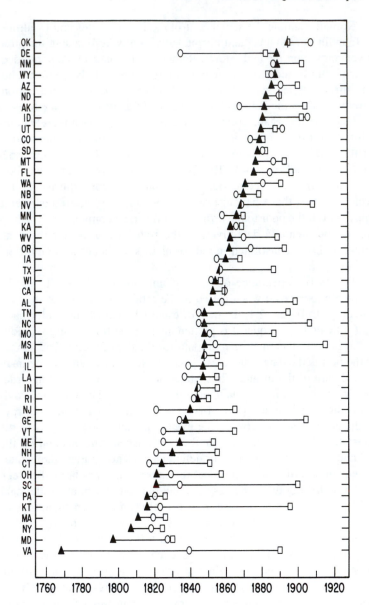

Figure 2.1 Residual Plot: Dates of Establishment for Asylums (triangle),
Hospitals for the Deaf (circle), and Reformatories (square)

the hospital for the deaf prior to the reformatory. In other ways Wyoming conforms, for it provided institutional care for the insane in neighboring Nebraska beginning in 1871.

The optimism that promoted the asylum and state hospital as correctives to defective individuals declined as institutional populations became more incurable and more culturally different. By the late nineteenth century, the educational optimism of the founding era succumbed to racial and ethnic mythology, spearheaded by a nativistic fear of the "menace of the feebleminded" and a professional turn to eugenic control (Haller 1963; Ludmerer 1972). Yet these changes reflected much more than a shift in popular tolerance and the rise of professional dominance; they assumed a fundamental growth in the coercive jurisdiction of the state (Mayer 1983, p. 31). This jurisdiction did not eclipse local communities, but coexisted above it, where state institutions defined a new and ascendant ideology of public over private, impersonal over domestic, institutional over traditional (Skowronek 1988, p. 41).

Signs of this ascendant ideology were evident by midcentury. Up to this time, the autonomy of local communities had been protected by what Robert Wiebe terms a culture of democratic "parallelism" (1984, p. 287), a concept denoting a climate of mutual tolerance that functioned to blunt the political effects of comparison between towns, cities, and states. New ventures would not be deemed late, but as innovations with the chance to catch and surpass those momentarily in the lead. This "fanning array of parallel ventures" was a source of renewable optimism that shielded an emergent national culture from the vagaries of local action and the strains of conflicting truths.

By the late nineteenth century, however, the self-sustaining climate of parallelism gave way to the "bifurcated" society, where "the translocal market increasingly challenged the family and community as a foundation for social order" (Bender 1978, p. 113). This new foundation relied increasingly on the classification of groups by criteria that defined participation in the translocal market and broader provincial culture. Enhanced by claims to scientific validity, classification schemes assumed a variety of uses, as a political rationale to discriminate new and old immigrants (Handlin 1957, pp. 74–110),[4] as a basis for jurisdictional claims made by the rising professions (Abbott 1988, pp. 303–306; Castel 1988, pp. 157–190), and for efforts to reorganize secondary schools to align with new conceptions of adolescence as a distinct age category. Delinquent misconduct, and mental and physical defect were now set apart as "at risk" categories with a broad, national recognition (Wollons 1993, p. xv). Debates over the best type of education were thereby narrowed, for the organizational form of the common school would not be troubled by populations of those of "unsound mind." In short, the movement to reform the world of the special classes "purified" the school-age population in advance of mandates for compulsory attendance at common schools, and indeed made it possible for compulsory attendance to be entertained.

Compulsory Education and Compulsory Attendance

The fact of high levels of school enrollments evident from colonial settlement confuses the distinction between compulsory schools and compulsory education, and the differences in the forms of the latter. The towns and communities of New England and southern colonies alike enacted laws for the maintenance of schools, supplemented by acts requiring parents and masters to educate their charges in preparation for a trade. As we have explored earlier, the requirements combining vocational preparation and secular instruction were embodied in "public enrollment of indenture," documents that recorded the mutual agreements or covenants that protected apprentices from neglect and abuses, while also symbolizing the town's collective presence to ensure this elementary education (Seybolt 1969, p. 23). The requirement that towns maintain a school expressed the responsibility of the state to make education available, but not to make attendance compulsory.

Compulsory instruction was, at first, the province of traditional agencies, with the debates and struggles over the organized form of education awaiting the middle and late nineteenth century. The need to make these distinctions was convincingly stated by Jernegan, a careful student of this historical sequence: "Compulsory education in the home, by parents or others, or by masters through the system of apprenticeship, with appropriate penalties for neglect, preceded by two centuries the modern idea of compelling pupils to attend organized schools for free education at public expense" (1931, p. 117). As Jernegan makes clear, the motivational basis for this original form of compulsory education was the problem of the "laboring and dependent classes." Through the principle of binding out, towns transferred poor, illegitimate, and orphaned children to agencies able to provide the rudiments of an education deemed compulsory, thereby minimizing the problem of dependency.

Within the confines of compact and homogeneous colonial communities, apprenticeship was an economical form of compulsory education. Where the focus of apprenticeship was on the problem of dependency, it produced the germ of a form of education operating parallel to the reliance on the traditional agencies of parents and masters. Children of the poor and laboring classes, subject to binding out, were in effect strangers within their own communities; their dependency threatened community solidarity. As communities grew in size and cultural diversity, the instrumental uses of binding out expanded, already legitimated as a means whereby state authority could enlarge its jurisdiction over children of dependent classes.

The dangers posed by these internal strangers were to become symbolically compressed into a single provocative term: truancy. Beginning around mid nineteenth century, the stigma of truancy was distinguished from criminal behavior, and variously defined as "voluntarily absenting oneself from school, or from employment," or acquired "from idle wanderings through public streets, frequenting saloons, skating rinks or shows, from consorting with thieves or other vicious persons, or found begging or receiving alms" (Laws of Wisconsin 1885). This moral transformation[5] of dependency to truancy was coincident with the sequence of institutional reforms, from the house of refuge movement of the 1830s (Hawes 1971, pp. 27–60; Schlossman 1977, pp. 18–32), to the reform and industrial schools between the 1850s and the turn of the century (Kett 1977, pp. 131–132; Sutton 1988; Schlossman 1977, pp. 33–54), to the Illinois Juvenile Court Act of 1899 (Fox 1970, p. 1207, passim).

The interrelationship of state reform and industrial schools, truancy, and compulsory education was particularly clear in the older, northeastern states. Exemplified most by Massachusetts and New York, the legal construction of truancy reflects the strained relation of the reformatory to the common school. The relationship was significant, for as Katz stated "the reform school is important because it was the first form of statewide compulsory education in the United States" (Katz 1968, p. 164; also Houston 1982, p. 135). The linked terms "reform" and "school" emphasize that this movement was at least as much educational as it was penal.

This view is more than interpretation. The reformatory and common school were linked intricately in the foundation case of *Ex Parte Crouse* in 1838. This decision concluded that commitments did not deprive one of civil liberty (as distinct from natural liberty) any more than did attendance at the common school (Pisciotta 1982, pp. 410–413). The reformatory and the common school were protected on similar legal grounds: both were educational places fulfilling community expectations affirmed in common law tradition. While this nonconfinement interpretation of the reform school would face challenge (most notably in *O'Connell v. Turner* in 1871, and *In re Ferrier*, 1882), the strategy of likening the reform school to the common school is key here. One outcome was the continued legitimation of state authority to intervene into conditions of youth dependency. At the same time, new and potentially threatening social innovations could be judged against the ascendancy of statute law (Hurst 1977, p. 35; Horwitz 1971, p. 309).

The sequential order placing the establishment of reform schools before the legislation of compulsory attendance is shown graphically in Figure 2.2. This figure graphs the two dates, plotting compulsory school attendance (indicated as a tick mark) against the timing of reform school formation (indicated by squares). The anchor for the plot is the date that each state established its first reformatory, beginning with New York in 1824, and ending with Mississippi in 1916. The pattern is clear: for all but eleven states, establishment of the reform school preceded enactment of compulsory school attendance at the common school. The simple correlation between these two dates is .41. It increases to .62 when the eleven "deviant" states are removed. With these states removed, the mean lag in years from reform school to compulsory attendance legislation is 21.4 years, with a standard deviation of 19.4 years. Eight of the eleven states that are "out of order" are far-western territories and new states (Arizona, Idaho, Montana, Nevada, New Mexico, Oregon, Washington, Wyoming). As latecomers to statehood, these territories and young states were without the "urban delinquent." In these cases, legislation of compulsory school attendance was largely a symbolic strategy to gain statehood (Richardson 1986). Only nine American states enacted compulsory attendance before achieving statehood, and seven of these are these deviant cases, of which six are far-western territories.

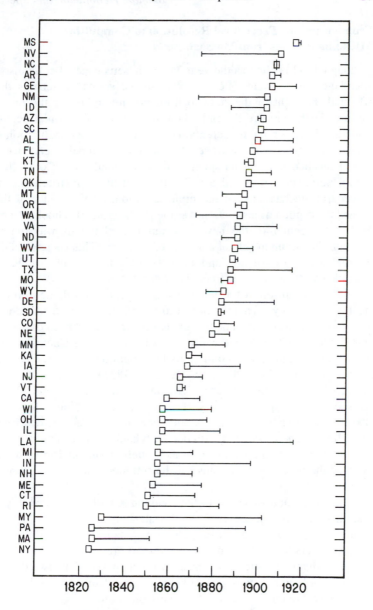

Figure 2.2. Residual Plot: Dates of Establishment of Reformatory (square) and Date of Enactment of Compulsory Attendance (mark)

Truancy and the Procedural Resolution to Compulsory Attendance: Notes from Massachusetts

Although 1852 is cited as the year Massachusetts enacted compulsory attendance, this single date can obscure the series of debates that affirmed the right of the state to limit private rights for the public welfare. Such was already embodied in the original colonial acts of 1642 and 1647 stipulating parental responsibility for the instruction of children (Clews 1899). However, the notion to compel attendance at school reached beyond the spirit of these original laws. Compelling school attendance required a refined definition of instruction, and procedural mechanisms for its implementation. At the center of this refined conception of instruction was the public issue of school truancy. And at the center of the new procedural mechanisms was the tie between the common school and the reformatory. This tie reveals the 'moral career' of truancy and its legal redefinition, out of which compulsory attendance was framed and enacted.

Early definitions of truancy were largely neutral, denoting a "technical truancy" from school enrollment. Absences from school were inoffensive and accountable, explained by parental need or gainful employment. After 1833 the practice of committing truants to the reformatory declined and complaints by schoolmasters to the Boston School Committee began to mount (Emerson 1831). Even after the first law restricting the employment of children in factories passed in 1836, rates of truancy persisted. By the 1840s, the problem of school absenteeism assumed a moral connotation; truancy was now described as "habitual" and associated with depravity and adult criminality. This moralization of truancy widened it as a public issue, and in so doing exposed the procedural weakness of the common school in relation to civil authority.

The procedural weakness of the common school was its inability to sustain complaints made by schoolmasters against parents for the habitual truancy of a child. The only sanctions available to schoolmasters were "admonition and corporal punishment." The habitual truant, enrolled but absent without parental knowledge or gainful employment, was soon likened to the "stubborn child," the older referent to one living an idle and dissolute life.

The association of the habitual truant with the stubborn child was made, nonetheless, on perceptual and not procedural grounds. The offence of growing up in idleness, without parental supervision and support, or without gainful employment, was not always the offense of truancy. The unwillingness of justices to equate truancy with stubbornness was a prophetic barrier. As the mayor of Boston noted in 1848: "If we can punish them for crime, it surely should have the power of preventing them from committing it, by giving them the habits and the education that are the surest safeguards" (Philbrick 1861, p. 219).

The legal basis that would sustain a complaint of habitual truancy was the focal concern for both schoolmasters and civil authorities. Institutionally, it was a matter between the common school and the reformatory. If commitment to a House of Refuge is defensible on preventive grounds, the implication was a redefinition of the reformatory as an "educational," as well as correctional, place. The discourse of instruction overlapped with the practice of reformation.

The power to commit youth to the reformatory on preventive grounds was the key to resolving the procedural dilemma of the common school. The combination of the common school and the reformatory served to distinguish incorrigible and delinquent youth from those enrolled in and attending the common school. As an early report on truancy noted in 1846 (Philbrick 1861):

> If the law, on the one hand, provides schools to which all the children of this city "may" go, on the other, it provides another institution to which certain children may be "made to go." Here, then, are institutions for those who 'will,' and for those who "will not" be instructed; and under one or other of these classes all our children may be arranged (pp. 212–213)

In the *Act Concerning Truant Children and Absentees from School* passed by the General Court in 1850, section 3 authorized judicial officers to place truants proved to be "without the benefit of education" in "such institution of instruction, or house of reformation as may be assigned . . . for the purpose." In the same year Boston interpreted this section with concrete procedures by affirming that "the House for the Employment and Reformation of Juvenile Offenders is hereby assigned and provided as the Institution of Instruction, House of Reformation, or suitable situation, mentioned in the third section." The resolution was an explicit redefinition of the reformatory as an adjunct educational site, linked to the common school by the criteria regulating school attendance.

With the designation of the reformatory as the adjunct educational institution, the legal basis was established for compelling attendance at the common school. This basis was founded on the union of two elements: parental responsibility and the institutional alignment between the common school and reformatory. The law of 1852 revived the spirit of the original colonial act of 1642 and its ideal of compulsory instruction. Beyond that, the principle of compulsory attendance was sanctioned by the prior regulation of truancy embodied in public acts.

The role of truancy in defining compulsory attendance continued well beyond the 1852 general statute. While the assignment of the House of Employment and Reformation as the procedural option was crucial to mandating school attendance, the linkage maintained a correctional orientation to truancy. Common schools became reliant upon municipal authorities to sustain their complaints against truant children and their parents. But this tie was an effective remedy for only the largest cities and towns. Not until 1862 did the General Court make it mandatory that all towns provide arrangements for truancy. One effect was to sharpen the distinction between habitual truancy and absenteeism. Yet more importantly, the effect was to create the "union truant school" as an alternative to the reformatory. As a consequence, truant officers became the agents of town school committees instead of municipalities (Perrin 1904–1905, p. 221–222).

The "procedural career" of truancy underscores how the formalization of common schooling was less the concern of compelling attendance and more the concern of controlling admission. As the case of Massachusetts demonstrates, the problem of truancy played a significant role in the internal differentiation of common schooling. Distinguishing truancy from crime strained the ability of common schools to enforce compulsory attendance. But the differentiation of truancy from criminal behavior was neither swift nor uniform across states. The inconsistency of continued reliance on the state reform or industrial schools for the management of noncriminal school absences contributed to the formation during the 1880s and 1890s of "truant" or "parental" schools as alternatives to reformatory commitments. These parental, or "family schools" (MacQuery 1903) became adjunct arrangements to both the reform and common school, designed to absorb truant youth by fostering an environment that would combine vocational training with common school subjects.

Although these schools shared many of the features of the reformatory, in particular, commitment for a specified length of time, they were designed nonetheless to promote the inclusion of "juvenile disorderly" youth within the boundaries of the urban school (see Report 1901; Hiatt 1915). More importantly, they evinced an important change toward the "degree of culpability" for delinquent acts (Report 1901, p. 92). By its very name, the parental school sought to replicate the family in physical design (cottage system) and in moral values. Seen this way, these schools presaged the juvenile court movement and foreshadowed the incorporation of the delinquent and special worlds in common schooling.

THE LEGACY OF THE CHILDREN'S AID SOCIETY: CHILD SAVING AND THE JUVENILE COURT

Much like the design of the parental school, the Illinois Juvenile Court Act of 1899 was passed to "regulate the treatment and control of dependent, neglected and delinquent children." This Act was as consequential for the reformatory as it was significant for the education of delinquent youth. The formation of a juvenile court and probation system bore similarities to the intent of Charles Loring Brace's Children's Aid Society, for it represented a turn away from the dominant penal approach to delinquency, attacking both the rationale and practice of institutionalizing youth. What was novel, however, was the principle of *parens patriae* that expressed the interests of the state to intervene authoritatively on behalf of children to protect their welfare. Sanctioned by this principle, the enlarged power of the state was nonetheless cast in a discourse that subordinated the delinquent or criminal act to the consideration of prior circumstances that contributed to that conduct. The suspension of due process cannot, however, be interpreted as a coercive strategy of social control. On the contrary, the turn away from confinement was a turn toward rehabilitation and prevention, a "legalized paternalism" with the family and school serving as primary models (see Grossberg 1993, p. 121). As Donzelot aptly summarized: "The educative vocation of the judicial apparatus arose when it became obvious that the penal system was inadequate to halt the substantial flood of "problem children," of all those adolescents who poured into the interstices between the old family order and the new educational order, taking advantage of the spaces that still remained in the junction of the two" (1979, p. 116; also Hogan 1985, p. 64). The popularity of the juvenile court movement derived from its success as a compromise of interests: the reach of state powers into the welfare of children was extended while the traditional authority of families and communities was preserved.

Yet beyond the lead of Chicago and other cities, the discourse of the juvenile court movement offers little explanation for the spread of this innovation across states. As Sutton (1985) has demonstrated, the rate or propensity of states to adopt the juvenile court, indicated by the timing of statute legislation, was not propelled by structural or "modernization" variables (such as percent urban, value of manufactured goods, rate of juvenile incarceration, number of state government officers). Nor was its diffusion propelled by the strength of a state's charity organization system (having a Charity board by 1900, level of social welfare spending). Rather, the diffusion of the juvenile court accelerated through time; as more states adopted the court, others were induced to adopt it as well.

In light of these findings, Sutton proposes that adoption of the juvenile court was not so much a real substantive change in the legal status of children, as it was a change in the "ceremonial" relation between state authority and delinquency. In his terms, the juvenile court "was primarily a shell of legal ritual within which states renewed and enacted their commitment to discretionary social control over children" (p. 142). Yet this interpretation must not dispel the arguments and struggles of the child-saving movement or of charity organization reformers. Rather, the discourse of rehabilitation and prevention, and of traditional family authority, provided the rationale for the changed relation between state authority and delinquency. As Sutton phrased it, the importance of the juvenile court "lies in the fact that it provided a setting in which the routine practices of child-saving established in the nineteenth century could be continued in a more legitimate form" (p. 108).

But the setting of these practices is not confined to the juvenile court. This is suggested by one finding in Sutton's analysis: against the weakness of structural and organizational variables, the level of school attendance has a strong and resilient effect on the rate of adoption. This suggests that the level of school attendance sets the parameters for the continuation of this "discretionary control" over children. The legal and procedural changes between delinquency and state authority take much of their content from "common schooling," conceived here as a trinary system of three worlds.

CONCLUSIONS

The formalization of common schooling was defined by the enactment of compulsory attendance. These laws were not a uniform event but were, as this chapter emphasizes, passed across a 66–year span of time, beginning with Massachusetts in 1852 and ending with Mississippi in 1918. This variation in the timing of enactment is a significant point of American educational history, for the date of legislating this law committed a state, or territory, to enlarging a common education on a nonvoluntary basis. It is with some paradox that the cessation of voluntary schooling brought the need to define the boundary of a school system to the forefront. Because compulsory attendance laws had little to do with enlarging attendance, their real social and legal intent was to define the rules of access to a publicly supported education. The formalization of a common schooling, the fulfillment of Horace Mann's vision, was nonetheless founded on the specification of powers to exempt exceptional children and to expel delinquent youth.

The enactment of compulsory attendance defined the boundary of a common school system by way of these powers. The institutional boundary of common schooling embraced the "three worlds" of those admitted into common schools, those committed to reformatories, and those residing in schools for exceptional children. In effect, Samuel Gridley Howe's vision of a "chain of common schools" was formally enacted. The circles of this chain were, however, quite unequal. Compulsory attendance laws were explicitly designed to protect admission to public schools.

With language that defined the rules of access, compulsory attendance laws signified a new discourse that centered around who was educable and who was not. Again it is with some paradox that the intent of these laws contravened so directly the beliefs and reform efforts of Mann and Howe. Against their beliefs in a universal educability, in a continuation of abilities as opposed to a hierarchy of "natural divisions," the formalization of common schooling set into motion a new focus of debate. The specter of an institutional society was no longer a distant fear; it was the preoccupation of the late nineteenth century. With compulsory attendance, the specter became the concentration of youth with incompatible capacities and conditions.

Against the vision of Mann and Howe, if those of limited capacity were allowed admission to common schools, their "dispersion" among normal children would not mitigate their condition but undermine the purpose and functioning of a common schooling. If the dawn of special education came with a defiance against natural divisions, the field of special education arose with a youthful embrace of classification and division. The site of this incipient field was the special class constructed as a means to absorb the unanticipated consequences of formalizing the ideal of a common schooling.

I now turn to the first decades of this century and build the narrative of this construction of special classes. As special education assumes its place within this trinary structure of common schooling, early categories are stamped by institutional linkages, specifically delinquency and the ties to male reformatories.

NOTES

1. Foucault's precise concept is *discursive formation*. The merit of such a concept is how it captures the unity of seemingly dispersed conditions and events that is made over time through "rules of formation" (Foucault 1972). Foucault's imagery of dispersion is crucial, on both conceptual and methodological grounds. While intentionally abstract, the imagery of dispersion is nonetheless demandingly empirical, for the "objects" composing a discursive formation occupy different locations in both space and time, change at different rates, and possess different capacities to relate to other objects in the "field" of discourse.

In his empirical study of the medical clinic (Foucault 1975), Foucault demonstrated how series of conflicts "passed through" different arenas, one through medical technology, another through political consciousness, another through the economy (see Lemert and Gillan 1982, p. 36). Similarly, the debates and conflicts that preceded the passage of compulsory attendance reflected the historical long-term erosion of traditional mechanisms that integrated local communities to the state. Yet as these traditional mechanisms eroded, conflicts and struggles over schooling now passed through disparate arenas. The debates over school attendance became symptomatic of the state's jurisdiction over once local matters of economic dependence and social deviance. These long-term struggles expanded the boundary of discourse over schooling and instruction, emerging by late nineteenth century as a *formation* that joined previously disparate arenas and their specific practices.

Crucial to the "unity" of a new discourse are the *rules of formation*, of which Foucault identified four: rules for the formation of objects, of enunciative modalities, of concepts, and of strategies. Space does not permit an elaboration of these, but only to note again the useful parallels between these rules and those events that formalized the boundaries that distinguished, while at the same time integrated, the common, delinquent, and special worlds. The mandate of compulsory attendance is but one rule of formation. The language refining the educability of the delinquent and the special *relative* to the pupils in the world of common schooling represent rules of enunciative modalities, and of concepts of equal significance to compulsory attendance. While this discourse about educability was to become highly formalized with mental testing and pupil classification, its historical beginnings are much earlier. As Canguilhem revealed about the origins of Norm and Normal, "But the very term normal has passed into popular language and has been naturalized there starting with the specific vocabularies of two institutions, the pedagogical institution and the hospital whose reforms, at least in France, coincided under the effect of the same cause, the French Revolution" (1991, p. 237). As institutions are sequentially related, so are their vocabularies.

2. The technique of "residual plots" for historical data is used by Sutton (1988). Similarities of topic and analysis enhance comparisons of this work with his. For a discussion of sequential analysis of historical events, particularly as they move toward a later "convergence," see Abbott (1983).

3. The dates for state insane asylums are taken from Hurd (1973), volumes 2 and 3. The year in which a state hospital or asylum was opened marks the establishment of an actual institution within the boundaries of the state. Although an accurate timing for physical sites, this is a conservative measurement for some states that supported the institutional care of their insane in neighboring states. Dates for state provisions for the deaf, dumb, and blind are taken from Best (1914).

4. With reference to old versus new immigrants, Ludmerer notes: "The late nineteenth century witnessed the beginning of social discrimination in America and the rise of 'society' to exclude the new" (1972, pp. 24-25; also 87-90). This "rise of society" or "translocal market" becomes an ideological reference, a tool for eugenic interests to classify and segregate defective populations.

5. We speak of "moral transformation" for it captures the focus and intent of common schooling relative to the growing problem of economic dependency. In his analysis of the crisis of apprenticeship in France, Colin

Heywood refers to the "moralization" of the working class and how "the institution destined to fill the moral and intellectual void allegedly opening up in the lives of working class children was the elementary school" (see Heywood 1988, p. 202; also Johnson 1970, p. 116). The moral power of the elementary school was also invoked to promote the passage of child labor legislation, as a theme of broad appeal to parents, manufacturers, and governmental officials.

A similar instance of moral transformation is the British case, where social class divisions penetrate deeply into the structure of education. For Britain, the "dame and common-day school" was the criterion of popular education, but against this the extensive network of working-class private schools was little seen and undercounted. The consequence was an estimated discrepancy of 135,893 enumerated "scholars" between the Education Census of 1851 and the Population Census, the "product of a series of encounters between two distinctive, class-based educational cultures" (Gardner 1984, p. 71). This discrepancy in census enumerations of scholars was symptomatic of deeper constraints on what constituted a "school." The implications of this accounting error reach into scholarly interpretations of mass education itself. The obscurity of working class private instruction and its network of schools reinforces an exaggeration of the 1870 Education Act as the beginning of mass education, and subsequently "[we] extol the expansion of publicly provided schooling after 1870 while we have remained ignorant of the catastrophic decline in private elementary schooling in the same period" (Gardner 1984, p. 189). The implementation of the Education Act implied a "moral transformation," for it proceeded against working class schools by evaluating their "efficiency," relying on local sanitary authorities, and making such judgments with laws regulating public health rather than with educational criteria (pp. 190-194). For matters of scholarly accuracy, the Education Act of 1870 marks the *formalization* of mass education by imposing state authority over working class private schools, while judiciously protecting middle class counterparts. The British system of mass education, commonly said to begin in 1870, is "late" only if the scope and efficiency of working class schooling is ignored.

CHAPTER 3

The Dilemma of Compulsory Attendance and the Construction of the Special Class

INTRODUCTION

The impact of compulsory attendance legislation on special education was direct. As Chapter 2 demonstrated, the words "compulsory school attendance" are misleading, for these laws had little to do with compelling attendance. Enacting these laws established the institutional boundary of a state system of public education, doing so by exempting physically and mentally exceptional children and authorizing schools to expel juvenile disorderly youth.

Thus when schooling ceased to be voluntary, state (and territorial) authorities became directly concerned with defining the conditions for admission to public schools. Yet it is important not to attribute an immediate impact to these laws (see Tyack 1976). If much of their immediate influence was symbolic, this itself is relevant to the "failure" of schools to successfully detect and exclude exceptional and delinquent youth. Precisely because the rules defining admission to a public school were more symbolic than enforceable, schools established the "special class" as the means to absorb those who entered but who could not move easily through the graded curriculum.

We have spoken of the "dawn" of special education, and have explored the essential prompt to its organizational beginnings. In this chapter, I examine in more detail the historical construction of the special class for the instruction of exceptional children within public education. Indeed the initial force behind this construction was the legislation of compulsory attendance, signifying a mandate that states receive all eligible children of school age. From this act forward, states increasingly confronted the problems of pupils unable to progress as expected by their age. Precisely because of the democratic vulnerability of a common schooling, the deviancies of physical and mental handicap persistently intruded upon instruction, however indirectly. As I have shown, the legislation of compulsory universal education occurred only after these boundary dilemmas were solved by the development of state-funded institutions for physically, mentally, and socially exceptional children. The organizational dilemmas of a democratizing public education heightened concerns and sharpened conflicts over the efficiency of city schools, and promoted a wide interest in plans for student classification and grading that could accommodate a diverse school-age population. In spite of a number of alternatives which were proposed and in practice, the special class emerged as the dominant strategy and by 1917 was bolstered by the scientific promise of intelligence testing.

This chapter elaborates upon the organizational dilemmas generated by enacting compulsory attendance. The focus is the first two decades of the twentieth century, which compressed a series of events that gave institutional recognition and meaning to the initial category of a special education: the Backward child. The construction of this category marks the "genesis" of special education as a pedagogical enterprise, situated as I have argued, between the residential population and the school population of exceptional children. I do not speak of the "origins" or the "rise" of special education (cf. Tomlinson 1982; Lazerson 1983; Carrier 1986b; Milofsky 1986). Rather, the term "genesis" intends to emphasize the contingent nature of historical events and circumstances that secured the special class and the education of exceptional children within the common school. Although the events constituted a long series that extended across the nineteenth century, the critical circumstances were compressed into the first two decades of the twentieth century. The broader context was the antinomy between a democratic access to common schooling and the requirement for efficient school organization. The focus is deliberately "partial," concentrating on the crucial decades that defined the early categories of special education.[1] From this focus, however, we learn the roots of features that persist to the present. One of these features is the degree to which gender was made a part of the structure and content of special education.

From this historical foundation, the chapter closes with a state-level statistical analysis of variable levels of Backward children. Of particular interest is the gender content of this initial category, how it was informed by a cultural and instructional prejudice toward "bad boys" and strengthened by an institutional tie between urban schools and male reformatories. I explore this with data on male and female Backward children for 1927.

THE HISTORICAL NARRATIVE: MANDATES, CONFLICTS AND TURNING POINTS

The Nineteenth-Century Institutional Order: Links in the Chain of Common Schooling

The decline in the capacity of apprenticeship to care for and protect poor and defective minors foretells the sequence of events that established the "institutional state" (Katz 1978). As a theory of pedagogy, the long-term influence of apprenticeship is evident in the persistence of vocational and scientific education. In much of European educational history, vocational and scientific education developed in separate schools and institutes outside of a liberal education, whether private or state supported. In the American case, however, the decline of apprenticeship was not followed by the creation of hierarchically separate, specialized institutions devoted to manual and industrial training.[2]

During the 1880s, the case for a broadened role of industrial education dominated debates at yearly conventions of the National Educational Association (NEA). What is significant is the pedagogical defense of manual training on grounds that it was an integral part of a youth's general intellectual development, and not a distinct mode of learning. Against claims that manual training was a unique mode of learning, different from a liberal education in both content and instructional form, its defense was anchored in references to the historical function of apprenticeship generally, and to its educational purpose specifically.

The motivation to establish hospitals for the physically and mentally defective, reformatories for the delinquent and a broadened curriculum to encompass manual training resulted in an institutional order that was more differentiated than hierarchical, resting on the relative administrative autonomy of local trustees. This loosely coupled array of schools encompassed a range of private and semipublic facilities, varying in name from home to public boarding school to state institution. As noted, such residential schools resisted becoming "asylums" for incurables, assiduously maintaining their place in Samuel Gridley Howe's desired "chain" of a common schooling. Their essential purpose was educational, bolstered by an optimistic ideology that viewed the feebleminded as "improvable." As such, the deaf, blind, and feebleminded were pupils.

The growth of this chain of schools and institutions throughout the nineteenth century followed a discernible pattern, initiated first through private and philanthropic efforts, then to state institutions, and finally to city school systems (McDonald 1915, p. 104). As private and philanthropic efforts inherited the traditional functions of apprenticeship, which were then transferred to state institutions, the authority to intervene on behalf of the child was increasingly assumed by the state. The path from apprenticeship to state institutions was in many respects a "rationalization" of binding out, a transposition of this traditional authority into formal institutions. In doing so, the reach of this authority was extended to populations that were not effectively accommodated by traditional arrangements.

Gender, Deviance and Classification: The Reform School as Model

With the passage of compulsory school attendance, the boundary of common schooling was affirmed in ways that voluntary enrollment could not achieve. By specifying physical and mental deviations as grounds for exemption, states affirmed the boundary between residential facilities for exceptional children and a common school education. By specifying circumstances of poverty or distance from a nearest traveled road, schools modified their responsibility to problems of economic dependency and public welfare.

As long as schooling remained voluntary, there was little need to devise organizational means to accommodate diverse, disorderly, or uneducable pupils. Yet once states mandated attendance, there was at least the formal command that schools accept all children of legal age. To meet the formal dictates of compulsory attendance, school created the "ungraded class." Poor, physically unkempt, and disorderly children

were assigned to ungraded classes as a proper exercise of in loco parentis. The ungraded class was common to urban school systems during
the late nineteenth century (Van Sickle, Witmer and Ayres 1911;
Tropea 1987) and later become the "special class" for exceptional children.

Compulsory attendance necessitated a shared responsibility
between parental and school authority, based in the concept of "in loco
parentis". Schools were required to conduct a census of those enrolled
and to monitor their attendance. Parents were charged with the
responsibility of bringing their children to school, and were subject to
fines for failure to do so. In spite of this mutual responsibility, the
enforcement capacity of schools was weak, diminishing any threat
against parental noncompliance. As a consequence, the status offense of
"habitual truancy" emerged to contend with those children who defied
both parental and school efforts to bring them to school. Once
attendance became compulsory, absenting oneself from school took on
a potential legal consequence. Truancy was never sharply defined, for it
overlapped delinquent illegalities with educationally relevant moral
misconduct. Initially, those youth who were "vicious and immoral" in
character, found begging or frequenting immoral places, could be
excluded from attendance and committed to the state reform or
industrial school.

In their classic study of the Chicago schools, Abbott and
Breckinridge (1917) distinguished between truancy and nonattendance.
There could be several reasons for nonattendance, including sickness,
family death, church attendance, or work at home. Truancy, which
accounted for only some 5% of the total number of nonattendance cases
in Chicago schools, was a willful absence from school without the
knowledge or consent of the parent. Truancy belied a significant gender
difference. Out of a total of 5,659 youth brought to the Chicago
Juvenile Court in 1917 as truants, only 37 were girls. "Habitual
truancy" was linked to the Juvenile Court, which in turn was the
referral agency for commitment to the Parental School. As the
intermediate institution between the common school and the
reformatory, the Parental School was designed for "truant boys," for
"no provision was made for girls" (Abbott and Breckinridge, p. 208).
For girls, absence from school was largely excused by reason of
"helping in [her] father's shop, taking care of the baby, caring for her
sick mother, or doing some other household task" (Abbott and

Breckinridge 1917, p. 206). Such reasons for nonattendance and truancy were more often deemed socially benevolent and attributable to parental failings.

By century's end, these deviations were compressed into the morally resonant category of the Backward child. The resonance of this new category lay in its capacity to elude precise definition. The Backward child was many things: slow in mind and often defective in body, poor in family background and lazy but defiant in school. But above all these things, the Backward child was "bad" and male. Backwardness and badness were now seen as causally related, with the direction eminently clear: "A boy is Backward because he is bad" (Holmes 1915, p. 83; also Wallin 1924, pp. 75–85). This causal relation was the link back to habitual truancy.

The observations on truancy and nonattendance reported by Abbott and Breckinridge for Chicago reflected a broader pattern of how gender influenced the definition and treatment of delinquent and criminal deviancy. This difference in perception and treatment is evident in the timing of separate institutions established for males and females. A state's legislation for its first reform school was almost exclusively for white males. For girls, the formation of the "industrial school" was the institutional counterpart to the male reformatory.

The need for separate institutions stemmed from the putative differences in nature between boys and girls. Where the boy is "bold, aggressive, active, gregarious," the girl is "self-centered . . . having a less vital grasp of the real and practical world," but possessing a "strong idealizing sense" that should be wisely directed (Dewson and Hart 1910, p. 28). These differences called for alternative treatment strategies that could not be implemented if the sexes were committed to the same institution:

> The girl needs a separate school, an individual room, studious development of her individuality, training in self-protection, initiative, in wise spending of money, housewifery, domestic science including plain sewing, dressmaking and millinery, the care of the sick, and the care of infants. (p. 29)

Principles of rehabilitation and vocational guidance were ushered in with the Juvenile Court in which the treatment of delinquency broke from the penalogical emphasis of early institutions. But the spirit of these new principles was itself guided by the conceptions of proper gender roles. For boys, the reform school should be organized around the mastery of skills that were largely mechanical and that would lead to employment and economic independence. For girls, the industrial school should be likened after the home, instructing girls in those domestic skills that "came early to the young housewife." As Brenzel has shown for the Lancaster Industrial School for Girls (Massachusetts), the initial purpose of reform and education was "dropped in favor or jobs," turning it into a "British-style vocational school" (Brenzel 1983, p. 146).[3]

The transformation of the reformatory and industrial school toward a vocational purpose was a change as significant for the common school as it was for reformatory institutions. The broader implications of the life and administration of reform schools was articulated by David Snedden in a doctoral thesis submitted to Columbia University in 1907. Snedden would soon become a prominent national figure in American education, through his many writings as a professor at Columbia and from his position as Commissioner of Education in Massachusetts (1909 to 1916). In his doctoral thesis he advanced a bold thesis: the "educational work" of the reform school had achieved much that could be of benefit to the common school. This early thesis extended into his subsequent work and kindled his practical efforts to reform the organization and administration of American education generally.

Two points were of particular relevance. First, the fact that delinquent boys were separated from parents and friends required reformatories to develop a pedagogy of broader scope than found in the common school. Instruction had to attend to the whole child, joining literary instruction to practical and vocational training. It was the latter especially that was deficient in the common school.

Second, out of this contrast in pedagogy Snedden advanced a proposition that would become the cause celebre of educational debate and reform in subsequent years. Snedden proposed that the reform school had evolved a system of classification that was superior to the simple divisions by grade found in the common school. For the reformatory, the "group" was the unit, and the bases of classification were differences in moral character and physical or mental capability. The reform schools had "discovered" the effectiveness of grouping boys who were "slow," or who were "hardened and vicious," and to tailor educational instruction to them as a unit. The guiding principle behind these classification was "contagion," for segregation was necessary to protect against the spread of moral depravity, and to separate along obvious physical and mental difference.

The classifications developed within the reform school were mirrored in the common school's ungraded or special class for truants and incorrigibles. This organizational connection was given some national priority by the Commonwealth Fund's forceful promotion of the "Program for the Prevention of Juvenile Delinquency" in 1921 (Smith 1922, pp. 168–174). The supportive base of this effort was far reaching, linking the Public Education Association of New York (PEA), the National Committee for Mental Hygiene, the New York School of Social Work, and the Joint Committee on Methods of Preventing Delinquency (see Cohen 1964, p. 120). Such a national strategy to prevent delinquency was to be entrusted to visiting teachers and psychiatric social workers, both of whom would operate in local schools to change attitudes and practices toward the socially maladjusted student. The child guidance clinic was the experimental arm of this strategy, and served as the intermediate bridge between delinquency and the common school (Martens 1939). Although by 1930 the Commonwealth Fund had formally abandoned its role in delinquency prevention, and the visiting teachers movement had waned as well, the legacy of these progressive reforms was in place: public schools had been sufficiently socialized to the precepts of intervention and treatment of social maladjustment (Thomas and Thomas 1928, ch. 5; also Eliot 1925, p. 74).

Resolving the Antinomy of Democracy and Efficiency: The Alliance of Vocationalism and Mental Testing

At the beginning of the visiting teachers movement in 1906, the prospect of vocational education and guidance serving as institutional mediator between the industrial training of juvenile reformatories and the general instruction of common schooling was as yet too early to foresee. As Snedden himself observed, "It is yet too early to say just what form industrial work will finally assume in the public school system" (1907, p. 382). As debates were beginning over vocational education, city school systems began to recognize and attend to inefficiency in pupil classification and promotion. The presumed inefficiency of city schools became an issue that resonated with alarming consequences (Callahan 1962). The 1909 statistical survey of school inefficiency by Leonard Ayres, published as *Laggards in Our Schools*, was especially influential. From his survey of city school systems, Ayres estimated that nearly 34% of all elementary school children were "retarded," defined more than two years older than the expected age for each grade. The statistical investigations by Ayres and others (cf. Thorndike 1908; Strayer 1911) informed policy decisions that would help guide the reform of schools, one of which was the call for the "special class."

The national stature of these investigations was further stimulus to a systematic academic inquiry into the problems of retardation in city school systems. Most representative of this was the ten-volume "School Efficiency Series" edited by Paul Hanus of Harvard (see Hanus 1913). With an initial prompting from the Committee on School Inquiry of New York, these volumes addressed problems of school supervision and organization with an eye to their commonality across cities and states. Despite differences across city school systems, one problem seemed to unite them most: the problem of detecting and classifying mentally defective pupils. The significance of this issue was made most clear with the volume submitted by Henry Goddard, then Director of the Department of Research of the Training School for Feebleminded Children in Vineland, New Jersey (Goddard 1915). Goddard's volume inserted the problem of feebleminded school children directly into the issue of school efficiency, and did so with two specific policy recommendations.

First, pupils must be classified into four categories. Goddard drew divisions between normal and supernormal (gifted) pupils, and between the "merely Backward" and the "feebleminded." The "merely Backward" were pupils whose school problems were tied to environmental conditions. To improve the efficiency of schools, the need was pressing to identify and remove feebleminded children. As Goddard noted, this could be effected only by those familiar with this population, and trained in the new Binet-Simon scale of intelligence. Second, for Goddard the only viable policy option was to retain these children *within* the city school, and to entrust their supervision to a Superintendent of Schools and Classes for Defectives.

Henry Goddard set a precedent for the significant stage in the genesis of special education (see Zenderland 1987). This stage was the mental testing movement generally, and its success in installing a pupil classification system that carried the legitimacy of science. The figure most central to this was Stanford University's Lewis Terman who both popularized and institutionalized Alfred Binet's work with the concept of IQ.

The breadth of Terman's influence upon the testing movement is well established (Marks 1974; Fass 1980; Chapman 1988). Terman confirmed the statistical presence of feebleminded children among the pupil population. From his surveys of California school systems, Terman reported a ratio of 2% or higher, consistent with figures estimated by Goddard for eastern cities. Thus California was no exception, but foreshadowed the problem of feebleminded children as a "menace" of national scope.

The entirety of Terman's academic work was on the measurement of human differences, especially the exceptional cases of mental subnormality. But for Terman the promise of intelligence testing in schools was founded on a larger social purpose: to identify the feebleminded is to distinguish those who lack the hereditary potential to acquire moral conduct from school knowledge (see Marks 1974, p. 342). Here Terman's imagery of a statistically small but disproportionately menacing number of feebleminded children complemented the Progressive Era's alarm over inefficiency. If the capacity to engage in moral conduct is given by the heritability of intelligence, the problem of "inefficiency" is a matter of finding those who are uneducable. From Ayres's "retardation" to Terman's "feebleminded" there is effected an important conceptual transformation. A term once denoting organizational inefficiency was now redefined as intellectual incapacity.

Terman's quest to distinguish those who could not profit from school knowledge led him, like Ayres, to promote the special class. But with the scientific guidance of intelligence testing, the traditional mechanism of an ungraded or special class took on new meaning. For Terman the larger concern was the "conservation of talent," the need to reorganize schools such that instruction would conform to the variety of individual differences. This required a differentiated school curriculum, a system of tracks that would at once segregate the mentally subnormal while protecting the intellectually gifted.[4] Terman's ideal and practical vision of mental testing in schools offered some resolution to the historic conflict that has shaped American education: the antinomy between democratic access to a common schooling, yet one administered with organizational efficiency.

However, mental testing was not sufficient, by itself, to resolve the antinomy. Resolution required a rationale for pupil classification directed beyond the immediate needs of schools. This was given by the renaissance of vocational education, now redefined as vocational guidance in a changed occupational world (Sears 1925, ch. 13). As Terman himself advised the San Luis Obispo school system, the remedy of the special class was "good argument for the introduction of manual training [and] domestic science" (Terman 1912, p. 137). David Snedden's observations of 1907 seemed prophetic indeed. The form "industrial work" would finally assume now hinged on whether it would be outside or within the public school system.

The resurgence of vocational education during the early years of the twentieth century would certainly profit from the attacks on school inefficiency. Yet the immediate roots of this resurgence were in the settlement house movement. Out of this reform movement was born the National Society for the Promotion of Industrial Education (NSPIE) in 1906, which had such well-known figures as Jane Addams as originating members of its board of directors (Stephens 1970, pp. 53–67; also Cohen 1968; Fisher 1967). Its first secretary was Charles Prosser, who left his work under then Commissioner Snedden in Massachusetts. The NSPIE exerted a national influence, but this national focus on vocational education was secondary to its role in defining the location of vocational education.

Amidst the attacks on school inefficiency, and against the context of an expanding industrial economy, the construction of a "dual system" that would distinguish trade and academic instruction re-emerged as a topic of debate, and in a climate of concern over school efficiency it represented an attractive option of reform. In its review of manual training programs in Massachusetts, the important Douglas Commission ended with a recommendation for "distinctive industrial schools separated entirely from the public school system" (Lazerson and Grubb 1974, p. 75). Such prominent figures as David Snedden and Harvard President Charles Eliot, contrasting figures in other respects, advocated separate systems of instruction, one to impart trade and industrial skills, another to impart academic preparation. Snedden contrasted an education for "consumers" with an education for "producers," introducing a dividing line between a literary or general education and a practical or vocational education. The contrast between consumers and producers was a fundamental one, for the content of instruction was basic to where one was destined to be in life.

Charles Eliot's call commanded the most attention, for it became the focal point of the political debate over vocational and academic education. In his address to the NSPIE delivered in 1908 (Eliot 1908), Eliot advocated a system of trade schools that would be separate from the public schools and that would meet the practical demands of a diversifying occupational system. These demands were not being met by a school system that emphasized liberal, academic instruction to the neglect of skills that must prepare youth to be actual "journeymen for the trades." But Eliot's call for a separate system of trade schools enlarged the debate beyond even his own inclinations. The new and pragmatic dilemma facing schools was how students would be selected into a trade and vocational preparation. To this question Eliot introduced the crisp but volatile notion of "probable destiny," connoting a tone of determinism between a student's background and his or her appropriate occupational placement. With the notoriety given to Eliot's address, the specter of a "separate system" of trade and vocational schools gained national attention.

Over the next few years the debate over vocational education centered on the locus of authority, whether the state public school system would extend provisions and retain control, or local boards would be empowered to initiate vocational schools independent of state powers, both regulatory and financial. The practical outcomes of the debate ranged from models of state partnership with local boards, as exemplified by laws in Massachusetts (1909) and New York (1910), to Wisconsin's Act of 1911 establishing a "dual system" that invested full control over vocational education in the hands of a State Board of Industrial Education (Wirth 1972, pp. 61–62; also Bennett 1937, p. 541). While Wisconsin was an exception, the salience of this struggle was broad enough that in its annual meeting of 1913 the NEA defined it as "unit vs. dual control."

The proposals for a separate system of trade schools were met by concerted opposition, most convincingly from academic figures like John Dewey (Dewey 1913) and from organized labor (Lazerson and Grubb 1974, pp. 101–115). But the struggle over trade schools came to a test case in the celebrated Cooley Bill introduced in Chicago in 1914 and 1915. Inspired by the Wisconsin Act, and sponsored by the

Commercial Club and other business organizations, the bill explicitly sought a dual system, one general and another vocational (Krug 1964, p. 147; Wirth 1972, p. 211). In spite of its strong base of support in business and manufacturing interests, it was nonetheless defeated. The defeat of the Cooley Bill may be taken as a significant turning point in the institutional direction of American education (Rubinson 1986, pp. 541–542), for the defeat signaled that vocational education should properly be located within public schools and should coexist with academic instruction.

With the defeat of the Cooley Bill, the momentum turned to the public schools and the viability of expanding vocational preparation as elective courses and programs. The culmination of this momentum was the federal passage of the Smith-Hughes Act in 1917 marking a national commmitment to vocational education within public schools.[5] The federal sponsorhip of vocational education released support to states that would augment the role of schools in pupil guidance generally, and guidance toward careers particularly. By implication, such sponsorship contributed to the retention of students who often entered school late, were laggard in their progress, and departed early. The problems of "over-age" and truant pupils, those of Backward social origins, and those of "subnormal" ability, became confounded with the vocationalization of education. The historically older "ungraded class" assumed an organizational use with vocational guidance. And in so doing, the practice of managing school deviance assumed an organizational function with the more purposeful policy of career guidance. The distinctive purpose of career guidance was stated most eloquently by the intellectual scion of American education, John Dewey: "An occupation is a continuous activity having a purpose," and "education through occupations consequently combines within itself more of the factors conducive to learning than any other method" (Dewey 1916/1929, p. 361).

The "vocationalization" of education modified a time-honored causal relation espoused by earlier manual and industrial education (Grubb and Lazerson 1975). The claim that the imparting of skills was the antecedent preparation to a trade was now modified, for the volatility of the job market greatly jeopardized that claim. Preparation must be more adaptive to the unpredictable demands of the job market (Kantor and Tyack 1982, passim).

This necessary deference to the job market once again highlighted the role of gender in vocational education. The return of gender to vocational education came from the home economics movement and through the powerful American Home Economics Association (AHEA), founded in 1908. The rise of home economics was a response to a changing job market that opened new occupational avenues to women. But much like the differentiation within juvenile reformatories, these occupational avenues were cast in traditional terms, to protect against job competition between males and females. For the years prior to Smith-Hughes, the focus of a vocational education for women was on the skills of "domestic science," preparing girls to enter homes of their own. After Smith-Hughes, the skills of domestic science were extended to secretarial and related office work, consciously preparing girls "for work in distinctly feminine occupations" (NEA 1910; also Rury 1991, pp. 141–147; Fritschner 1977, p. 230). The association of home economics with the politics of vocational education ensured that its curriculum would be differentiated along gender lines. As office work became feminized, female enrollments in commercial education rose sharply (Weiss 1981, p. 413), drawing a gender distinction between commercial and industrial education (Kantor 1988, pp. 59–65). The concentration of girls in commercial classes appeared to aggravate the already low retention of boys in secondary schools. This "boy problem" (Hansot and Tyack 1990, ch. 7) heightened the motive for a vocational reform of the curriculum generally, but one that would serve the different occupational needs of male and female students.

The alliance of AHEA with the NSPIE forged the political base necessary for passage of Smith-Hughes. In spite of an initial reluctance by the AHEA to identify home economics with legislation for vocational education (Palmer 1989, p. 92), the alliance solidified the precarious unity of the NSPIE, business (National Association of Manufacturers —NAM), labor (American Federation of Labor—AFL) and education (National Education Association—NEA) to achieve federal funding for three vocational areas: agriculture, arts and industries, and home economics.

Theoretical Summary: The "Age" of State School Systems

Passage of compulsory attendance marks the turning point in the institutional genesis of special education (Sarason and Doris 1979). The attendance laws committed state school system to the support and administration of a *system* of public education. Although these laws had no intention to compel attendance and were largely unenforceable at first (Tyack 1976), their significance was to be considerably more than some symbolic expression of state authority. In spite of legislative second thoughts and pockets of local resistance, the law compelled efforts to be coordinated and to distribute a common schooling to a school-age population with increasing economic efficiency. Enactment of compulsory attendance defined the "birth" of a state school system; the time of enactment marks the *institutional age* of state school systems (Richardson 1984). Accordingly, Massachusetts is the "oldest" state school system by enacting first in 1852 and Mississippi is the "youngest" by enacting last in 1918. Each state school system has, therefore, an *institutional age* defined by its date of passing compulsory attendance. In addition to this absolute year, however, is the position a state has within the 66–year time period that elapsed before all states formalized school attendance. To pass the law near the lead year of 1852 is to be closer to the ideas and arguments that inaugurated this "movement" in Massachusetts. To be "late" in the duration time is to do so with more remove from these ideas, or with more accumulated forms of resistance. Most exemplary is the South, for all but two southern states passed compulsory attendance legislation after 1900 and many with considerable reluctance.

By conceiving of compulsory attendance as measuring the age of state school systems, special education is reconceived: its own growth is a function of the "temporal distance" from the date of enactment. The democratic obligation to receive (at least nominally) all eligible children of schoolage made conspicuously visible those pupils who could not move easily through the grades. During the early years of this century, when nearly all states had enacted compulsory attendance, the inefficiency of "laggard" students in city schools was amplified as a national concern. Importantly, a major part of the solution to this problem was imported from outside the common school. By adapting the classification scheme long practiced by juvenile reformatories, public schools began to accommodate the truant and incorrigible pupil, as well as the Backward and feebleminded. By relying on the reform school as the institutional model, the "ungraded class" was implanted as the core unit of a special education for exceptional children.

Ultimately, the successful genesis of special education hinged on the 1917 Smith-Hughes Act extending federal aid to states for vocational education. The significance of vocational education derives from its placement within state public schooling. This placement permitted the continuation of nineteenth century events and their most logical outcome: the expansion of special education within public schools.

Throughout this historical timeframe, perceived gender differences influenced the construction of pupil classification and instructional content. While conceived as part of a practical adaptation to the problems of democratic admission, the character of the special class, that content which linked it to the general growth of state school systems, was shaped by debates over the control of gender differences in deviant behavior. A primary association was forged regarding the "bad boy" as the Backward child. In turn this construction generated consequences of even wider institutional reach. Specifically, the early conceptions of habitual truancy and Backwardness linked the special class within the common school to the control of male deviance in the juvenile justice system. From its implication in the control of male Backwardness, the genesis of special education was linked to the parallel system of male reformatories.

In terms that describe the general context that all state school systems faced, the special class arose as a strategy to accommodate the dilemma of formalizing school attendance as compulsory and nominally universal. From the event of enacting compulsory attendance are a number of general processes of growth that all states experience over time. As part of an earlier enactment of compulsory attendance is a higher level of pupil expenditures, an expanding secondary enrollment, and an earlier participation in vocational education. In more specific terms, *the special class was constructed as a resolution to the antinomy between the political mandate for democratic access and the practical requirement for institutional efficiency.* The potential void between the abstract statutory language of the state level and the immediate constraints of cities was minimized by a consensus over the social control of school deviance as founded on gender. The role of gender conditionalizes, as it were, the largely correlational thesis that stops at an explanation for the "origins" of special education with the passage of compulsory attendance. The policies formed to distinguish and control male and female deviance provided an educational purpose to the organizationally informal "ungraded class". The confirmation that vocational education would remain within the common school transformed an antiquated practice into a system of special instruction, now linked to the different occupations which male and female students were seen as destined to enter.

AN EMPIRICAL INQUIRY: INSTITUTIONAL LINKAGES AND THE CATEGORY OF BACKWARD CHILDREN

As demonstrated in chapter 2, institutional linkages follow the nineteenth century events, from establishing the state (lunatic) asylum, the reform school for boys, and the industrial school for girls to the enactment of compulsory school attendance. From the date of enacting compulsory school attendance, varying from 1852 (Massachusetts) to 1918 (Mississippi), flow institutional effects that bear on early categories of special education. The timing of compulsory attendance embodies general processes of growth as state school systems mature over time (Richardson 1984). An earlier passage of compulsory attendance is strongly related to higher levels of (both male and female) secondary enrollment and to levels of pupil expenditure.

As the historical narrative suggests, the early category of Backward children was an immediate consequence of mandating compulsory attendance. Moreover, as the narrative proposes, the category should be empirically linked to the growth of vocational education as part of general growth within common schools, and to the system of delinquency outside of common schools. In the final section of this chapter, I turn to a test of these proposals, with a particular eye to the linkage between male delinquency and the level of males in classes for Backward children.

Empirical Results

The completeness of data is determined by the reporting of figures for special education categories. For the category of Backward children in 1927, data are not available for 17 states, yielding 31 cases for analysis. Of the 17 states for which no Backward Children are reported, 9 are southern states, 5 are far-western, 2 are mid-western and 1 is from New England. (See Appendix A for actual states.) The analysis here is conducted on male and female Backward children. With this gender dis-

tinction, we are able to contrast the specific linkages between a male
(and female) delinquent population and a male (and female) Backward
population.

While the absence of "full" data for the early special education
category of Backward children presents problems for the empirical
analyses, these patterns are to be taken as a reflection of the historical
development of special education itself.[6] For Backward children, the
fact that one-half of non-reporting states are from the South is some
reflection of their "youthful" institutional age.

Table 3.1 gives the results of hierarchical regression analyses that
explore the levels of Backward children in 1927 with measures of
general institutional growth (the date of enacting compulsory
attendance and enrollments in vocational education) and to the
institutional linkage of male and female delinquents in 1917 (see
Appendix B). The initial equations with date of compulsory attendance
(equations 1 and 5) exhibit a predictive strength that is essentially equal
for both males and females. For both males and females, the addition of
vocational enrollment levels increases R^2, and reduces the magnitude of
compulsory attendance as well. The reduction in compulsory
attendance emphasizes the meaning of vocational enrollments as a
measure of general processes of growth in state school systems.

In contrast to this general institutional growth, the addition of
delinquency reveals a sharp gender difference in the category of
Backward children. For male Backward children, the addition of
delinquency in 1917 raises the R^2 and emerges as the strongest
predictor (equation 4). Its addition essentially eliminates the initial
contribution of compulsory attendance. For female Backward children,
no such effect of delinquency is found. For girls, the timing of
compulsory attendance and the level of vocational enrollments remain
as the predictors of female Backward children in 1930. The measure of
Backward has the closest historical affinity to the mandate of
compulsory attendance and to the subsequent problems of school
laggards. In effect, it is a category most infused with social and cultural
attributions and defined by the particular institutional responses
generated by the school efficiency movement.

**Table 3.1. Predicting Rates of *Backward* Children in 1927:
Results of Hierarchical Regression Analyses (standardized
coefficients reported)**

		Independent Variables		
	Comp Attend	Voc-ed 1930	Delinq 1917	Adj R^2
Males [n=31]				
1	-.57*			.31
2	-.39*	.33*		.38
3	-.43		.44**	.46
4	-.25	.33**	.42**	.54
Females [n=28]				
5	-.61**			.35
6	-.53**	.31*		.41
7	-.47**		.08	.27
8	-.22	.31*	.05	.33

* $p < .05$ ** $p < .01$

CONCLUSIONS

This chapter has argued that the genesis of special education was
marked by the construction of the "special class" within city schools as
a means to absorb the growing diversity of students. The special class
was an organizational strategy born of the enduring conflict between
the ideal of a common schooling and the practical demands for
efficiency in meeting this ideal. However, special education did not
arise as an automatic response to this conflict, but as a purposeful
enterprise legitimated by the functional and intellectual alliance
between intelligence testing and vocational education.

The genesis of special education began at the city level and
centered on the problem of school "laggards" as the symbol of school
inefficiency. The symbolic resonance surrounding the overage pupils in
city school systems contributed to a reform impulse that was fed by a
diverse range of interests, from business and labor, to academic and
political. Despite this diversity, and likely because of it, attempts to
distinguish and segregate a manual and industrial education from a

public system failed. As a consequence, vocational education was anchored inside the public school.

Because vocational education was now to remain within the public school, its own historic function became entwined with the organizational means to control deviant pupils. As the moralization of compulsory attendance met the vocationalization of schooling, school guidance stood parallel to the ungraded class. At the core of the genesis of special education was the intersection of vocational education with the formalization of public schooling.

This intersection would bring with it "broken promises" as schools embodied the growing conflict between public goals and private ends (see Grubb and Lazerson 1982, p. 134). As one indicator of this conflict, the genesis of special education was significantly stamped by a gender difference. This difference was rooted in nineteenth century institutional origins and persisted through the return of vocational education. As the empirical analyses reveal, two relatively separate institutional paths are discernible. The male path relates reform school formation and the male delinquent population to the special education category of Backward (and Truant) children. With this path we see the historically constructed association of the "bad boy" with the Backward child. In contrast, the female path relates the formalization of public schooling to vocational education, reflecting the more manifest purpose of common schooling. In contrast to the bad boy, the working girl was closer to the avowed function of vocational instruction. As a consequence, the vocational education of girls may have served to protect them from both the external label of delinquent, and the new internal classification of Backward.

To the extent that the "bad boy" was a gender description of a pupil from the poor and laboring classes, the genesis of special education was stamped by a cultural prejudice as well. The original category of Backward was certainly implicated in the prevailing cultural antagonisms of the time, principally the division between native and foreign-born. As this division fades by midcentury and is "replaced" by the divisions of race, special education will become implicated in the cultural transformations of urban school systems.

By midcentury, the strategic role of special education in defining the rules of access shifts to its crucial place in defining the rules of passage. These rules define passage through an increasingly entrenched structure of tracks. As the transformation of urban schools intersects with the structure of tracking, the post World War II expansion of special education becomes "spoiled" by the tempest of racial overrepresentation in classes for the educable mentally retarded. I turn to this "non-normative" expansion next.

APPENDIX A

The states that lack data on Backward children are: [South] AL, AK, DE, FL, MY, MS, OK, SC, VA; [Farwest] AZ, ID, NV, NM, WY, ND, SD; [North] VT.

APPENDIX B

The major independent variables are indexed accordingly: *Comp Attend* is the year states enacted compulsory school attendance; *Voc-ed* is the enrollment levels of males/females in vocational education, indexed as the number enrolled per 1000 of the state school-age population enrolled in school in 1930; *Delinq* is the population of males/females in respective reformatories or industrial schools in 1927 per 1000 of state school-age population; Backward is the number of male/female students in special classes for Backward students, per 1000 of the state school-age population enrolled in 1927. Due to the extreme range of these latter measures, both are log transformed.

NOTES

1. The adjective "partial" is borrowed from Gianfranco Poggi's lucid summary of Max Weber's classic thesis linking Puritanism and capitalism. In emphasizing Weber's own insistence that his work did not seek the causal origins of capitalism, but only its "genesis," Poggi notes: "I call Weber's argument 'partial' because it addresses a single, distinctive and (relatively speaking) minor aspect of a very large historical problem: how to account for the genesis of modern capitalism" (Poggi 1983, p. 79). Poggi further notes that Weber's work was "complex" insofar as a reasonable account of capitalism "comprises a number of discrete points, connected by a corresponding high number of steps or transitions" (p. 81). Taken together, the emphasis on partial relations *strengthened* understanding of the complexity of the problem, thereby giving the account a greater theoretical leverage ("momentous") in view of its wider implications. The emphasis on the genesis of special education shares Poggi's summary of Weber's methodological intent.

2. As England exemplifies, pressure for an expanded secondary education resulted in the creation of "junior technical schools" as set out in the 1902 Education Act. The decision to establish new educational structures is a persistent feature of British educational history, for "the creation of new, lower-status structures protects and even enhances the status of existing structures," namely the grammar schools and elite universities (Silver 1983, p. 156).

3. This vocational emphasis introduced a division within female deviance, isolating "sexual precocity" as most serious and subject to severe punishment (Schlossman and Wallach 1978). In turn, this division contributed to the creation of prison-like female reformatories which exacted this punishment as "partial justice" (Rafter 1985; see also Lekkerkerker 1931, ch. 5).

4. Experimentation with a differentiated curriculum had been undertaken by a number of city school systems. Often bearing the name of the city in which they were utilized (e.g., Cambridge, Batavia, Chicago), several distinct plans for the classification and promotion of students were known and debated. For all plans the routine of age-graded system was a "Procrustean bed," compelling the bright and advanced to move at the same pace as the slow and unable. Against this organizational flaw, the various plans experimented with flexible grading, discretionary promotions by individual teachers, and different schemes of tracks for average and gifted pupils (Department of the Interior 1923). Yet in spite of the acknowledged flaws of age-grading, actual practice appeared to follow the most economical path. The results from a national survey of superintendents, principals, and teachers reported in 1910 (Hartwell 1910) confirmed a dominant reliance on group teaching and ungraded classes, demonstrating that mechanisms that involved the "least amount of structural reform . . . achieved the widest use" (see Chapman 1988, p. 51).

5. There is some need to modify the claim here that Smith-Hughes was "decisive" in defeating or terminating the debates over unitary versus dual control. In many respects, the debates over unitary or dual control went on among friends, where familiar names would represent the interests of business and manufacturing, while educators and intellectuals would present counterarguments. While Wisconsin had gone the furthest toward dual control by its Act of 1911, various forms of dual control had existed in states well before Smith-Hughes. By the 1890s there were a considerable number of trade and vocational schools in place across the states. Moreover, these schools were "separate" from the public schools. Nonetheless, two points are relevant to the assertion that Smith-Hughes was a decisive event.

First, these vocational schools varied in name, including intermediate trade schools, independent industrial schools, industrial training schools, and manual training schools. This variation in name belie important differences *within* the vocational education movement itself, expressing significant contrasts in pedagogical philosophy. These contrasts were often deep and bitter (see Krug 1964), and to this extent weakened collective efforts to establish dual control as a national priority.

Secondly, the growth of vocational education within public high schools was dramatic much before Smith-Hughes. As given in the Report of the Commissioner of Education, in 1900 there were 540 public high schools reporting "technical or manual-training" courses, enrolling 68,440 students. By 1915 the number of schools reporting such courses had increased to 2,442, enrolling 125,807 students. Moreover, by this year, the Report now gave numbers for courses that framed Smith-Hughes, namely agricultural and domestic economy. What this suggests is that Smith-Hughes did not inaugurate vocational instruction within public schools, but rather legislated what was already well in place.

6. This uneven entry of states into the data set parallels the analysis of nations reporting evidence of school enrollment levels that constitute measures of "mass education." As states enter the "modern world system," they produce these data and report them to international bodies that are, like the Reports of the Commissioner of Education, the sources from which researchers on cross-national mass education draw their data. (For an example of this as a substantive issue see Meyer, Ramirez and Soysal, 1992, p. 133.)

PART II

Constructing the *Rules of Passage*

CHAPTER 4

The Non-Normative Expansion of Special Education

INTRODUCTION

As I explored in Chapter 3, the conception of Backward children gave form to the original category of an incipient field of special education. This category was crucial to the "takeoff" of special education less because its criteria were objectively clear but more because they were subjectively open. The category was, therefore, adaptive to the organizational dilemmas exposed by enacting compulsory attendance.

When states established a compulsory system of primary education, schools lost a measure of control over admission, and the composition of students became more diverse. This diversity was economic and cultural, but was highlighted by physical and mental differences. A response of schools to this diminished control was the construction of an ungraded or special class that gave to public schools a measure of control within their jurisdiction and secured a "site" for the development of special education categories. Yet the dilemmas presented by enacting compulsory attendance were not confined neatly to common schools. Viewed more broadly, more institutionally, the field of special education arose between two populations of exceptional children: those in separate, often residential institutions, and those who gained admission into public schools. Insofar as exceptional children were "diverted" to separate schools, the jurisdictional responsibility of public schools was delimited.

The more "objectively" exceptional conditions of the deaf and blind posed less of a dilemma than the characteristics subsumed under backwardness. While even this difference is by no means sharp, it is the root source of the expansion of special education. In more definitional terms, Tomlinson (1982) distinguishes between normative and non-normative categories. The former would include those conditions that have the greatest consensus: deaf, blind, crippled, severe mental handicaps. The latter includes those conditions that have much less consensus: backward, feebleminded, socially maladjusted, emotionally disturbed, or learning disabled. In Tomlinson's words, "the major sociological interest in the categories of special education lies in the *conflation of normative with non-normative conditions*" (p. 65, my emphasis).

This distinction provides a way to explain some or much of the postwar expansion of special education (cf. Booth 1983; Tomlinson 1985; Fulcher 1989). It is clear that much of the expansion cannot be attributed to a legitimate extension of provisions to accurately diagnosed exceptional children. As Table 4.1 shows, the category for Backward children accounted for nearly 40% of all children in special education up to 1932, when the category became Mental Deficiency. Aside from Speech, the greatest categorical expansion has occurred in Learning Disabled, rising exponentially from 1% in the 1950s to one quarter of the total special education population by 1975. By 1995, it had reached nearly 50% of all exceptional children in public schools.

As Chapter 3 demonstrated, the category of Backward children was conflated with behavioral deviancies, specifically that of male delinquency. The population of children in special education classes for backward children was conflated with the shifting population of males in state reformatories. In effect, this institutional tie carried the early expansion of special education. From the beginning the expansion of special education was spoiled.

In this chapter, I extend our view into the legacy of this awkward expansion and build on our narrative that links historical origins to contemporary patterns and consequences of change in special education. The particular focus is the expansion of the non-normative categories of Educable Mentally Retarded (EMR) and Learning Disabled (LD). The EMR category was the site of substantial "racial overrepresentation" in classes for the educable mentally retarded discovered in the mid 1960s. As Tomlinson noted from the evidence in British schools, the overplacement of West Indian children in non-normative categories "is related to the way particular groups are regarded as potentially troublesome," and this perception was linked to

Table 4.1: Percentage Distribution of Special Education Categories, 1932–1995

Category	1932	1948	1978	1985	1995
Backward	*	-	-	-	-
Mentally Deficient	41	-	-	-	-
Delicate	15	5	-	-	-
Epileptic	-	.1	-	-	
Socially Maladjusted	9	4	-	-	-
Crippled/orthopedic	10	8	2	4	1
Visual	3	2	1	6	1
Hearing	3	4	2	2	1
Speech	14	48	33	26	19
Mentally Retarded	-	23	25	16	11
Emotionally Disturbed	-	-	8	9	8
Learning Disabled	-	1	26	42	46
Multiple Handicaps	-	-	-	2	2
Other	-	-	4	2	2
Total (thousands)	164	378	3751	4315	5440

* "Backward" was the category as reported in 1927; the category was changed to "Mentally Deficient" in 1932. The numbers differ by only 1,296.

the immigration of black children into the education system in the early 1960s (Tomlinson 1982, p. 155). With strikingly similar timing, black and Hispanic children were found to be overrepresented in EMR classes in all American cities with sizeable minority populations (cf. Mercer 1973; Kirp 1973; Richardson 1979; Reschly 1988c). This widespread (and comparative) evidence of disproportionate placement persisted in spite of significant court challenges, legislative reforms, and a heightened professional and lay awareness.

Racial overrepresentation spoiled what had been a dramatic postwar expansion of special education (Dunn 1968; Christoplos and Renz 1969). Accounts and explanations have been varied, from largely consensual (Hobbs 1975), to conflicting (Elliott 1987) and acrimonious (Gordon 1980). Despite this "tempest in a teapot," special education profited some, for public and legal scrutiny contributed to a strengthening of due process checks that moved special education away from its often marginal place in schools. Nonetheless, racial imbalances displayed an intransigence, apparently shifting from one categorical site to another (Tucker 1980; *see also* Argulewicz 1983; Wright and Criz 1983).

The instance of racial overrepresentation is certainly an outcome of compact micro-social interactions. But above the countless individual encounters and local schools have been historical trends that may be felt and appreciated but little understood. When such trends intersect, the visibility of their combined effects can be reduced or obscured, and the capacity to appreciate these effects is commonly attributed to "unintended consequences" (see Mehan, Hertweck and Meihls 1986, p. 53).

The more relevant question, if not a preceding one, is how racial overrepresentation could have happened at all. The timing of racial overrepresentation alone suggests the role of trends whose intersection generated such common results. Two trends are suggested here. The first is the development of school tracking, the sequential arrangement of the curriculum that becomes linked, intentionally or not, to different postsecondary destinies. By midcentury, a hierarchical structure of tracks was firmly in place across urban (and indeed most rural) school systems. What grounded and rationalized this structure was the non-college-bound general track, and at the base of this was special education.

The second trend is the closing of the era when high school was a terminal enterprise, ushering in what Martin Trow aptly termed the "second transformation" of American secondary education (1973). The development of tracking predates this transformation of secondary education, but by the 1960s the two had become intricately associated. Additional pressures cemented their organizational symbiosis, however. Among these has been the unrelenting legal challenges that are in one way or another informed by *Brown v. Board of Education;* another has been the ongoing demographic transformation of urban school systems. The pressures brought by *Brown* against the organizational and legal defenses protecting racial segregation across schools defined full inclusion into regular education as the acknowledged goal of educational reform. Yet, as an unanticipated outcome, the combination of legal pressures for desegregation, the consolidation of general tracks, and the growth of special education provisions all contributed to the occurrence of racial overrepresentation.

This chapter first sketches the development of school tracking as the necessary context within schools for the occurrence of racial over-representation in special education. What gave to tracking its particular interpretation and rendered it susceptible to racial (and class) abuse was the ideological articulation of a "theory of general education." The de-mographic change of urban school systems is the additional, although not sufficient, trend. As these two trends intersected, they pulled urban school systems in opposite directions. While tracking was rationalized by the second transformation of secondary education, it was solidified by a changed composition in the cultural and economic backgrounds of students. As secondary education "moved upward" toward higher edu-cation, it did so as groups historically exempted and segregated from regular education "moved in." As these groups moved in, their partici-pation in regular education presented challenges to the curricular struc-ture, instructional methods, and counseling practices that sustained the vertical system of tracks. In effect, their increasing presence and inte-gration exposed the historically constructed *rules of passage.*

Special education was caught in the middle. Especially vulnerable for colonization by a theory of general education and a developed track structure was the non-normative category of "mildly mentally retarded." And especially vulnerable for misclassification were members of groups historically segregated from mainstream, general education: black and Hispanic students. And yet, the susceptibility of these groups to overrepresentation was not uniform across states. We may more accurately speak of the susceptibility of state school systems to engage in overrepresentation. As I will explore, the *institutional age* of state school systems has shaped this vulnerability well into this century. Specifically, the expansion of the non-normative categories of EMR and LD is an extension of the formalization of common school systems that inaugurated the timing and pace of growth in special education. Thus, when states would enter upon the expansion of these categories will define both the timing and extent of overrepresentation.

THE THEORY OF GENERAL EDUCATION AND THE TRIUMPH OF SCHOOL TRACKING

In the years following the World War II, the topic of "adjustment" seemed all consuming. The debates over the role of schools in a postwar world were triggered by an apparent consensus about the profile of the secondary school population. The initiating event was the presentation in 1945 of results from the study Vocational Education in the Years Ahead sponsored by the Office of Education. In his now famous summary of the conference proceedings, Charles Prosser, a long-time major figure in vocational education, advanced the claim that 20% of the high school population was oriented toward vocational studies, another 20% were preparing for college, but fully 60% was filling the courses of general education with little specific direction.

In light of this presumed distribution, Prosser called for a "life adjustment training" to meet the needs of this majority. Concretely, Prosser called on the federal level, requesting that the Commissioner of Education and the Assistant Commissioner for Vocational Education convene a series of regional conferences to address the issue. The Commissioner of Education, John Studebaker, responded favorably, convening national conferences, thereby inaugurating what soon would be a virtual national movement for "life adjustment education" in the schools.

Paralleling the regional and national conferences on life adjustment education was the publication of two significant reports that can read as "pointing in quite different directions" (Kliebard 1987, p. 245). The first, published in 1944, was a report by the Education Policies Commission, a body appointed in 1935 by the NEA and the American Association of School Administrators. Entitled *Education for All American Youth* (EAAY), this report anticipated the Prosser Resolution by its delineation of ten "imperative educational needs of youth" and its translation of these into a "common learnings" curriculum. The ten needs were distinctive, for they were largely nonacademic. They included such common learnings as developing salable skills, knowing how to purchase and use goods and services intelligently, being able to use leisure time, and understanding the significance of the family and of cooperative work with others (Educational Policy Commission 1944, pp. 225-226).

The report drew the distinction between "differential" and "common" studies in secondary schools. While acknowledging that students differ in occupational interests and plans, in ability and achievement level, the ten needs formed a common framework for all students. As the report noted, the critical time was the tenth grade, for it was then that the first of the "imperative educational needs"- the need to be equipped to earn a living in a useful occupation - be the focus of schools (p. 232).

The need for many students to earn a living certainly accounts for some of the wide attraction that life adjustment education gained. The problems faced by schools in the postwar years were considerable. But the real effects of this movement on the structure of general education can easily be obscured, for it generated its own countermovement. Pointed attacks on the anti-intellectual character of the life adjustment movement were voiced by prominent historians Arthur Bestor and Richard Hofstadter. Bestor was unrelenting in his attacks, taking issue with the 60% figure claimed by the Prosser Resolution. To Bestor, such a claim was as antidemocratic as it was empirically suspect. After citing other studies which gave quite different figures, Bestor dismissed the discrepancy as "not of particular moment," for life adjustment is "not a matter of statistics, it is a philosophy of education" (Bestor 1985, p. 82). As Bestor noted, this philosophy of education was one that would condemn some three-fifths to unskilled occupations on the presumption that they lacked the intellectual ability to achieve otherwise.

While the debate raged over life adjustment training, a second major report was published in 1945 by a Harvard committee, entitled *General Education in a Free Society* (GEFS). The committee, appointed by then President James Conant, was charged to examine the great majority of secondary school students who will not attend college. While the topic of the two reports was identical, their styles were quite different.

The GEFS advanced a "theory" of general education, making no mention of life adjustment training. The core of this theory was a conception of liberal education as "an earlier stage" of general education, "similar in nature but less advanced in degree" (Harvard University 1945, p. 52). In a democratic society, a general education must embody the ideals of a liberal curriculum, but now must extend these ideals to all. While opposition to a liberal education stemmed from historical causes, opposition to a general education now arose from the demands of specialization. Along with a general education, a "special education" must train students for a given career or occupation. Where a special education "enhances the centrifugal forces in society," a general education was a balancing force. In light of the fact that in most states the whole population of high school age was in school, the balancing task of a general education was all the more imperative.

Like the *Education for All American Youth*, the need to extend a general education to a diverse range of students was fully acknowledged. Yet unlike EAAY, the Harvard report addressed the issue of differentiation as a historical problem, recognizing "the welling up of talent and energy which has historically accompanied the decline of privilege and the rise of submerged classes" as a "release of powers suppressed or dormant" (p. 81). This large and dormant range of individual differences was divided into an "inner" and "outer" sphere. The inner sphere of mind and outlook involved intelligence, expectations, and fidelity to purpose, whereas the outer sphere involved opportunity. The problem of differentiation was the discrepancy between the two: the fact that many who are able to go on to college, by intelligence and outlook, nonetheless lack the opportunity. On the basis of "slender evidence," the report estimated that that 3% to 5% of the age-eligible population, some seventy-five to one hundred and twenty-five thousand, "are of college caliber and would go to college if they could but are prevented by poverty" (p. 88). Yet there was a remedy, which the report cast in metaphoric terms: "general education at high school is like the palm of a hand, the five fingers of which are as many kinds of special interests [which] would stretch for all beyond the common core, and all would follow one or more than one" (p. 102).

By their contrasting styles and timely coincidence, the two reports may suggest that a climate of debate over general education filled the postwar years. While true to an extent, it is more instructive to note points of consensus that gave form to a national perspective on general education. Both EAAY and GEFS underlay their inquiries with a commitment to the democratic ideal of education for all youth; both distinguish between a common and a differentiated or "special" education; both acknowledge the latent abilities of the majority who will not likely attend college; both distinguish the diversity of interests, academic and occupational, from the diversity of ability; and both view, in different ways, a general education as a continuation of the liberal education tradition. For both, continuation of a liberal education tradition is grounded in the moral priority of a common citizenship, not in the distinctions of privilege.

The full meaning of these similarities should not be lost by accounts of these postwar years as "battles" over a national curriculum (Spring 1976, pp. 1-51). Rather, these reports, and the life adjustment movement in particular, are continuations of "already established versions of progressive education" (Ravitch 1983, p. 67). The reports provided the "theory" of a general education that was conceived as national in scope and applicability. Two implications best summarize the similarities that unite the reports into a theory of general education, and were consequential for curricular grouping. First, in a free society, equality of opportunity falls upon schools and they must therefore provide a differentiated curriculum that can accommodate the expanded diversity of a secondary school population. Individuals should select, with appropriate guidance, the curricular subjects that best fit their interests and abilities. Secondly, the framework that would ensure the historical continuity of a liberal education should be subject-based. A subject-based structure resolves, in part, the problem of a diverse population in a democratic society. Because achievement in one subject is not transferable to others, curricular grouping should occur within and not across subjects.

Both assumptions are evident in the influential "Conant Report" issued in 1959, as *The American High School Today*. In Recommendation 4, Conant (1959a) was explicit about ability grouping:

> In the required subjects and those elected by students with a wide range of ability, the students should be grouped according to ability, subject by subject. . . .
>
> The middle group might be divided into two or three sections according to the students' abilities in the subject in question. This type of grouping is not to be confused with across-the-board grouping according to which a given student is placed in a particular section in "all" courses. Under the scheme here recommended, for example, a student may be in the top section in English but the middle section in history or ninth-grade algebra. (p. 49)

Yet two years later, in *Slums and Suburbs* (1961), there is a decisive change in Conant's position:

> In my first report I also recommended individualized programs. . . . There would be no classification of students according to clearly defined and labeled tracks. . . . In some schools the student has little or no choice in determining his high school program. He is assigned to a particular track with its outline of courses he must study. . . . At this point, tracking and ability grouping become synonymous, since all the pupils of given abilities will be found in the same track. (pp. 64-65)

While confessing to being unable "to take a stand on tracking in the large cities," Conant nonetheless saw three reasons for its emergence: the great number of students, the problem of challenging slum children of high ability but low aspiration, and the problem of Latin for the slum child who cannot read English. While the last of these reflects Conant's elite values, the first two were more broadly shared. As he concluded, the initiation of a tracking system in large cities "may indeed have merit," where "the system of rigid tracks may be the only workable solution to a mammoth guidance problem" (p. 66).

Conant's change of position does not reflect his own personal rethinking. Rather, the "theory" of general education led to, if not facilitated, the construction of vertical tracks in many large cities. Much like the discrepancies between the pedagogical ideals of the comprehensive high school and its curricular realities that had been challenged earlier (see Counts 1922), the realities of tracking during the 1950s and 1960s would conflict with the theory of general education as formulated in the 1940s (see *Hobson v. Hansen* 1967).

From General Education to General Track: Notes from Detroit Schools

Like the image of the comprehensive high school, the theory of general education was rich with promise, but lacking in empirical verification. As Counts (1922) had demonstrated, parental background influenced these processes deeply. For the theory of general education, no similar scrutiny is available that matches the scope of Count's pathbreaking study. Nonetheless, evidence of tracking in the Detroit schools for this period is available, and provides some way to understand James Conant's shift in favor of tracking.

The first source is the publication in 1961 of *Education and Income* by Patricia Cayo Sexton. Sexton's study of "Big City" was undertaken in light of the prevailing national concern over American education prompted by the successful launching by the Soviet Union of Sputnik 1 in October of 1957. Such critics as Admiral Hyman Rickover, "father" of the nuclear submarine, helped to focus attacks on the comprehensive high school and its failure to protect the education of an ability elite (Spring 1986, p. 292; Ravitch 1983, p. 228). Sexton's study was begun with a rebuttal to these fears. Like Counts did forty years earlier, Sexton proposed that social class, augmented by race, accounted for the differences in measured ability and performance in high schools.

As a measure of social class, Sexton analyzed six broad income levels and, with divisions within these, she produced a finer gradation of seventeen levels. In her analysis of "the selecting and sorting process," she provides direct evidence on school tracking in the high schools. Three tracks structured the curriculum in these high schools: college preparatory, business and vocational, and general. While the first two were designed to prepare students for specific occupations or careers, the "general" track embraced the more open electives proposed by the reports on general education.

Sexton demonstrated a strong relation between the six income levels and enrollment in the three tracks. Concretely, with each increase in income level, she revealed a virtual linear increase in enrollments in the college preparatory track, rising from 15% to 79%. Fully 49% of the lowest income level was in the general track, compared to only 10% for the highest income level.

As an important addendum to her analysis of track assignments, Sexton showed further that income level was strongly related to "students requesting transcripts" as indicating plans to attend college. While only 23% of the lowest group sought transcripts, 81% of the highest group did so. Yet, this behavioral act of requesting transcripts conflicts, in part, with her analysis of "planning for college" now or later. Here the differences across the income levels were not as great, for 63% of the lowest level stated they planned for college. Nonetheless, the fact that track assignments are so rigid, with very little movement up or down, highlights this discrepancy. As Sexton concluded: "In this school social system, the college preparatory curriculum is the upper class, the vocational curriculum the middle, and the general curriculum the lowest. . . . Once assigned to a curriculum and status level in the high school, students seldom change to other curriculums and class categories" (p. 179).

Sexton's early work on Detroit gave little attention to the historical roots of curriculum tracking. Her analyses provide a sharp picture for 1961 only. Yet recent accounts of the "rise and fall" of Detroit schools show how early Detroit introduced a tracking system, and how it has been sustained in a context of racial and class diversity.

As Mirel notes (1993, p. 70), the three track system, begun in 1919, was in fact "equated with democracy," introduced with claims that "a differentiated curriculum offered expanded educational opportunities to students who otherwise would have shunned the classical high school of the nineteenth century." Yet despite this early introduction of tracking, the more consequential period for Detroit, as a fair reflection of American secondary education generally, was the postwar years that saw the growth of the "needs-oriented" general track (Angus and Mirel 1993, p. 178). Spurred by the depression, a loss of confidence in vocational education led educators to emphasize the "custodial" function of schools. Of Detroit's four tracks, college preparatory, technical, commercial, and general, the latter was the least demanding. It was, therefore, a means to accommodate a growing number of students whose apparent abilities and prospects did not suit them for either a college, technical, or commercial curriculum. Most conspicuous among these numbers were African-American students, who increased in presence, becoming nearly 45% of the school population by 1957.

As Angus and Mirel show, the response of the schools was to "relegate black students to the needs-oriented rather than the goals-oriented curriculum," so that black students were disproportionately assigned to the general track (p. 186). By the end of the war, the general track enrolled more than half of the students in the Detroit schools.

The traditional interpretation of this pattern has been one that stresses the injurious effects of the life adjustment movement, and its collapse in the face of severe criticisms. Yet contrary to this account, what Angus and Mirel demonstrate was the resilience of the curricular offerings. As they succinctly note: "In light of these data, the Life Adjustment Movement appears to have legitimated changes that had already taken place a decade earlier; its effect was to solidify these changes and make them relatively impervious to the waves of attacks that would occur in the 1950s and 1960s" (p. 189). The subject-based structure of the curriculum remained essentially unchanged. What did change, however, were the requirements for graduation.

The historical account of the rise and decline of Detroit's schools gives both necessary and critical knowledge to Sexton's sociological evidence for 1961. Shorn of its historical antecedents, the vertical grouping of students into curricular tracks appears as an insidious mechanism employed by elites to maintain their control, or in Sexton's terms, to maintain an educational "caste system" more severe than what exists outside of schools. Yet such an interpretation gives undue weight to tracking *per se*, failing, as Mirel concludes, "to recognize the importance of the general track as the primary vehicle for the dilution of academic standards and the increase in educational inequality" (Mirel 1993, p. 400). The root of inequality is not the tracking structure in its entirety, but the particular function entrusted to the general track, and the "philosophy" that nourished its growth: the theory of general education. But in addition, the function of the general track as an organizational residue for failing or underachieving students is itself conditioned by specific historical contexts. When the coalitions that temporarily bind over the divisions of social class and race lose their hold, the fragile consensus that instills a moral rationale for the support of schools deteriorates, and political struggles over key financial resources ensue.

The two decades following the war were turbulent years for urban school systems. As blacks underwent a second migration out of the South to major mid-western and western cities, many of these cities witnessed a qualitative transformation in the cultural and economic composition of the school-age population. Yet in addition, a legal transformation was initiated with *Brown v. Board of Education* in 1954, which struck at the traditional authority of the local level. The combined pressures of demographic change at the immediate district level and of legal mandates from the federal level forced schools to respond in a relatively short time. Instead of devising new organizational provisions, or introducing bold academic changes, many schools relied on existing structures. One strategy was to rely on the general track, a strategy that aligned the tracking structure with the divisions of race and social class. Another strategy was to utilize the placement process of special education.

From General Track to Special Education: Delinquency, "Divergent Youth" and Educable Mentally Retarded: Notes from California

Much like the leadership role of Massachusetts in nineteenth-century school reform, California has been a leader in the development of special education provisions in this century. The earliest reference to special instruction is in 1921 where the state Education code specified that city school districts may establish separate classes for "pupils who would profit more from a course other than the regular course of study" (sec 1661). In 1931 the Code mandated attendance at some state school for deaf children "unable to benefit materially by the methods of instruction in use in the public schools" (sec 17251). Despite these early declarations, the authority to exempt classes of children "whose bodily or mental conditions are such as to prevent or render inadvisable their attendance upon a school or class" persisted until 1947. In that year, the permissive language of earlier statutes became mandatory with the formalization of "special classes" for the education of mentally retarded minors (sec 9801). Provisions for physically handicapped minors, and intellectually gifted students, were formalized in 1959, and in 1963 similar provisions were formalized for educationally handicapped youth. For California, the formalization of special education was anchored in 1946 when a constitutional amendment reorganized the State Department of Education by creating a Division of Special Schools and Services, and a Bureau of Special Education (Simmons 1972, p. 99).

During these postwar years, the pressures to formalize special education provisions mounted. Most conspicuous was the growth in population, enlarging the size of school districts and bringing qualitative change in their social and cultural composition. Between 1950 and 1960, California's school-age population nearly doubled, from 1,181,106 to 1,561,366. By 1960 it had nearly doubled again, reaching 2,826,339. By 1970 it more than doubled again, reaching 5,699,187. These demographic changes were sharpened, however, by a decisive legal change in 1947: the repeal of the "separation of races" clause that had remained unchallenged from 1883. The successful challenge came with *Mendez v. Westminister School District,* a suit arguing that Mexican-Americans were not members of the "great races of man," and thus the separation of races policy did not apply to them. The court agreed, thereby repealing the long- standing policy that could sustain segregation by race. In that same year, the provision of special classes for "educable mentally retarded" minors was formalized.

The propitious timing of *Mendez* and the formalization of the EMR category reflect more than a historical accident. The legislation of formal provisions for mentally retarded minors owed much to the impact of delinquency reform that lead to special education by way of county-level vocational guidance. The rationale for the tie between delinquency and school guidance was articulated most by Norman Fenton who, as director of the California Bureau of Juvenile Research with headquarters at the Whittier State School, sought to extend the child guidance clinic to the public schools. At the invitation of a public school, probation department, or county superintendent of schools, a traveling child guidance clinic would go into a local community. From psychological tests and medical examinations, conducted by both school and community personnel, a simplified and practical model of mental hygiene could operate at the school level, effectively joining vocational guidance to delinquency intervention (Langston 1950, pp. 46-49; Richardson 1989, p. 105-106). As a psychologist, Fenton was well versed in diagnostic and therapeutic work with delinquent youth. But his real contribution came from his broader, "theoretical" sensitivity to the historical relation between delinquency, public schooling, and the local community environment.

This theoretical sensitivity was elaborated in his influential textbook *Mental Hygiene in School Practice*, published in 1943. A professor of education at Stanford University, Fenton defended this historical relation in scholarly terms. As he noted, "Legend has it that Horace Mann improved his prospects of obtaining a program of public education from the Massachusetts Legislature by predicting the end of crime in that commonwealth if and when all the children of all the people were given a common school education" (Fenton 1943, p. 370). This intimate association between delinquency prevention and common schooling became the philosophical core of the original juvenile court. From this philosophy the relation between delinquency and public schooling exhibits a "temporal sequence" which leads from an initial reliance on the individual judge (1900-1910), to the diffusion of child guidance clinics (1910-1930), to the community or coordinating council (pp. 372-383). As the fullest expression of child welfare, the coordinating council would intervene against "socially maladjusted youth" through formal ties between lay and professional groups and the public schools. Like the juvenile court, the coordinating councils were visualized as more contemporary replications of earlier apprenticeship arrangements for the education and welfare of children. As a culmination of this temporal sequence, the permissive authority granted to county superintendents to provide guidance services was formalized in the 1947 act to mandate direct services to mentally retarded minors.

The formalization of special classes for mentally retarded children in 1947 served the mutual needs of urban educators, child guidance personnel, and the new profession of school psychology. Yet subsequent years presented additional pressures on local schools by increasing the population of new students who again could not pass easily through the graded curriculum. This new school deviance was identified by school officials and legislators as *Divergent Youth*. Throughout the 1950s and early 1960s, youth "divergency" was evidenced by the increasing reliance of local schools on the long-term suspension. A report by the California Assembly Committee on Education relative to the use of suspension found that long-term suspensions had increased seven-fold faster than the normal expectancy due to increased average daily attendance in secondary schools. In a three-year period prior to 1964, the number of long term suspensions rose by 84% from an initial base of 3256 to 6000 in the reporting local school districts. In this same period, the average daily attendance rose by only 9%. Significantly, the major reasons for this wide discrepancy had little to do with statutory reasons for suspension as outline in the Education Code. Rather, for 1963-1964, more than 60% of all long-term suspensions were given for "nondeportment" reasons (Report of Senate 1963). The increasing assignment of non-deportment causes indicated a changing conception of suspended students, from one previously viewed in behavioral terms entirely, to one viewed in terms of low motivation, poor adjustment, and other forms of withdrawal. As a culmination of hearings and investigations into youth divergence, the special education provision for "educationally handicapped" minors was formally enacted in 1963.

The tension presented by Divergent Youth that led California to pass special education legislation bears a similarity to the dilemma over truancy that led Boston to enact compulsory attendance. In both instances, traditional means to accommodate school deviance were strained and for both, a conceptual distinction contributed to the formalization of new means. For Boston, the moral connotation of "habitual truancy," as distinct from absenteeism, limited the traditional means available to schoolmasters to control nonattendance. For California, the distinction drawn between deportment and "non-deportment" reasons for youth divergence, broadened the problem of school failure beyond the traditional mechanism of suspension. For the Boston case, the distinction permitted the identification of the reformatory as an educational site. For the California case, the distinction permitted assignment to a special education category.

Summary

As an institutionally older school system, California's introduction of EMR provisions coincident with its repeal of the separation of races clause can be interpreted as a deliberate reform to absorb challenges to educational access. Yet, it may also be interpreted as the coincidence of reforms that were each part of a longer momentum of institutional change beginning decades earlier with the enactment of compulsory attendance legislation. Similarly, the particular dynamics of Detroit, its "rise and fall," are not wholly particular to it as an illustrative case. Rather, the capacity to make and sustain coalitions that bind across divisions of race and class derived certainly from the favorable economic and political climate of immediate post-War Detroit. Yet, it came also from a state school system that was institutionally mature enough to accept and to incorporate these coalitions into public instruction. The context external to Detroit schools interacted in a particular way with a curricular structure that could be utilized to meet a number of educational objectives.

SOME EMPIRICAL ANALYSES OF EXPANSION: THE CONTINUITY OF NON-NORMATIVE CATEGORIES

As noted at the outset, Tomlinson's distinction between normative and non-normative categories provides a useful way to explain much of the postwar expansion of special education. In my focus on the institutional genesis of special education, the original category for Backward children exemplified such non-normative content. Specifically, the number of Backward children in state school systems for 1927 was explained largely by gender and by the level of male delinquents in 1917. By 1930, the category of Backward children had developed along the "impure" lines of cultural and behavioral deviance.

In 1932, the category of Backward children virtually disappears. In its place the category of Mental Deficiency (MD) emerges. Significantly, the total number given for Backward children in 1928 nearly matches that given for Mentally Deficient in 1932; they are different by only 1296. The change in name is by no means trivial, for now Mental Deficiency implied a more biological classification. Nonetheless, the continuity between Backward and Mental Deficiency also implies an inheritance of the institutional links that defined these categories as non-normative.

Table 4.2: Predicting Rates of Mentally Deficient, 1940. Results of Hierarchical Regression Analyses (betas reported).

		Independent Variables			
eq	Comp attend	Expend	Voc- ed	Back- ward	Adj R^2
1	-.31*				.07
2	.09	.57*			.23
3	.07	.51*	.08		.21
N = 31					
4	-.35*	.19	.04	.44*	.74
5	-.45*			.53*	.74

* $p < .05$

To underscore this non-normative legacy of the Backward child category, I initially analyze the variation in levels of Mental Deficiency in 1940. In Table 4.2, the effects of historical antecedent variables that embody the formal and early genesis of special education are tested: the timing of enacting compulsory attendance legislation (Comp attend), the expenditures per pupil (Expend), and the number enrolled in vocational education classes in 1930 (Voc ed). As the hierarchical analyses demonstrate, the inclusion of all three produces an R^2 of .21, with expenditures emerging as the strongest predictor. (See the Appendix for the definition of all variables used in the analyses conducted.)

My particular interest here, however, is the continuity of a non-normative content that links the Backward category of the early decades to the Mental Deficiency category of midcentury. As shown by equation 4, the addition of the levels of Backward children in 1927 increases the predictive strength dramatically. While the prior level of Backward children is the strongest predictor, the independent strength of compulsory attendance legislation returns while expenditures is diminished. Thus, historical antecedents exert their influence on the growth of special education well into this century. What may remain largely unchanged are the institutional linkages that transfer the cultural and behavioral deviancies associated with one category to the other. The early decades of the genesis of special education imprinted, as it were, a code of linkages that may persist across a considerable span of time.

We may carry this evidence of early institutional linkages over to the analysis of the EMR and LD categories as primary carriers of this expansion. By the end of the 1950s, the category of Mentally Deficient underwent a further division between educable and trainable. While the trainable retarded category may fit Tomlinson's normative definition, the category of educable mentally retarded inherits the legacy of non-normative content. As such, it would be linked to Mental Deficiency in the 1940s, and thus rooted in the original construction of Backward children. The EMR category ought to have "traces" of this non-normative legacy; it ought, therefore, to be institutionally susceptible to changes in what defines this non-normative content.

To explore this hypothesis of non-normative continuity, I first examine the cross-sectional effects of institutional and contextual variables on EMR levels in 1957 and 1978. These results are given in Table 4.3, which compares standardized coefficients. In the regression analyses, variables are examined against a baseline model that consists of the timing of compulsory attendance, levels of pupil expenditures, and a control for southern states. The initial comparison shows a sharp difference in predictive strength; the R^2 for 1978 is three times that for 1960. Revealing is the change in sign for expenditures per pupil. In 1960, it alone reaches significance, constraining much of the information in compulsory attendance. Yet for 1978, the direction reverses: states spending less now had higher placement levels. This change in direction is suggested for establishment date of the state reformatory. For 1960, states that had established the reformatory earlier had significantly higher placement levels; for 1978, the effects of this antecedent were essentially gone. In contrast to the significance of these measures of school system formalization, none of the measures for residential populations has any effect at all. It is *institutional age* that defines the rate of special education placements.

Table 4.3: Predicting Rates of EMR Placement: Cross-Sectional Analyses, 1960 and 1978 (betas reported)

| | |-------*Baseline Model*-------| | | |
	Comp Attend	Expend	South	Adj R2
[1978]	.25	-.25*	.36*	.54
[1960]	.06	.59*	.18	.18
Predictors added to Baseline Model				
Mentally Deficient, 1940 [n=44]				
[1978] -.18	.18	-.10	.42	.49
[1960] .66*	.29	.15	-.13	.44
Reformatory legislation				
[1978] -.11	.26	-.31*	.35*	.54
[1960] -.54*	.12	.37	.13	.43
MR residential population				
[1978] -.16	.23	-.27	.34	.55
[1960] -.19	.01	.63	.20	.16
Juv Delinquent residential population				
[1978] -.16	.20	-.30	.38	.56
[1960] -.09	.08	.59	.16	.17
Neglect residential population				
[1978] .07	.25	-.24	.36	.54
[1960] .03	.05	.59	.20	.16
% Black of the school population				
[1978] .42*	.12	-.29*	.12	.60
[1960] .03	.05	.59*	.14	.18

* $p = < .05$

The interpretation of these effects as measures of formalization needs be made in relation to regional contrasts. The timing of enacting compulsory attendance is confounded with the regional distinctiveness of southern states, where all but two enacted after 1900. And consistent with the institutional sequence, the establishment of state reformatories is intertwined with the timing of enacting compulsory attendance. For

1960, institutionally older school systems were also in highly urban states; for 1978, the location of higher EMR placements was not only in southern states but in less urban ones as well. Thus, the interpretation of these measures simultaneously involves the institutional sequence and the ascendancy of institutionally younger school systems. A significant proportion of these systems is the southern region; a contrast that defines these state as more homogeneously "young."

Between 1960 and 1978 these states were "thrust forward," in part by *Brown* and in part by their own institutional growth. The significance of this regional contrast is emphasized by the impact of the percent black of the school population. For 1960, this measure had no effect at all; for 1978, however, it is the most significant predictor. From this change we are given some insight into the dynamic of racial overrepresentation. While we cannot make inferences about the composition of EMR classes from this ecological correlation,[1] the associations permit interpretations about the behavior of state school systems. The evidence of overrepresentation revealed in the 1960s was concentrated largely in major cities outside of the South. The occurrence of overrepresentation in these cities was a consequence of the sequential development of their larger state systems. By the end of that decade, however, these state systems and their larger urban schools accelerated the decline in their EMR placements and began the expansion of the LD placements. Southern states, with institutionally younger school systems and sizeable Black student populations, entered the expansion phase of EMR placements. They did so as a predictable pattern of institutional growth as well as a strategic response to external pressures for racial desegregation. One response was the utilization of Pupil Assignment Laws to prevent the "mixing" of races (Peterson, Rossmiller and Volz 1969; see also Bersoff 1979, pp. 35-39; Smith 1983). A reflection of this was the utilization of the EMR category as an available within-school status, however remindful of educational segregation.

Finally, as some evidence of the continuity of non-normative content, the level of placements in the Mentally Deficient category in 1940 is a significant predictor of EMR levels in 1960. For 1978, however, this predictive strength is gone, interrupted by the inclusion of LD as a new special education category. As older state systems exhausted the line of expansion from Backward to Mentally Deficient to EMR, a half century of relatively continuous expansion, they began the categorical shift to LD. And as LD became the new site for the continuation of this non-normative legacy, institutionally older state school systems commenced this change.

We may amplify these cross-sectional patterns by turning to analyses of the rate of expansion for both EMR and LD. For EMR, I focus on the period from 1960 to 1978; for LD, I focus on the years from 1976 to 1985. For LD, the significant period of its expansion occurred from the early 1970s to 1985.

Table 4.4 presents the comparative results of panel analyses for both EMR and LD. For these analyses, the baseline model is composed of two measures: the level of EMR in 1957 or LD in 1976 (Prior Level), and the total enrolled school population for those years (School Enroll). Against this baseline, institutional and contextual variables are added. In addition, I explore the full range of regional contrasts, introducing dummy variables for northern, southern, mid-western, and far-western states. (See the Appendix for the indexing of each variable.)

What is most instructive from this comparison is the inability to predict variation in levels of LD placements. The non-normative continuity is evident, yet is intertwined with *institutional age*. States with higher levels of MD in 1940 experienced lower rates of EMR expansion between 1957 and 1978. The inverse relation between the two is determined by *institutional age:* the expansion of LD was carried by the downward decline of EMR, begun by institutionally older andnationally prominent state school systems. Between 1957 and 1978, California, Pennsylvania, Massachusetts, and New York alone declined in EMR placements; yet they also led the nation in the rise of LDplacements. While we have seen that such states had higher EMR levels by 1960, this analysis of change detects the beginnings of their withdrawal from EMR and their leadership in the rise of LD. Such an interpretation is suggested by the contrast of regions. Southern states exhibit a significantly positive impact on the rate of expansion; by contrast, northern and far-western states exhibit a strong and negative impact. Northern and far-western states enacted compulsory attendance laws comparatively early and, relative to southern states especially, they have been "ahead" with regard to the institutional direction of change in special education categories. In short, the inverse relation between EMR and LD is a continuation of the sequential dynamics that link non-normative categories across time.

Table 4.4: Predicting the Expansion of EMR and LD (betas reported)

		|---Baseline Model--|		
	Effect on Baseline	Prior Level	School Enroll	Adj R2
EMR				
Baseline prediction		.58	.24	.61
Additional Variables				
Expenditures	-.45*	.65	.29	.81
Compul Attend	.43*	.47	.36	.79
% Black sch pop	.43*	.53	.21	.79
MD, 1940	-.36*	.86	.07	.73
Reformatory	.36*	.74	.26	.71
MR resid, 1960	-.25*	.48	.28-	.66
Juv Del, 1960	-.10	.54	.24	.61
Neglect resid, 1960	.06	.62	.20	.61
North	-.24	.59	.26	.66
South	.40*	.54	.27	.77
Midwest	-.02	.59	.24	.60
FarWest	-.23*	.45	.31	.65
LD				
Baseline prediction		.49	.48	.82
Additional Variables				
EMR, 1978	.38	.33	.35	.89
Compul attend	.18*	.45	.54	.85
% Black sch pop	.18*	.46	.47	.85
Reformatory	.09	.50	.52	.83
MR resid, 1960	-.13*	.48	.47	.83
Expenditures	-.08	.48	.51	.82
Juv Del, 1970	-.10	.45	.49	.82
Neglect resid, 1970	.01	.50	.48	.82
North	-.06	.48	.50	.83
South	.16*	.45	.52	.84
Midwest	-.09	.49	.49	.83
FarWest	-.02	.49	.48	.82

* p < .05

A close look at the coefficients for the expansion of LD points to a simplified interpretation: historical and contextual variables do not explain the variation in state levels of LD. Put differently, the variation is explained only by prior levels and by the size of the school population. In essence, states may have heterogeneous histories, but by the late 1980s they have become "institutionally isomorphic" (DiMaggio and Powell 1991) around the dominant special education category of Learning Disabled.

LD and Delinquency: A Glance at "Reversed" Expansion

Special education has attained a "pedagogical high road" in recent years. Owing to the greater diversity across the population of exceptional children, particularly the combination of different cultural backgrounds with handicapping conditions, special education has moved far from its historically marginal location. The challenges that special education must face and answer pragmatically promote curricular and instructional innovations that flow from its resource rooms and research models into general education. One is reminded of Horace Mann and Samuel Gridley Howe's mutual belief that a common schooling could learn much from the education of the deaf and blind.

The contemporary stature of special education derives, in part, from its lack of power. The very absence of defenses forces special education into the foreground of the social and cultural problems facing urban schools. Far from the "dumping ground" for behaviorally deviant students, special education presents conceptual and working models for the *retention* and *education* of such students. If the reformatory was the model for the construction of the original special education category of Backward children, the expansion of learning disability, as a theory of learning as well as a diagnostic category, is the contemporary model for delinquency.

In Table 4.5, some results are given that explore this reversed causal influence: the relation between earlier levels of LD on the proportion of delinquents in diversion or detention homes. As shown, LD levels in 1976 are inversely and significantly related to the proportion in diversion in 1980: states with higher placements in LD classes have a lower proportion of their delinquent populations in diversion four years later. And as we see, no other additional variable, whether it be measures of school system formalization   (compulsory

Table 4.5: Variation in Proportion of Delinquent Populations in
***Diversion* Programs, 1980: Results of Regression Analyses**

		|-----Baseline Model-----|		
		Prior level	Age pop 10-17	Adj R^2
		.14	.17	.01
Predictors added to Baseline Model				
LD, 1976	-.38*	.20	.06	.12
Comp attend	-.14	.14	.15	.01
EMR, 1978	-.11	.12	.15	.01
% Black school pop, 1970	-.18	.15	.20	.02
State pop, 1970	-.18	.15	.35	.01
Number of banks in state, 1970	.04	.15	.15	.01
South	-.10	.14	.17	.01
North	.09	.14	.17	.01
Midwest	.02	.14	.17	.01
FarWest	.06	.14	.17	.01

attendance enactment) or contextual measures (percent black of the school population, size of the state population, or a measure of the economic strength of the state with the number of banks), has any predictive effects on state variations in diversion.

While this association is suggestive, it must be cautiously interpreted. Diversion itself is a measure of delinquency reform, an indicator of the size of "status offense" relative to criminal offenses within the delinquent population. What is suggestive here is that the expansion of LD within schools may diminish this subpopulation within delinquency, retaining status offenders within public education who otherwise would remain confined in state reformatories or detention homes.

The affinity between public schooling and delinquency is most evident in the current reform cycle to deinstitutionalize juvenile justice by distinguishing "status offenses" from delinquency. Under various designates, the jurisdiction of status offenses encompasses a range of conduct from ungovernable, school truancy, dependency, and neglect, to sexual molestation. Empirical research has found much of these reforms wanting, demonstrating that status offenses and delinquency are not distinct populations (Zatz 1982, pp. 42-50), that designations vary across states and are often reordered to encompass different behaviors and populations (Stapleton, Aday and Ito 1982; Gough 1977), and that diversion may in fact widen the net of delinquency and contribute to the discretionary abuse of the PINS (Persons in Need of Supervision) jurisdiction at various levels (Nejelski 1973; Miller 1979; Klein 1979; Rosenberg and Rosenberg 1976, pp. 1110-1121).

Yet these failures belie their real significance. The designation of status offenses is not a reform wholly internal to delinquency. Rather, the changes wrought by significant court cases, principally *In re Gault* (1967) situate noncriminal, status offenses interstitial between public schooling and delinquency. Violations of school rules regarding dress, sexual comportment, or political disposition join conditions of dependency and offenses of incorrigibility *to form a continuum of noncriminal infractions.* One or a combination of behaviors may be claimed by either delinquency or public schooling.

The communication between delinquency and special education is in several respects direct. Much of the intent of the *Juvenile Justice and Delinquency Prevention Act* of 1974 (JJDP) mirrors that of *The Education for All Handicapped Children Act* of 1975 (EAHC). Both share a core concept: "least coercive disposition" for juvenile justice, and the "least restrictive environment" for special education. Both have established national-level organizations; both require monitoring of state practices, the reporting of statistical information to the federal level, and the formulation of standards for the assessment of legislative intent. More specifically, the intent of JJDP to remove status offenses from the jurisdiction of the juvenile court impacts many youth to remain within general education. This reform overreaches the boundary of juvenile justice; it exerts a defining influence on the construction of special education categories and their implementation and composition. Standards 3.11 to 3.21 bear on education generally, but 3.14 links juvenile reform to bilingual and bicultural education, and 3.17 concretely links the problem of delinquency to the diagnostic category of LD (National Advisory Committee 1976, pp. 101-126). As this "glance" at the reversed effects of LD levels on diversion populations suggests, this link may indeed be effective.[2]

CONCLUSIONS

The real institutional growth of special education occurred over the past three decades. In numbers of students provided with special education instruction within public schools and in the size and scope of the administrative delivery of these provisions, the expansion of special education has been nothing short of dramatic. Yet most of this expansion has been in non-normative categories, emphasizing that the legitimate extension of provisions to truly exceptional children cannot adequately explain this growth. For England and the United States at least, much of this expansion has been inspired by defensive responses from general education directed at groups seen as threats to established curricular policies and instructional practices, or, in our terms, threats to established *rules of passage*.

The expansion of special education thus has two major parts: the growth of placements and the elaboration of categories. The two are clearly interrelated, yet may be analytically distinguished. That is, the categorical structure of special education may be viewed as a temporarily stable system, a finite number of classifications across which a shifting population is distributed. The categories of special education are slow moving, for their number and definitions can remain relatively stable for a good period of time. The population of students is fast moving, rising overall while changing the number, size, and composition of categories.

Physically and mentally handicapped children may legitimately be brought into public education, bringing them away from an otherwise home- or residential-based education. The argument for conflation involves the exaggeration of or inappropriate reliance on characteristics that are not essentially pertinent to educational potential or performance. Being of West Indian origin or speaking Spanish as a primary home language are traits that became conflated with diagnostic evaluations of mental retardation.

This chapter has argued that conflation is historically conditioned. The historical continuity of non-normative categories, from Backward to Mentally Deficient to EMR and LD, is a defining thread that runs through time, through periods of relative stability and through periods of tumultuous change. From this perspective, the expansion of special education followed a determinant sequence, where each succeeding category inherited the population size and composition of students from its predecessor but altered the criteria that defined its formal boundary. These criteria defined, as it were, the *rules of access* to particular provisions of special education; and in so doing, they defined the *rules of passage* within general education for those students placed.

The historical sequence continuing from Backward to LD bears a likeness to the "formal sequence" in the history of art. In his critique of the placid notion of style, George Kubler showed how the patterns of change in art forms may be seen as "linked solutions" to problems of technical design or aesthetic appreciation (1962, p. 33). Such chains may be closed or open; they may exhaust the possibilities and problem sources for continued innovation, as has Greek vase painting, or they may invite new innovations and replications that extend the duration of linked solutions, as with Australian Aboriginal bark-painting. The continuity across non-normative categories illustrates an open sequence of linked solutions: the problems that gave form to the original category of Backward children were "solved" by the reformulation of the category as Mentally Deficient, embracing the momentum of the intelligence movement. In turn, new problems led to the differentiation of EMR, which contributed to the subsequent definition of LD. The entirety of this sequence comprises a "form class," which in Kubler's terms, "may serve as a scaffold which [it] may be convenient to discard later on, after it has given access to previously invisible portions of the historical edifice" (p. 36).

In this case, the formal sequence that more properly fits Kubler's imagery of a *scaffold* would be the sequence of institutional foundings: from the lunatic asylum or hospital for the deaf, to the reformatory, to compulsory attendance. This sequence was indeed constructed by linked solutions and once completed it "occupied time" as an original scaffolding from which subsequent expansionary sequences derive. We may not want to discard it; but it does provide access to "previously invisible portions of the historical edifice."

Formal sequences, in cross-section, are composed of a network or "mesh of subordinate traits." Thus, if examined during the late 1920s, the mesh for special education was composed of the ties that linked Backward classes to male delinquency; if examined during the late 1950s and 1960s, the mesh involved the ties that linked EMR to black migrations into urban school systems. As the empirical analysis of LD suggests here, the mesh has become increasingly invariant as state differences are worn smooth by "institutional isomorphism" and by the dictates of federal legislation. A contemporary cross-section suggests a mesh where the expansion of the LD category is spilling over to influence juvenile delinquency.

Formal sequences have a "fiber-like structure of temporal stages, all recognizably similar, yet altering in their mesh from beginning to end" (pp. 37-38). As Kubler notes, French gothic architecture illustrates a sequence of linked solutions but is not strictly a "formal sequence"; rather, it is an ecclesiastic category and a reflection of administrative conception in canon law. Similarly, the sequence from Backward to LD is not a true formal sequence. Rather, it is better viewed as documenting the alterations in educational discourse, particularly the transition from a discourse about *rules of access* to *rules of passage.*

In the next chapter, I turn to a theoretical reflection upon this by exploring the "structure of temporal stages" as a sequence of *pedagogic frames.* We are now able, in Kubler's terms, to "discard" some of the scaffolding of nineteenth-century formalization and focus more deeply on the impacts it has had on the sequence of ideas that constitute the theoretical transitions of special education.

APPENDIX

The variables that enter into the analyses for Tables 4.2, 4.3, and 4.4 are indexed as follows:

Dependent Variables

MD, EMR, LD: The number in such classes per 1000 of the enrolled school-age population.

Independent Variables

Comp Attend. The year states enacted compulsory attendance legislation.

Expend: Per pupil expenditures: 1957 for EMR analysis; 1975 for LD analysis.

Reformatory: The year states established the first state reformatory.

Juv Del: The number of juvenile delinquents in reformatories per 1000 of the 10–17-year-old population.

Neglect resid: The number of Dependent and Neglected in residential institutions, per 1000 of the 5–17-year-old population.

MR resid: The number of mentally retarded in residential institutions per 1000 of the 5–17-year-old population.

% black sch pop: The percent of the school-age population black.

Regions

Entered as dummy variables: (1=states within the region, 0=all other states).

NOTES

1. These state level analyses are conducted as tests of our theoretical perspective on *institutional age,* and are not directly interested in the composition of EMR classes. Some previous empirical research does, however, provide some reason to infer composition in these classes, specifically black overrepresentation. In their study of "second-generation educational discrimination," Meier, Stewart and England (1989) use school district data, and using the "representational index" constructed by Finn (1982), they demonstrate both black student overrepresentation and the effects of various measures on the placement of black students in EMR classes. Their analyses are, however, a series of four cross-sections from 1978 to 1984, not an analysis of expansion. Other analyses confirm the correlation between the size of the black (school) population and the variation in state levels of mild mental retardation (Patrick and Reschly 1982; Gelb and Mizokawa 1986). While Patrick and Reschly found that variations in educational criteria were not related to levels of mental retardation (p. 358), it may be that such criteria are indeed peculiar to each state, "loosely coupled" and subject to change in short periods of time. The educational criteria in these analyses are conceived as more historically enduring. Some (compulsory attendance, reformatory) constitute the nineteenth-century *rules of access*; others (pupil expenditures, residential populations) constitute their twentieth-century residues, exerting their influence as the *rules of passage.*

2. More recently, the U.S. Office of Juvenile Justice and Delinquency Prevention's (OJJDP) publication, *Comprehensive Strategy for*

Serious, Violent, and Chronic Juvenile Offenders (1993) identified schools as among the strongest of core institutions, and as the best means to address the "crisis" of delinquency. This portrayal of schooling as the best means to reform delinquency is given considerable support in social scientific research. In a meta-analysis of criminological research on schooling and delinquency, Maguin and Loeber (1996) underscored the consistent finding that general school failure predicts delinquency for children across all socioeconomic levels and racial groups. As if echoing this as established truth, the OJJDP's *Guide for Implementing the Comprehensive Strategy for Serious, Violent, and Chronic Juvenile Offenders* (1995) cited the various educational programs and instructional innovations which are seen to reduce delinquency by way of improving school performance.

CHAPTER 5

The Dramatistic Sequences of Special Education
A Theoretical Reflection

INTRODUCTION

As the field of special education expanded and matured, a corpus of literature developed that awakened many to its breadth and significance. Nonetheless, this literature is distinguished by a considerable division between work that is "indigenous" to special education, and work that originates from "outside." Within the field, there is the ongoing research that is informed by the practical needs of exceptional children and directed toward policy. Companion to this literature are critical reviews and studies addressing substantive questions that often originate from legal challenges and court decisions (cf. Wang, Reynolds and Walberg 1987, vols. 1–3; Sigmon 1990; Hehir and Latus 1992; Skrtic 1991a, 1995).

Outside the field, a body of research has profited by its immunity from practical constraints. Historical research has detailed comparative differences in origins (Sutherland 1981; Lazerson 1983; Tropea 1993; Carrier 1986a), special education"s relevance to current policy (Franklin 1987; Wollons 1993), and its strategic role in educational stratification (Carrier 1983, 1986a; Mehan, Hertweck and Meihls 1986).

In spite of this divide, persistent themes minimize the distance between the two sides. Throughout the literature there is the theme of deviance, founded on real physical and mental differences. The theme of deviance takes research into matters of cultural perceptions, social labeling, and stigmatization. There is the theme of educability and access to instruction, for the exceptional child presents a real challenge to the professional division of labor in public education. Such themes as deviance, educability, and access comprise cornerstones for a unifying theoretical perspective.

This chapter reflects upon the historical genesis and non-normative expansion of special education and joins them by means of *dramatistic* sequences. Special education is particularly suitable to such a perspective, for the historical treatment of exceptional children, from the legality of their exemption to the mandate of their inclusion, is indeed an unfolding drama. Classroom enactments of this drama are revealed in the contested jurisdictions of referral and placement. As our focus on the sequential expansion of non-normative categories established, the growth of special education has not been fully explained by the successful incorporation of truly exceptional children. These categories of exceptional children are historical constructions, and the various motives, which play out in the process of referral and placement, are as much culturally bounded as they are informed by authoritative knowledge.

Our use of the dramatistic perspective adds substantive content to the transition from *rules of access* to the *rules of passage*. Across this past century, the "architectonic history" of this transition has been structured by the sequential shift in dramatistic ratios, where each shift in turn signals a change in the defining trope, from metaphor to irony. But the shift in dramatistic ratios has not proceeded in some abstract way as a broad, national pattern. Rather, I anchor these dramatistic sequences to what have been the dominant referents for the defense of exclusions and exemptions. Defining these as Pedagogic Frames, I argue that these referents have been three, changing sequentially from *culture,* to *character,* to *health.*

Moreover, the pace of these sequential shifts has been defined by *institutionally older* state school systems. As sites of the significant court cases over "racial overrepresentation," cases that have impacted so much of the reforms in assessment procedures and instructional innovations, such states as Massachusetts, California, Pennsylvania, and Illinois, have also been leaders in the contemporary debates over "full inclusion." I end this chapter by a closer examination of the "long shadow" of racial overrepresentation, and explore how the cumulative reflections on this event mirrors the sequential shifts writ large from the late nineteenth-century to the present.

DRAMATISM IN THE WORK OF KENNETH BURKE

The framework for this theoretical summary is provided by the dramatistic analyses in the work of Kenneth Burke (esp. Burke 1966, ch. 7; 1969). Specifically, Burke's *dramatistic pentad* of scene, act, agent, agency, and purpose, and the derived dramatistic ratios, guide this analysis.

Developing these ideas primarily in *A Grammar of Motives* (1969), Burke proposed his "five key terms of dramatism": Act, Scene, Agent, Agency, and Purpose. A given act is emitted or conducted by a particular agent, and the place wherein the act or acts occur is the scene. The conduct and substance of the act by the agent is performed by some means, or agency. Finally, it is an act, rather than an accident, when there is a purpose (see Burke 1969, p. xxiii).

The power of Burke's pentad lies in the "collective interrelation" of each element to the others. Thus, particular scenes condition specific acts: we may expect certain behaviors or levels of performance within the confines of particular scenes. Further, social definitions of particular scenes may condition expectations about given acts when conducted by different agents. Whether a purpose is reached or not may be conditioned by the relation between act and agent.

Burke's pentad yields the construction of "ratios," specific pairings that imply or define a given causality or sequence. Burke's ratios imply or define "propriety," "suitability" or "compulsion" between paired elements, social qualities that reveal a "mutual round of requiredness among them" (Signorile 1989, p. 81). Thus in the scene-act ratio, the core ratio, a proper act is "implied" in a given scene, which in turn is actualized by the appearance or perception of the act. In the act-agency ratio, the activation of a given response may be required, as it is linked to a particular act by social convention or legal mandate.

As Burke noted, the ratios are "principles of determination" (Burke 1969, p. 152). The nature of the relation, its "requiredness," is not only different across the ratios, but this difference holds implications for subsequent action (see Gusfield 1989, pp. 152–153). That is, the ratios differ in their "circumference," a measure of the scope of the ratio. While given scenes may contain particular acts, historical changes alter the circumference of the ratio, and thus alter the grammar of motives that prevail at any given time.

The Outline: Pedagogic Frames, Dramatistic Ratios, and the Master Tropes

By themselves, each of Burke's terms is applicable to education. Certainly a classroom is a constraining scene, wherein certain acts are expected. Additionally, within such a scene, expected levels of academic performance may be "contained" differentially, along lines of gender, race, cultural status, and age. Enactment of the scene-act ratio is everywhere in education. Violations of this ratio, and others, are especially revealed by special education.

This chapter explores special education through the relationship between a Pedagogic Frame and its prevailing Dramatistic Ratio. A Pedagogic Frame defines a time period wherein a referent dominates to provide professional and lay explanations for school performance. Three Pedagogic Frames are identified as developing sequentially, spanning the decades from the 1870s to the present: culture, behavior, and health. School performance may be explained by reference to a pupil's cultural background, to behavioral qualities or deficiencies, or to biological or neurological conditions. For the decades of the late nineteenth-century and early twentieth, cultural background was a pronounced referent, centering on the relation between foreign-born groups and backwardness. With the beginnings of the intelligence testing movement and vocational guidance, attention turned to school truancy and juvenile delinquency, and behavior became the dominant referent and character education the dominant Pedagogic Frame during the inter-war years. From 1950 on, the shift has been to health as a referent for school performance. A Pedagogic Frame of health has come largely with the dramatic expansion of special education placements, from only 1% of the school-age population in 1950, to over 12% in 1995. With Learning Disability becoming the predominant category of special education by 1975, a Pedagogic Frame of "neurological dysfunction" is the predominant reference for school failure.

Each of these Pedagogic Frames promotes and is promoted by a defining dramatistic ratio. Moreover, each embodies a master trope. For the frame of culture, the prevailing ratio was scene/agent, and the prevailing trope was the metaphor of cultural distance. For behavior, the ratio became act/agent, and the defining trope was metonymy. The case-study methodology that probed the various "parts" of an individual delinquent's past led the way to subsequent statistical measurements that formed the empirical foundation to character education. For the frame of health, the ratio is now purpose/agency, and the trope is synecdoche. With learning disability theory, problems in school performance are symptomatic of breaks in a normal sequence of development, where each stage defines an integration of new experiences into an emergent whole. Yet over the past twenty-five years much of the legal and policy challenges that have embroiled special education reflect the role of irony as the pedagogic frame of health became caught in the discrepancies between authoritative knowledge seeking certain purposes, and unintended outcomes from specific dramatistic actions.

A dramatistic analysis of special education focuses on the manner in which a prevailing Pedagogic Frame constructs our understandings of disability and difference in relation to common or public schooling. In Burke's term, the historical sequence of pedagogic frames is in large measure a reduction in the circumference (a term borrowed from William James) of the scene/act ratio. Indeed, much of contemporary research, as well as the legal quagmires that have embroiled special education, are confined to the narrowed circumference of "handicapping conditions" as scenes of school deviance.

A Brief Note on Method

A "dramatistic history" of special education takes language as its primary source. The focus is on exemplary figures and events that were, and are now, especially influential in defining the pedagogic frames of culture, behavior, and health. Professional writings are variously informed by the prevailing Pedagogic Frame; accordingly, the discourse of practitioners should reflect the reduction in the circumference of the scene/act ratio.

There is no claim that each Pedagogic Frame is a qualitative shift distinct from the others. On the contrary, the shift from one frame to another was made through debates over the relative contribution of each. The frame of culture, for example, was deeply infused with extant beliefs about the behavior and medical condition of exceptional children. Both the retention of previous elements and the anticipation of succeeding ones constitute the "dialectics" of Pedagogic Frames.

THE HISTORICAL SEQUENCE OF PEDAGOGIC FRAMES

Culture as Pedagogic Frame: Metaphor and the Exceptional Child

As the late nineteenth-century grappled with the new immigrants from eastern and southern Europe, academic and popular preoccupation was with different racial "stocks." It was widely held that racial differences were rooted in biology, through the genetic transmission of different traits and capacities. The Spencerian metaphor of "survival of the fittest," grafted onto the more neutral Darwinian scheme of evolution, was made to order for the political moment. The cultural inferiority of foreign-born racial stocks was due to inferior biological inheritance. From this equation grew a popular interpretation of racial and class inequalities.

The politics of immigration was but one arena of the debate over biology. In addition to racial and ethnic groups, there was a growing awareness of the "special classes" of the deaf, dumb, blind, and feebleminded. With the 1890 census, the first national enumerations of these groups were given. Concurrently, the educational jurisdiction of state school systems was enlarged by the formalization of compulsory school attendance.

The problem of absorbing children with physical, mental, and/or behavioral deviancies was indeed an organizational dilemma created by formalizing attendance. Yet these deviancies were neither discovered nor invented by schools. Rather, they were used by them to effect the organizational change from voluntary to compulsory attendance: *schools relied on what were already established societal categories: the deaf, dumb, blind, feebleminded, and juvenile delinquent.*

Of these categories, feeblemindedness signified a potential threat. Deaf and blind children presented unambiguous limitations, and their care and education had been seen as a proper obligation of states by the early nineteenth-century. This obligation was discharged through state residential institutions, not by extending access to common schools. In contrast, mentally defective children presented ambiguity. As one observer noted, "It is being more and more recognized that the line between a defective and a normal child cannot be drawn hard and fast, and that many a child who appears dull and stupid in school is in some measure defective" (Allen 1899, p. 5). Indeed, appearances were deceptive, and what constituted "in some measure" became a focus of considerable preoccupation.

American schools were thus facing their own politics of immigration, now complicated by mandates to protect the normal child. The exceptional child symbolized to schools what the new immigrants symbolized to American life. In both instances, the symbolization was cultural distance.

The Dramatistics of Cultural Distance: A Scene/Agent Ratio

That the "line between a defective and a normal child" could not be drawn with certainty was all the more haunting as schools faced compulsory attendance. The specter of students appearing dull and stupid but who were in fact mentally defective led to the depiction of feeblemindedness as a "menace." With the implied metaphor to a contagious disease, feeblemindedness could spread with little detection or warning. Feeblemindedness as menace likened the organizational dilemma facing common schools to the broader political debates over immigration.

Yet the metaphor of the feebleminded as menace was at odds with the fact that mental defectives were largely confined to custodial institutions. The real problem was not that appearances of dullness and stupidity belied feeblemindedness, but that such appearances were indeed real and not fully explained as mental deficiency. Herein lay the "origins" of the exceptional child, and of special education itself.

If the student in school who appeared dull and stupid was not feebleminded, he was nonetheless behind his peers. As noted earlier in chapter 3, in Leonard Ayer's influential report on "retardation" (1909), the problem of "laggards" in city schools was statistically confirmed. Ayer's term for these students did not stick; what did was the term Backward. As a term specifically relevant to schools, Backwardness was soon distinguished from feeblemindedness. In *Backward Children,* Arthur Holmes offered a crisp definition: Backwardness was "not a mental defect, nor a physical defect, nor a judgment of Providence, nor a quality of the individual inherited or acquired"; rather, "it is merely a relation" (1915, p. 13).

With such a definition, Holmes proposed a crucial, albeit "simple and untechnical classification": he distinguished the "temporarily" and "permanently" backward. The former designated children whose retardation derived from "removable defects"; the latter referred to the "growing army of unfortunate little people whose defects are deeply seated within their very being beyond the present philosophy of man to understand" (p. 24). For Holmes, the need for schools to make such a distinction was crucial; failure to do so would simply aggravate the hopeless efforts of teachers who sought "to teach their charges things impossible to learn."

Holmes' book was "an inductive study of backward children." It was soon joined by a growing literature on exceptional children, on their relation to normal students in school and to the broader standards of American culture itself.

An exemplary portrayal of the backward child as a mark of cultural distance is found in the works of Maximilian Groszmann, an early influential advocate for the education of exceptional children. Groszmann's practical work was conducted at the Herbart Hall, the laboratory school of the National Association for the Study and Education of Exceptional Children at Plainfield, New Jersey.[1] In contrast to Holmes' simple and untechnical classification, Groszmann presented an elaborate system of classification, locating backwardness in a "deductive" scheme encompassing all exceptional children.

Groszmann's *The Exceptional Child* (1917) may reasonably be considered the first text-length excursus on the range of "atypical" children and on the role of special education. The core of Groszmann's perspective was "cultural-epoch" theory, first formulated by Johann Herbart, and taken by Groszmann to be "essentially true" (1917, p. 40). This theory proposed that individuals progressed from infancy to adulthood by passing through a number of "developmental stages" that represented the stages of civilization through which human societies have passed. The stage of infancy was likened, metaphorically, to the behaviors of savages and the ancients. The "biological laws" that determined the development of the mind were replicas of the sequential development of the "race" as a whole. While acknowledging that no child in fact is an Indian, an Assyrian, or an Egyptian, it was the corollary to these "civilization levels" that was Groszmann's refinement upon Herbart. Of central importance was the claim that individuals and groups express this correlation in different ways and at different rates. This variation in manifesting "civilization levels" was seen as due to both environmental and hereditary causes.

From this cultural epoch theory, Groszmann advanced the first classification scheme to embrace types of exceptional children. In graphic format, each type was portrayed as a concentric circle, with the genius and normal child marking the center, and atavistic individuals and primitive races deemed "outside of human society," or on the "fringe of modern civilization" (p. 64). Groszmann's classification scheme was entitled a "Diagram of Social Strata," for exceptional children were highly correlated with specific cultural groups, which in turn were strikingly representative of prior civilization levels. These social strata represent "survivals of obsolete types" or are "typical reversions to earlier periods of civilization" (p. 49). Groszmann's real concern was not with "degenerates" or the feebleminded, for these were genetically determined deficiencies that were beyond the reach of society. His focus was on "atavistic" individuals who were members of "deeper levels of culture" which, like geologic strata, are "often times brought to the surface" during times of societal reorganization.

As examples of these atavistic cultures, Groszmann gives particular mention to "colored children," citing reports that find a majority of black children to be exceptional or backward as confirming evidence. Other groups with high numbers of exceptional children included children of "backward types," principally Native-Americans, certain foreign-born groups, and native stock found in the "backyards of Virginia, Tennessee, Kentucky and the Carolinas" (p. 64). These groups, owing to isolation and oppression, were nonetheless "fragments and relics of bygone times," "left untouched by the progress of civilization above and about them" (p. 51).

Within this classification scheme, the exceptional child was on the periphery of the common school, and largely beyond its established pedagogic means as well. Where cultural difference is a dominant referent for school performance, the scene that defined the exceptional child was cast in group terms. These groups were societal categories of race and national origin. Both had become major dimensions of popular thought and were reinforced as census categories, which gave them an apparent facticity with numerical counts. They were outwardly cultural but conceived as inherently natural entities. In Groszmann's terms, they represented distinct civilization levels that comprised a hierarchical order argued to account for the capabilities and motives of individual children. Yet while Groszmann gives repeated attention to individual variation, this variation was determined a priori by the place of an individual's group in the order of civilization levels. Thus, the incapacities of atypical children were inherited properties, detected in psychological, mental, and behavior deviations. The range and severity of these deviations were implied by, or contained in, the broader scene of civilization levels. The circumference of these scenes was indeed large, embedded in epochs of time. They could not be undone within normal school provisions, nor remedied with the normal pedagogics of common schooling.

Insofar as the deviations and incapacities of children were agents of civilization levels, the strategies for the care and treatment of atypical children were likewise viewed in natural, if not necessary, terms. For Groszmann, the exceptional child would be examined in the separate experimental setting of the "psychological clinic," and their education is best limited to "training" within separate residential placements. The ungraded or special class was temporary at best, suited only for the "pseudoatypical" child. For the truly exceptional child, only the residential home setting was the natural counterpart to the scene from which their deviation arose.

The segregated treatment of exceptional children, with eugenic undertones, was a logical extension of Groszmann's scheme of civilization levels. From this scheme, Groszmann sounded words of beneficence and promise, if not utopian in design. In the context of the "sad future of the race if deterioration be allowed to go on unchecked," Groszmann added:

> We must revise our methods of approach in sizing up the social misfit, the disturber, the dead-weight. Instead of branding an individual, with a shrug of the shoulders, as a "misfit," we should try to discover how far he "may" fit, judging his position in the scale of social usefulness by the measure of his competency. This will show how much he is lacking, surely—but not through being "defective," but through being a representative of earlier forms of civilization. Thus we may rank him properly and discover methods of "fitting" him and raising him in the scale. (p. 38)

This is a remarkable statement indeed. While disparaging of common terms for exceptional children, his scheme of civilization levels committed him to a vision of social usefulness founded on efficient methods of allocation.

While Groszmann believed that the optimal education of the exceptional child was in segregated institutions, his "pseudoatypical" category would experience a remarkable growth within city schools. Only ten years after publication of *The Exceptional Child*, eighteen states reported the number of Backward children in special education classes.

Behavior as Pedagogic Frame: Metonymy and the Explanation of Delinquency

The shift from culture to behavior as the pedagogic frame paralleled the waning preoccupation with feeblemindedness. Paradoxically, the decline of the metaphor of feeblemindedness as cultural menace was hastened by the separation of delinquency from mental defect. The relation of delinquency and feeblemindedness had long been a part of both educational and popular thought. Juvenile delinquents were a captive population and at various points from court to reformatory they were scrutinized as individual cases, and these cases could yield aggregate profiles on family, medical, and psychological histories. As part of this scrutiny, it was common practice to look for feeblemindedness.

And indeed feeblemindedness was "found" among delinquents. Yet estimates were as varied as they were unreliable. Estimates ranged from nearly one-half of cases examined (Doll 1917) to under 10% (Bronner 1917). The discrepancies in estimates were due, in part, to differences in methods of assessing mental capacity, ranging from reported IQ scores to verbal accounts by school and reformatory personnel.

Most of all, the problem of juvenile delinquency was confounded with school truancy. Criminal offense was not the sole definition of delinquency. The delinquent was most often an "habitual truant," but the causal relation between the two was unclear. At first this confusion appeared to be resolved by the prior condition of feeblemindedness. Yet this only complicated matters, for it led to conceptual distinctions in attempts to account for delinquency among those of normal intelligence. Out of this complication the delinquent who was not feebleminded emerged as the real problem. The "truly delinquent" was one whose deviance, whether school truancy or criminal offense, could not be traced to mental or physical defect.

Discussions of juvenile delinquency as a type of exceptional child continued to reflect the belief in mental defect as strongly correlated with, if not the cause of, delinquency (Horn 1924, pp. 178–187). Yet the distinction between delinquency and feeblemindedness was affirmed by some who were themselves influential figures in the study of mental subnormality. One figure especially was Henry Goddard, who departed academic psychology to work at the Vineland Training School in New Jersey and, armed with medical knowledge and practical observations, dedicated himself to the study of "psycho-asthenics," or feeblemindedness (see Zenderland 1987). In *The Kallikak Family* Goddard outlined the hereditary lineage of feeblemindedness, feeding the view of it as a menace. Yet in later years, now as Director of the Ohio Bureau of Juvenile Research, Goddard turned his attention to delinquency. In his *Juvenile Delinquency* (1921), he continued to be forceful about feeblemindedness: "We may regard idiots as intellectual monstrosities and as such bar them from our discussion. Omitting these, all human beings have intelligence" (p. 6). For Goddard, the delinquent must not be confused with the feebleminded; to do so was to confound moral weakness with mental weakness.

If not caused by mental defect, the causes of delinquent misconduct must lie elsewhere. Goddard's answer returned him to psychology: delinquency was the eruption of "primitive instincts" that were not symptomatic of a mental disease, but were the symptoms of "mental suffering." This suffering was termed psychopathy and was accorded its own classificatory distinction.

Psychopathy was a condition that may be associated with feeblemindedness, but was largely found among those of normal intelligence. The psychopathic child displayed behaviors that were legion among juvenile delinquents: [he] was nervous, forgetful and disobedient, cunning and shrewd, dishonest and lying, a sexual pervert and a consistent thief. In short, the psychopathic was "an irresponsible, nonadjustable, uncontrollable misfit in society" (p. 39).

As Goddard stated, the psychopathic was "in society" and, therefore, curable. Unlike the other defective classes, the delinquent presented an opportunity, for delinquency "can be largely eradicated." The means for this social redemption were well available: the public schools. In contrast to state institutions that were principally custodial in purpose, the common school was the opportune site for the intervention and eradication of delinquency. As Goddard saw it, the path was clear and determinant (1921):

> So modify primitive instincts that the group can function as a unit . . . like the organs of the body . . . each one must function in such a way as to fit in with the functioning of the rest to the end that the total functioning of the body may be that of the highest efficiency. (p. 113)

With the imagery of functional efficiency, Goddard sounded the tone of a metonymic explanation of delinquency. Once delinquency is distinguished from mental defect, delinquent behavior could be broken down into its component parts and understood first and foremost as malfunction.

The Dramatistics of Behavioral Deviance: An Act/Agent Ratio

Goddard's transition from his work in mental subnormality to delinquency came late in his career. As such, what he promoted in *Juvenile Delinquency* was neither original nor empirical. The definitive statement on delinquency, foreshadowing Goddard's essay, came six years earlier. In 1915, William Healy published his *The Individual Delinquent,* subtitled "A Text-Book of Diagnosis and Prognosis for All Concerned in Understanding Offenders" (1915b). As the Director of the Psychopathic Institute in Chicago, Healy would have the greatest single influence on the "diagnosis and prognosis" of delinquency. Unlike Goddard, Healy was a physician; but like Goddard, he worked directly with his subjects: Healy's laboratory was the Juvenile Court.

Healy was unequivocal about the relation between mental defect and delinquency. In parsimonious fashion, he stated: "as we go up in the scale of mentality we naturally find more ability to be an active delinquent." By reversing the commonly believed relation of mental defect and delinquency, Healy opened a range of anti-social behaviors that were as intentional as they were cunning. The delinquent, Healy often described, was often thoughtfully and provocatively engaged in his acts. The deviations and deceptions of the delinquent were not primitive instincts, as Goddard claimed. Rather, they were expressions of an intensely rich "mental imagery," whether about stealing, lying, swindling, or sex (Healy 1915a; 1915c). In contrast to normal behavior, the mental imageries of the delinquent are reflections of underlying mental conflicts which are often repressed (1923).

Healy's methodology of study was metonymic from the start. The beginning point was the individual case, "not in himself to be grouped according to any logical system, and mere classification of either the antecedent or the consequent of his tendency leads only a short distance along the path of scientific and practical aims" (1915b, p. 165). The intensive study of the individual delinquent must follow the "genetic method," the backward search for salient experiences or events that constituted the "intricacy of causality."

On the surface of this intricacy is the particular offense, arising as it were from a particular pathway of experiences. But this pathway was essentially specific to an individual delinquent. Again and again Healy emphasized how a given offense can be traceable to more than one "antecedent condition." But these causal links will vary across individuals. Explanation of delinquent acts increases as one traces back to unravel the constellation of prior experiences. Only by "disembodying" a delinquent's past can the best prognosis be devised. Yet while a prognosis can be made that best fits the constellation of experiences, this prognosis remains specific to the individual case. One does not, in short, return from the various experiences to a theory of delinquency (Healy and Bronner 1936, p. 159).

For Healy, delinquent offenses were intentional and willed; yet by tracing backwards from these acts to antecedent conditions, Healy's interpretation relies on a mechanistic language. The relations that link antecedent conditions to intentional acts are likened to paths or channels that are dug deep. These channels become, in Healy's apt phrase, the "mechanics of habit" (1915a):

> Now, what specific action, what type of conduct, is the outcome of the stimulus, may largely depend, even in very young persons, on the relationships and sequences that have previously been established between stimuli and action. The path once trodden beckons on. The force of habit pervades the whole of mental life and, indeed, is one of the main processes that regulate the association of ideas, the fundamental phenomenon of mental life. (p. 89)

Healy's analysis and explanation of delinquency employed both willful intention and the mechanics of subconscious forces. The delinquent's offense was a willful act enacted in present circumstances. The cunning and dishonesty of the individual delinquent were quizzical, for they were simultaneously intentional and habitual.

Delinquency was the enactment of an act/agent ratio. In contrast to Groszmann's metaphor of civilization levels that "contained" the exceptional child, the delinquent as agent does not contain his acts, or offenses. However, in Burke's terms, "its results may be said to 'pre-exist' within him" (1969, p. 16). As if with reference to Healy, Burke noted further:

> the act-agent ratio more strongly suggests a temporal or sequential relationship than a purely positional or geometric one. The agent is an author of his acts, which are descended from him, being good progeny if he is good, or bad progeny if he is bad . . . And, conversely, his acts can make him or remake him in accordance with their nature. (p. 16)

For Healy, the individual delinquent was indeed the "author of his acts" which were "descended from him." Nonetheless, what is "descended" does not derive from a distant cultural position. Misconduct, in contrast to backwardness, is situationally activated. For Healy, the circumference of the scene of delinquent misconduct is reduced to within the recent past of the individual. Accordingly, the data relevant to delinquent behavior do not lie in obscure civilization levels, nor in "racial characteristics."[2] Consequently, the education of delinquent misconduct is receptive to alterations in the immediate situation of the child, or student. On the other hand, the education of backwardness, however "temporary," must await the long-term mobility of civilization levels.

Healy's foundation work on delinquency forged a bridge between the psychological clinics and the public schools. The first psychological clinic for children was established 1896 by Lightner Witmer, a professor of psychology at the University of Pennsylvania. The design of Witmer's clinic was to examine the influence of truancy on the learning problems of school children. Healy's work at the Psychopathic Institute was similar in design, if not motive. For both, whether a child was in school or in the juvenile court system, some history of "maladjustment" was the root cause. For both, this history was largely situational, for neither biological inheritance nor racial ancestry were determinant. Their common thread was "clinical psychology," the definition given by Witmer for the practice conducted by child guidance and mental hygiene clinics.

While the practical benefits of the psychological clinics were attractive to public schools, their utility was limited by the methodology of case-study. In contrast to this time-consuming method, the statistical approach of the mental testing movement offered the means to assess behavior with reference to general patterns and distributions. During the inter-war years, the meeting of clinical psychology and mental testing converged on the matter of "character" and its school related consequences. One result was "character education." With character education the fund of delinquency research found practical implementation.

No effort represents the ascendancy of behavior as a pedagogic frame more than the three-volume work, *Studies in the Nature of Character*, by Hugh Hartshorne and Mark May. These volumes, published between 1928 and 1930, were the products of the Character Education Inquiry commissioned by the Institute of Social and Religious Research and conducted by Teachers College. The first volume, subtitled "Studies in Deceit," acknowledges the "illuminating work [of] Healy" who demonstrated the situational determinants of dishonesty. For Hartshorne and May, deception was a learned response and in particular situations, a reasonable one. With careful statistical methods, the Character Education Inquiry could unravel Healy's "causal intricacy" of delinquent behavior.

Indeed, the authors of the Inquiry held out great promise from "the statistical manipulation of large masses of data," for such manipulation could reveal "certain trends of association [that] can be detected which elude the most careful observation" and that can prove unfounded "imagined associations" that come from "folklore or superstition" (Hartshorne, May and Shuttleworth 1930, p. 371). The significant "trends of association" were defined in hierarchical order: the strongest determining factor was the school classroom and the experience of friendship; this was followed by factors of intelligence, capacity to resist suggestion, and emotional stability. Lastly was "the general and economic social background." Thus, much like Healy, but now compelled by "large masses of data," the Inquiry drew the circumference of the scene to the specifics of the situation. Broad cultural distinctions explained little of the differences in deceptive behavior or self-control; rather, "In proportion as situations are alike, conduct is correlated" (p. 373).

Beyond its theoretical contribution, the Inquiry lent its considerable influence on the "practicable measure of total character" by closing with recommendations for the school use of tests in five areas of student conduct: honesty, service, inhibition, persistence, and moral knowledge and attitude. With such batteries, teachers and schools could be assisted in their attempts to identify and treat the causes of behavioral misconduct and its impact on school achievement. Throughout the inter-war years, the number of such measurement techniques grew, elevating character as a dominant pedagogic referent for explaining academic performance and school behavior as well (see Thomas and Thomas 1928, pp. 273–294).

Health as Pedagogic Frame: The Synecdoche of Learning Disability

The "modern" era of special education is dominated by a pedagogic frame of health. The rise of this frame has not been a return to mental deficiency, nor has it been centered around the inclusion of deaf, blind, crippled students, or ones with speech defects. Its ascendancy was centered on the less visible and complicated arena of "learning disabilities" and school performance.

Certainly the ascendancy of a pedagogic frame of health is tied to mental handicap. The category of "mentally retarded" experienced dramatic growth in placements, accounting for 26% of all exceptional children in special classes in 1963. The expansion and contraction of this category is linked to the "dialectics" of a maturing system of special education, specifically, the decline of EMR, still evoking a genetic limit to intellectual potential, and the corresponding expansion of LD, a category founded on an emotional and neurological etiology but evoking the positive promise of normal intellectual capacity.

The theoretical core of learning disability was set forth some twenty years before its formal recognition as a handicapping condition. In the mid 1940s, Alfred Strauss and Heinz Werner (1942) drew the distinction between "exogenous" and "endogenous" mental defectives, associating brain-injury with the former, and genetic inheritance with the latter. With this division, a range of behavioral disorders were freed from interpretations long given for mental retardation. The behavioral disorders of the brain-injured child, or in pointed terms *The Other Child*

(Lewis, Strauss, and Lehtinen 1951), were especially troublesome in school settings, rendering the child slow in learning and often uncontrollable in the classroom. These children exhibited two consistent behavioral abnormalities: perseveration, or the tendency to persist in an activity without conscious purpose; and disinhibition, or the inability to control desires or to respond appropriately to social expectations. For Strauss and his colleagues, brain-injury could not be confirmed with objective, medical evidence. The occurrence of brain-injury could result from an infectious disease, an emotional disturbance, or a traumatic experience (Kephart 1968, pp. 11–14).

The key intervening condition from which the behaviors of perseveration and disinhibition derived was disturbance to normal perception, premised on damage to neurological capacities that alter how a child perceives both space and motion. It is not that the child does not see the shiny automobile; rather, he/she sees only that it is shiny. Perception is partial, and thus abnormal (Lewis, Strauss, and Lehtinen 1951):

> In normal perception, the whole is recognized at once and its parts in relation to it and to each other . . . When it is perceived, the whole becomes more than simply the sum of its parts. It becomes a meaningful configuration, capable of generating a response by the whole organism. (p. 22)

This failure to perceive the whole was the "psychopathology" of perception. In contrast to earlier, metonymic definitions of psychopathology, this new definition now meant the capacity to see the whole as "more than the sum of the parts."

This newer "synecdoche of perception" was an important claim, for it allowed a kinder judgment of behavioral deviancies. The brain-injured child was of normal intelligence and well intentioned, but perceptually confused. The LD child was thus unaware of how to behave properly. The numbers of such school children were estimated to be considerable, and their educational troubles were likely misinterpreted and, worse, wrongfully treated.

The early work of Strauss and Werner formulating "learning disability" as symptomatic of brain-injury was more fully articulated in the 1960s and 1970s. Leading the way were Strauss's co-workers, of whom Newell Kephart and William Cruickshank were the most prominent. Of the two, Kephart was the more theoretical, locating learning disability in a synecdochic model of the normal "course of development."

Kephart's theoretical refinement of learning disability is set out in *The Slow Learner in the Classroom* (1960). While the work offers a practical focus for training learning disabled children, such procedures are derived from a theory of normal development. The essence of Kephart's theory is an emergent view of growth, the starting point for which is the "patterned nature of the developing neural structure" (p. 16). The key term is *patterned*, for the unique qualities of the neural circuits do not arise from individual circuits, but from their "interrelationship." Much like the generation of a normal curve, the resulting aggregate pattern is neither willed nor anticipated by individuals. Similarly, the "data" of experiences are processed by a neural system and the resulting unique qualities are "imposed upon them." These new neural patterns are then observed in behavior.

Because neural systems are dynamic, so too is the course of development. The "normal" course of development is guided by two processes. One is normative, where behaviors are observed as quantitative measures of chronological age levels. Each succeeding age level is assumed to possess more skills and abilities, by virtue of accumulation. This process of accumulation is linear, with no "discernible breaks or points of inflection."

Paralleling this normative cumulation of abilities is a "step-like" process, adopted from Piaget, that is marked by breaks and points of inflection. The passage from one step or stage to another is both abrupt and qualitative, bringing a progressively greater conceptual generalization. For Kephart, achievement of conceptual generalization is the measure of real and normal development. At each stage, conceptual generalization is an integration of elements, constituting a unique form generalization. Each "constructive form perception" possesses an "emergent quality," for it is an abstraction from single elements. Thus, children may behave in classrooms "as if" they possessed form perception, but they may be simply "manipulating single elements or small groups of elements." Similarly, development is "unidirectional and irreversible," always "toward wider and richer perceptions" (Kephart 1968, p. 35; Strauss and Kephart 1955, p. 90). If a child regresses to lesser complex tasks, performance is affected by the emergent qualities gained by already achieving higher levels of form generalization.

The Dramatistics of Health Deviance: A Purpose/Agency Ratio

The dramatistics of contemporary special education are situated within a purpose/agency ratio. Special education has come of age. The defining moment of this maturation was the passage of the *The Education for All Handicapped Children Act* of 1975 (EAHC), a federal mandate that all school children, regardless of handicapping condition, be given access to education in a "least restrictive environment." With this legislation, special education secured a purpose that moved it out of the shadows of regular education. With terms akin to racial desegregation, the policy of "mainstreaming" of exceptional students enlarged the purpose of instruction to encompass physical and mental disabilities.

To implement this purpose, a host of agencies gained expanded roles. School psychology rose in prominence, for certified evaluation and testing of students referred was the legal basis for placement. Supplementary staff, including school counselors and nurses, became implicated in referral, diagnostic, and evaluation procedures. As court challenges to special education placements linked cities and states, the agencies of special education enlarged around concerns of due process. Special education hearings became a mandated part of placement procedures, designed to monitor the purpose of PL 94–142.

The ascendancy of LD as a category of special education, and as a dominant referent for school performance, has been due, in large part, to the expansion of LD as a field, rooted in broader societal changes (Franklin 1980) and promoted by effective political interests (cf. Carrier 1987; Sleeter 1987b; Franklin 1987). Yet the category of LD has been "carried" by the field itself, subordinated, as it were, to the purposes of PL 94–142 and by the agencies that have secured their places in relation to this Act (see Jepperson 1991). Within this context, the condition of LD has been the subject of considerable research, but the outcome of this work has produced little consensus. There is an acknowledged discrepancy between the theoretical basis of learning disability and supporting empirical evidence (see esp. Coles 1978; Ysseldyke, Algozzine, Ridley and Graden 1982; Ysseldyke, Algozzine Shinn and McGue 1982; Ysseldyke, Algozzine, and Epps 1983).

This evidentiary embarrassment is indeed striking. In one attempt to explain this, Kavale and Forness note in succinct terms, "the field of LD has become a victim of its own history" (1985, p. 18). In their interpretation, this victim circumstance derives from the continued acceptance of the fundamental assumptions set out by Strauss and Werner, principally their distinction between exogenous and endogenous defectives. Yet this distinction is not supported (Kavale and Forness 1984). As a consequence, Kavale and Forness propose that the LD field has not been able to make paradigmatic shifts necessary to accommodate social and cultural changes. In sum, both the success and failure of LD are simultaneously explained as a moment in the Kuhnian scheme of scientific paradigms.

Yet this explanation seems to provoke more questions. Are we to await more empirical studies, designed with greater methodological care? Yet if virtually all test batteries are lacking in validity and reliability (Coles 1978), would tighter research designs be the corrective? In light of inconsistent definitions of LD, conflicting measures of perceptual and behavior symptoms, of the documented failure to distinguish labeled LD students from non-LD students, how has the field achieved its prominence? What sustains learning disability as a dominant health referent for school failure?

Such questions should not be confined to LD, but may be asked of special education itself. How has special education achieved its prominence? And, in light of abundant evidence of misdiagnosis and inappropriate placement, what are its defenses against such evidence? Again, we must begin with purpose.

PL 94–142 broadened the circumference of special education to include all school-age children in all school systems. In defining the purpose of special education as national in scope, the Act functions, in Burke's term, much like a political "constitution." In their political form, constitutions are "agonistic instruments," where "the attempt is made, by verbal or symbolic means, to establish a motivational fixity of some sort, in opposition to something that is thought liable to endanger this fixity" (1969, p. 357). A motivational fixity is a dominant way of viewing things, be they facts or social relations. Constitutions condense and thus organize collective perceptions and understandings. Most of all, constitutions offer legitimacy to facts and relations, doing so by anchoring them in a presumed "natural" order. In doing so, "social inequality can gain the legitimacy of a grounding in what people see as natural inequalities" (Carrier 1982, p. 55). As a social constitution, PL 94–142 most certainly addresses inequalities: rights of access to education; recognition of educability and equality of opportunity.

Key to Burke's meaning of constitution is a conceptual reversal: in his terms, "social rights were first "ascribed" to nature, and then "derived" from it" (Carrier 1982, p. 54). That is, social rights are conceived as derived from a nonsocial, natural realm, but are understood and justified *against* an existing social order. In affirming the right of exceptional children to a public education, regardless of handicapping condition, PL 94–142 evoked a natural right against a formidable inequality of capabilities.

By constituting such a purpose, "the terms scene, act, and agent *fall away*, as we talk simply of purposes and the agencies proper to these purposes" (Burke 1969, p. 309, my emphasis). Thus, estimates of LD students vary across school systems as scenes, no composite behaviors differentiate LD students from non-LD students as acts, and psychologists and teachers cannot successfully distinguish LD students from non-LD students (cf. Johnson 1980; Algozzine and Ysseldyke 1983; Mehan, Hertweck and Meihls 1986; Ysseldyke 1987). Regardless of these empirical embarrassments, LD is sustained as an organizing principle well suited to the purposes of PL 94–142. Dramatistically, its very ambiguity is a source of its prominence, where "the very strength in affirming of a given term may the better enable men to make a world that departs from it," for "the affirming of the term as [their] god-term enables men to go far afield without sensing a loss of orientation" (Burke 1969, p. 54). In spite of its empirical embarrassments, learning disability provides a motivational fixity against an ever-present challenge: school failure; and against that which is liable to threaten that fixity: an increasing social and cultural diversity within public schools.

If the relationship between empirical evidence and the founding theory of learning disability is viewed synecdochically, the relation is "loosely coupled" indeed. The volume of evidence and the diversity of definitions and measures are allowed to vary across scenes, acts and agents. This decoupling of evidence and theory has not, in turn, done serious damage to the LD field itself.[3]

The immunity of the LD field may, in fact, derive from the weakness of supporting evidence and the diversity of definitions and measures. This decoupling of evidence and theory may be functionally adaptive to the organizational structure of contemporary American education. As Meyer and Rowan (1978) describe, the long- term change has been from a local exchange between families and schools, to an exchange among schools at the national level. Integral to this larger-level exchange are educational categories, such as LD. Regardless of the discrepancy between its founding theory and empirical support, the category is a concrete referent for agencies whose purpose is to regulate and explain school failure.

THE LONG SHADOW OF "RACIAL OVERREPRESENTATION": AN EXEMPLAR

It can be argued that much of the research focus in special education, and the tenor of its discourse as well, has been shaped by the tempest of racial overrepresentation in EMR classes first revealed in the 1960s. The scope of such evidence drew several parties into a prolonged exchange that has carried over into the present. In a number of ways, both the debates over mainstreaming during the 1970s and early 1980s, and currently over inclusion, are heir to the court struggles over IQ tests and minority bias that stemmed directly from these revelations. Yet debate is a weak term, if we want only to recount exchanges merely in serial, chronological form. If, however, we step back and contemplate overrepresentation as a cultural and intellectual drama, we see that it resonated widely and penetrated deeply into the very core of public schooling.

Indeed, the legal challenges, legislative mandates, and the changing contour of empirical research and formal discourse exhibit a correspondence to the sequential "grammar" of the master tropes. With the revelation of overrepresentation in the late 1960s, there was a general metaphorical awareness or collective mood that stimulated romantic ideals and motivated struggles against injustice and the prospect of real change. Out of this general consciousness began a metonymic phase of conflicts which reduced the abstract goals to narrower and more practical interests. After an accumulated history of conflict and debate, national calls for the reform of special education practices arose as a renewed, synecdochic mode of thinking. Finally, as the actual form of implementing the calls for (radical) reform was confronted, a new discourse emerged that is ironic in tone and content. This cumulative history "ends" with irony, for the resolutions of divisions and struggles produces a likelihood of outcomes that are often as unwanted as they are unanticipated.

The tropological sequences of racial overrepre-sentation bound it as an historical event within the long historical development of special education. Racial overrepresentation has been much more than debates over statistical evidence and assessment procedures; it has in fact been a drama with unfolding consequences that arise from earlier stages and carry over into subsequent stages. Seen in this way, the stages of racial overrepresentation in special education bear a strong likeness to the stages conceived by Marx in his classic *The Eighteenth Brumaire of Louis Bonaparte* (1968). Marx conceived of Bonaparte's ascendancy to power as an unfolding drama constituted by four periods: the February period, the period of the Constituent National Assembly, the period of the Legislative National Assembly, and the Second Empire, lasting from 1851 to the Paris Commune of 1871. Each period corresponded to the stages of the classical drama, and to the master tropes as well. Like Marx's analysis, we do not so much claim that the "drama of racial overrepresentation" was in fact demarcated by four periods. However, legislative events and key publications within and outside of special education mark transitions that reflect the semantics of tropological development similar to Marx's four periods.

Racial Overrepresentation as Metaphor: Warnings and Revelations, 1968–1972

The initial revelations of overrepresentation ignited a general awareness of bias and violation that linked special education placement to larger issues of educational opportunity. These first years were metaphorical in character, stimulated by intense commitments against the wrongs of test bias and misclassification. Like Marx's February period, the revelations were "a surprise attack, a taking of the old society unawares, and the people proclaimed this unexpected stroke as a deed of world importance, ushering in a new epoch" (Marx 1968, p. 18).

Early statements within special education by senior and leading figures published statements warning of inappropriate placements (Johnson 1962; Darrah 1967; Reynolds 1967; Dunn 1968; Christoplos and Renz 1969; Johnson 1969; Deno 1970; Lilly 1970; Garrison and Hammill 1971). Dunn's article was especially timely, for it resonated with a climate of civil rights and sensitized a younger generation of prospective special educators to the political relevance of special education placements. Dunn asserted that much of special education for the mildly retarded was not only unnecessary, but imposed harm by labeling and stigmatizing. Referencing a first generation of "efficacy studies" that presumably supported his claims, he added the reference that most of those labeled mildly retarded were black students and of low socioeconomic background. A double error was plaguing special education, the error of inappropriate diagnosis and the social-legal error of misclassification.

While Dunn's article has been rigorously critiqued for its selective use of empirical evidence (MacMillan, Semmel and Gerber 1994), it nonetheless signaled a shift in tone and focus. Two years after Dunn's warnings, Deno (1970) followed with a critique that combined an affirmation of special education's unique "retrieval vantage point" (p. 231), with a blunt proposition that special education ought to "work itself out of business" (p. 233). On the heels of these two articles, the practices of educational psychology and of special education itself were linked to issues of civil rights and national scope; they defined as "public issues" what may have remained isolated "private troubles."

An especially provocative and timely statement that captured the public dimension of private troubles was proposed from outside of special education by Jane Mercer in *Labeling the Mentally Retarded* (1973; see also Mercer 1971). Reinforced, in part, by the volatile political climate surrounding the revelations of ethnic overrepresentation and with the evidence of disproportion beginning to be challenged in courts, Mercer reported her research on the epidemiology of mental retardation in a medium-sized western city. At the core of her research design was the novel thesis that mental retardation is an achieved status, not a condition ascribed at birth. The discrepancy between evaluations within a school context and their absence within home and neighborhood contexts defined the condition of mental retardation as a situationally acquired label that is achieved by the "successful" application of a label. Thus, a child can occupy the status and learn to play the role of mental retardate in school, but vacate that label and occupy no such status elsewhere. The consequence is a misdiagnosis generated by the misalliance between the school and home as among the "social systems" individuals inhabit and traverse in their daily lives. The misalliance between school labels and other social systems emphasized scene as prior; and its priority yielded a bold presumption: an individual is not mentally retarded if not nominated and labeled. From this framework, those whose social systems were most discrepant were Hispanic and black school children.

The empirical strength and theoretical novelty of this work thrust Mercer into the center of an emerging agonic phase of special education and racial overrepresentation. Significant class action challenges against minority misclassification began to define lines of opposition; especially *Diana* (1970) and *Larry P.* (1972) in California; *Mills* (1972) in Washington, D.C., and *PARC* (1972) in Pennsylvania. In abrupt contrast to the "prologue" of revelations and warnings, where "nothing and nobody ventured to lay claim to the right of existence and of real action" (Marx 1968, p. 21), with the filing of class actions suits minority misclassification was metonymically reduced, from a general disaffection to alignments with particular group interests, from an abstract defense of rights to court disputes over test bias among expert witnesses. The transition reduced a general, "metaphorical" climate to the metonymy of individual ethnic and cultural differences that extended, as it were, with equal claims to the ideal of equality of educational opportunity.[4]

The Metonomy of Court Challenges and the Receding Significance of Scene: 1972–1979

A period of conflict and struggle commenced with the filing of class action suits on behalf of Hispanic and black students against city and state school systems. Like Marx's period of the Constitutional National Assembly, the law suits of this agonic phase represented the interests of "factions" that co-existed "contiguously," separated by their particular claims and the content of their causal arguments.

Diana v. California (1970) was one of the very first to challenge minority imbalance. The fundamental argument in Diana was that Mexican-American children assigned to EMR classes were not "legally" mentally retarded. At the extreme, the Mexican-American students were tested in English when their primary home language was Spanish. When Diana, then age 8, was retested by a Spanish-speaking psychologist, she improved by 49 points, giving her a score that disqualified her for EMR placement. The primary settlement in *Diana* stipulated that testing be done in both English and Spanish, and that norming procedures be undertaken for a test wherein the population would be comprised of Mexican-American students who live in California.

The claims of *Diana* served to highlight overrepresentation as a statewide problem; yet the settlement was narrow in scope. That is, the interpretation of Hispanic overrepresentation was closely tied to bilingualism (see also *Covarrubias v. San Diego* 1971; *Guadalupe v. Tempe* 1972). In contrast, the overrepre-sentation of black students elevated the challenge to cultural bias in the IQ test itself. In *Larry P. v. Riles* (1972), the much-watched class action challenge against IQ testing of black school children in San Francisco, the claims of inherent discrimination linked socioeconomic background to test bias, defining the scene of cultural background as an explanatory source of test performance. *Larry P.* won an immediate moratorium on the use of IQ tests with black students and initiated a decade long debate over test bias and special education placement.

The priority of scene appeared to dominate the period of court challenges (see, e.g., Hobbs 1975). In *Larry P.*, Judge Peckham was persuaded by the discriminatory bias in IQ tests as linked to socioeconomic background (cf. Sattler 1981; Elliott 1987; Reschly 1980). One consequence of this apparent consensus was a mandate for the construction of an instrument that would incorporate sociocultural background directly into the assessment of intellectual potential. Due in part to her critical role in *Larry P.*, Mercer went on to produce SOMPA (System of Multicultural Pluralistic Assessment) (Mercer 1979) as an alternative to the standard IQ test. The conceptual and technical dimensions of SOMPA reflect the priority attributed to scene: distance from the values of the core culture, determined by occupational and family measures, is the source of an individual's Estimated Learning Potential. Different social and cultural groups produce multiple normal distributions; evaluation against a single normal distribution is the source of the test bias that contributes to inappropriate diagnosis and placement in special education (Mercer 1979).

As the debates over IQ testing and bias, special education placement, and school tracking implicated parents, professionals, and school administrators in opposition to one another, the climate of exchange drew more fragmented. Most conspicuous, the apparent consensus about test bias and racial overrepresentation was broken by the discrepant outcomes between *Larry P.* and *PASE v. Hannon* (1980). While Judge Peckham declared the IQ test to be culturally biased,

Judge Grady expressed no such agreement. With most of the issues remarkably the same, *PASE* rejected the claim that IQ tests were inherently discriminatory, critiqued the claim that poverty was a source of IQ deficits and downplayed the significance of adaptive behavior for the measurement of intelligence or for life's challenges in general. As Elliot summarized (1987, p. 199), "Judge Grady was interested in the tests at a far more microanalytical level than Judge Peckham."

And so the reduction continued, and with it the priority of scene. Critiques of SOMPA appeared with some frequency, upon its technical validity (Oakland 1979, 1980; Brown 1979; Gutkin and Reynolds 1980, 1981), conceptual framework (Jirsa 1983) and remedial effectiveness (Reschly 1987, p. 35). An especially incisive and grounded critique was given by Goodman (1977; 1983), whose dissection of Mercer's account of racial overrepresentation and of its alleviation through SOMPA rested on a displacement of scene by an empirically forced respect for the "indeterminacy" of agency.

For Goodman, the discrepancy between school labels and nonschool contexts was not essentially relevant to the etiology of mental retardation. In fact, such information may harm more than assist. Goodman's critique proceeded from a rejection of the entrenched belief in the separation of mind and body and of *organicity* as an explanatory concept in particular. Ironically, SOMPA critiqued IQ but utilized it conceptually and technically. Herein lay its Achilles heel; its central fault was precisely its *diagnosticism*, "the proposition that pure cases of deficit originating in biology and relatively enduring can be determined by peeling away those instances in which retardation is a by-product of social circumstance" (1977, p. 204). The "diagnostic fallacy" is the belief that biology is recalcitrant to improvement and only culture is malleable. We can manipulate socioeconomic and cultural background as variable scenes that account for intellectual potential; but we cannot manipulate biology. In terms that were meant to be heuristic only, Goodman (1983) nonetheless reverses the causal logic of SOMPA:

> But let us assume, for the sake of argument, that the opposite is true: It is the consequences of culture which are more impervious to intervention than the effects of biological damage. One should then develop a test which calls learning potential the variation which occurs after equating children on organic parameters. This test would

assume that since biology is more changeable than culture, "true" retardation is the variance in low scores attributable to the environment. (p. 107)

Heuristic or not, Goodman exposed the irony that theories proposing to intervene on sociocultural differences embrace and uphold the incorrigibility of biology. With convincing evidence, Goodman detailed how the relationship between organic impairment and prognosis is not direct. A diagnosis of brain-damage does not necessarily explain the observed behavioral problems, for neurological evidence may be a result as well as a cause of the behavioral problems, or they may be essentially and practically irrelevant. The distinctions between mind and body, between endogenous and exogenous retardation, must simply be rejected. At minimum, the fallacy of organicity perpetuates a laissez faire attitude toward individuals with more severe handicaps and favors those whose "mild mental retardation" presumes to derive from the prior scenes of socioeconomic and family background. As she concludes, "organicity becomes a shorthand for statements about the sources and consequences of the problem, not its location, for all behavior is located in the body and all complex behavior in the cerebrum" (1983, p. 116).

Much like Marx's stage of the Constitutional National Assembly, amidst the flurry of court challenges the "foundation" for the educational rights of exceptional children was established by the passage of *The Education for All Handicapped Children Act*. The national machinery "represented" the rights of all children, regardless of handicapping condition. Like Marx's second period, where the aim was "to reduce the results of the revolution to the bourgeoisie scale" (1968, p. 23), the annual reports to congress were to account the results of state practices, reducing them to comparative measures that may be evaluated against the "scale" of federally defined standards. The potential for a healing of conflicts and for a correction of the injustice of overrepresentation was seen as the ideal and intent of the EAHC. From above the various challenges, the mission of the EAHC expressed the potential for a synecdochic reintegration, where the rights of exceptional children would be ensured by the monitoring of due process procedures.

The *Synecdoche* of Mainstreaming, 1979–1986

With the authority of a national legislation, the reform model of mainstreaming began a period that linked state special education practices and outcomes to federal-level monitoring. The instrumental intentions of EAHC, broadening the mandates of *PARC* and *Mills*, extended to all children the right to a publicly supported education and defined a number of procedures to ensure due process.

This third period is characterized by a tearing apart of the fragile unity that gave the multiple demands of court challenges a semblance of common purpose. As Marx described the third period of the Legislative National Assembly, defeats forced the proletariat "into the background of the revolution." Yet, "subsequent blows become the weaker, *the greater the surface of society over which they are distributed*" (1968, p. 24, my emphasis). Likewise, against the representation of the rights of exceptional children embodied in the EAHC, the implementation of these ideals across a *greater surface of society* confronted the realities of local and state practices, tearing at the professional framework of special education. Defenders of mainstreaming, as the unifying symbol of the revolution in educational rights, faced embarrassing empirical evidence that tainted the ideal of integration itself, and of due process protections as well.

Haunted by the specter of racial overrepresentation, the effectiveness of due process checks was held up for critical review and the findings were not kind: implementation of due process rights was fractured and often countermanded by the inertial force of local school culture (Kirp, Kuriloff and Buss 1975; Kirp 1976; Weatherley 1979), hearings were few, often costly and timeconsuming, and to many parents the right to legal and expert counsel was more an abstraction than a viable option (Kirp and Jensen 1983; Neal and Kirp 1986; Kirst and Bertken 1983). In short, attempts to implement the goals of mainstreaming accentuated the intransigence of *scene*: an unwieldy categorical structure was superimposed on local cultures that were, however, organizationally decoupled from evaluation.

This intransigence of scene became a basis for a class action suit challenging the overrepresentation of black students in the public schools of Georgia. In *Marshall et al. v. Georgia*, first filed in 1982, plaintiffs argued that overrepresentation resulted from violations of procedural protections and improper interpretation of federal and state standards and guidelines. Although many of the claims drew upon *Larry P.* as a precedent, the decision was, like *PASE*, strikingly opposite. The claims of misclassification were rejected, turning away the argument that overrepresentation arose from discriminatory conduct. Moreover, the statistical disparity in EMR placement may not be a result of procedural violations, for such occurrences were found for white students as well. As Reschly, Kicklighter, and McKee noted (1988a, p. 35; also 1988b), "the results of other EMR overrepresentation cases such as *Larry P.* might have been different if this test had been applied." As the claims first made in *Larry P.* are "distributed over a greater surface," the uniqueness of one racial or cultural group is diminished. The outcome of *Marshall* suggested precisely that.

Coincident with *Marshall,* in timing and conclusions, was the national report of the Panel on Selection and Placement of Students in Programs for the Mentally Retarded commissioned by the National Academy of Sciences (Heller, Holtzman and Messick 1982). The report signaled an important shift in focus, from the nearly imponderable question of why overrepresentation occurs, to the question of why it is a problem at all (see Reschly 1984; Prasse and Reschly 1986). The Panel reported substantial evidence confirming the extent of racial and male overrepresentation, but proceeded from the belief that unequal numbers do not by themselves mean inequity. Rather, the investigation turned the statistical issue around, directly acknowledging that "disproportion is very probably determined by multiple interacting factors that are inextricably confounded in any concrete instance" (Heller, Holtzman and Messick 1982, p. 4). What is inextricably confounded can vary across school district, state, and region, and across time as well. The remedy for overrepresentation was not to be found in the abolition of IQ tests or EMR classes, for overrepresentation was symptomatic of "deeper failings in the education and social systems" (p. 93). Remedies cannot, therefore, be quick; such solutions may simply relocate disproportion to another section of the educational system (see Maheady et al., 1990, pp. 90–91). While the Panel held out the promise of "fundamental change," given the inextricable complexity behind overrepresentation, the focus emphasized by the Panel was the validity of assessment procedures and instruction (Reschly 1988c, p. 317).

The Panel's major recommendations were entitled "Principles of Responsibility"(p. 94). Six recommendations were formulated, with each specifying the locus of responsibility for assessment and instruction. As the prelude to the recommendations, the Panel cautioned that fundamental change in special education "will take time, and procedures *must evolve* in response to practical experience" (p. 93, my emphasis). To assist the evolution of these procedures, "broad principles, rather than detailed administrative prescriptions" composed the Panel's recommendations. The principles were broad indeed, distributing responsibility widely. As the authors summarized:

> Although we have focused on the participants in the placement and instructional processes—notably teachers and administrators—responsibility for bringing about these changes must be shared by all concerned with educating children: parents, school boards, state education agencies, and the federal government. To ask for major institutional change and to ask public institutions to support such change is to ask a great deal. (p. 94)

Such a diffusion of responsibility was adopted rather than "direct mechanisms for the elimination of disproportionate special education placement rates" (p. 112). The reluctance to assign particular responsibility appeared consistent with the overall, if not lofty reference to the ultimate responsibility, the best possible education for *all* children. The persistent elevation of *all* children above the fray of inextricable complexity was, nonetheless, haunted by the Panel's own recommendations for continued research on the efficacy of assessment procedures and placement decisions. Belief that more valid procedures must evolve, or that they would evolve, necessitated routine monitoring and evaluate research.

The monitoring of assessment procedures and placement decisions leading to overrepresentation paralleled empirical assessments of the logic and accuracy of classifications for the mildly retarded. Empirical findings were sobering, raising doubts about the "efficacy" of the very data used in placements (Ysseldyke 1987). Factors such as gender, low socioeconomic status, and physical appearance were shown to affect referral decisions (Ysseldyke, Algozzine, Ridley and Graden 1982); teachers were shown to be poor judges of candidates for special education intervention and students identified as LD could not be distinguished from underachieving students (Ysseldyke, Algozzine, Shinn, and McGue 1982; Algozzine and Ysseldyke 1983; Epps, Ysseldyke, and McGue 1984). Such evidence reinstated the memory of Dunn and Deno, as some claimed that nearly half of students in LD classes may be inappropriately classified (Shepard 1987; also Lilly 1986), unjustifiably "burgeoning" the masses (Algozzine, Ysseldyke and Christenson 1983). The result was a renewed "schism" between regular and special education.

While the empirical merits of these and other studies met with methodological and conceptual critiques (Gerber and Semmel 1984; 1985), such could not stop the image of an "evolution" toward fundamental change drawn by the Panel on Selection. As Assistant Secretary for the Office of Special Education, Madeleine Will hastened this evolution in her call for a "shared responsibility" between general and special education (Will 1986). While special education programs were historically "designed with the best of motivations," their continued existence promoted a conceptual and verbal language of difference and separation. No doubt haunted by the specter of overrepresentation, the proposal for a Regular Education Initiative that would dissolve the separation between general and special education was born.

Beyond Mainstreaming: Irony in the Call for Full Inclusion, 1986–2000

Marx reserved his most biting analysis for the final period, the ascendancy of Louis Bonaparte to dictatorial power in 1851. In contrast to the previous periods that conferred power in established offices, the succession of power to Bonaparte reified the mystique of an individual person who stood over all classes in the name of the nation. The transition from the Legislative National Assembly to the Second Empire witnessed the "betrayal" of the very ideals espoused by the bourgeoisie as it ascended to power. In Marx's penetrating words (1968, p. 67) "by now stigmatizing as "socialistic" what it had previously extolled as "liberal," the bourgeoisie confesses that its own interests dictate that it should be delivered from the danger of its own rule."

The betrayal of the ideals of 1789 was magnified by the betrayal of the very groups that elevated Bonaparte to power. It was the marginal and disfranchised small-holding peasants that Bonaparte proclaimed to represent and yet soon abandoned once securely in power. The synecdoche of the Legislative Assembly gave way to the farcical irony of the Second Empire.

No strict parallel can or should be made between the events shaping special education since 1986 and the final period of Marx's *Eighteenth Brumaire*. For one, there has been no dictatorial ascendancy to power. For another, recent events may be more profitably interpreted as a new beginning than as a final period. What has defined the years since 1986 is indeed the momentum of mainstreaming; yet this very momentum spawned forces of resistance. The parallel to Marx's final period, however loose, is reflected in the elevation of professional discourse to the abstract plane of *all* children. As a consequence, the most prevalent population of mildly handicapped children was "disaggregated" as the vision of a unified public education emerged as the dominant theme (Kauffman 1995, p. 202).

The momentum of mainstreaming brought advocates to avow the "limits" of initial arguments, or in the words of Lipsky and Gartner (1989, p. 271): "'Mainstreaming' . . . *slides together* two concepts worth keeping separate (my emphasis)," the concept of least restrictive environment combined with de facto placement in a special class setting. Although crafted with the best of motivations, the two concepts are, more accurately, antinomous: the growth of mainstreaming highlights awareness of difference and heightens this with a cascade of provisions that are no less prominent than a categorical system.

Again reminiscent of Dunn's warnings, the call for a unitary system of full inclusion cited the failure of research to confirm the "efficacy" of special class placement. Yet the calls drew on a more compelling source of support: the identification of special placement with "segregation," and by extension, the association of critics with "segregationism" (Wang and Walberg 1988). The combination of an empirical and moral imperative would erase the issue of racial overrepresentation. As Gilhool succinctly stated (1989, p. 247): "It may be argued that *everybody* is overrepresented, and the crucial problem is that there are separate "special classes" for *any* child said to be disabled." Overrepresentation will disappear if provisions could be "distributed over a greater surface of society."

Nonetheless, this professional and moral optimism soon met resistance on precisely the same grounds. The empirical base for the vision of a unitary system may be as porous as the early efficacy studies that informed Dunn. As Kauffman, Gerber, and Semmel (1988) have detailed, the "assumptions" of the Regular Education Initiative may be questioned on logical grounds and contrary empirical evidence may be cited as well (see also Hallahan et al., 1988). But the moral implications of full inclusion are likely of greater consequence. If the empirical feasibility of full inclusion is rendered suspect by virtue of methodological weaknesses in cited research, the claims of its moral imperative may be the real "illusion" (Kauffman and Hallahan 1995). Borrowing from Marx, "stigmatizing" critics as "segregationist" may be a way to "deliver" one from the "dangers" of realizing full inclusion. To presume that *all* students, whether "high" or "low" incidence groups, can be educated in regular classes substitutes "appealing images" for the complexity of established social and cultural differences, and for the subtlety of ideas (Kauffman 1995, p. 198).

What may be appealing may also be paradoxical. By dissolving the boundaries between a general and a special education, the vision of full inclusion presumably strips away provisions and resources that are "intermediate" between the two. Yet the melding of special and regular education *beyond* a partnership is organizationally condescending insofar as the direction of consolidation is away from special education and *into* general education.[5] Full inclusion is organizationally paternalistic as well. The presumption that regular education represents the superior educational environment diminishes the long-established residential schools. As Bina aptly notes (1995, p. 271): "Residential schools do not segregate or restrict in a discriminatory manner, but rather positively and purposefully bring together *children as do science, math, and music magnet schools,* which consolidate students with special interests and aptitudes" (my emphasis). As special education is denounced as segregation, "magnet" schools are praised.

Harlan Lane goes further. Deaf children who "do best in school," whether mainstreaming or residential, do so having learned American Sign Language (ASL) from their deaf parents (Lane 1995; see also Sacks 1988). The acquisition of ASL is the key to better adjustment and learning potential. Yet it may also be best utilized in "segregated," residential settings.

The image of a unitary system, however appealing, conflates the established differences, in history and culture, between residential and public schools. To presume the superiority of the latter not only slights the proven strengths of residential schools; it minimizes the very significance of place. As Kauffman succinctly states (1995, p. 196): "Place, as a set of coordinates in the physical world, is a central issue in identity or belonging." By itself, this would attract little challenge. But Kauffman elaborates in a way that isolates a major presumption of full inclusion:

> One might assume that what is likely to happen socially and academically in one place cannot be assumed to be equally probable in any place . . . we understand relatively little about how students' placement determines what is possible and what is probable as far as instruction and its outcomes are concerned. There is a lot of "noise," or unexplained variance, in the available data regarding place. In any given study, the "noise" might be an artifact of outcome measures, a confound of place with what actually happens instructionally and socially in various places, a function of the heterogeneity of student characteristics, or some combination of these and other factors. (p. 196)

The belief that, if we abolish special education, racial and other forms of overrepresentation will cease interprets the "noise" of available data as a product of organizational separation itself. By eradicating scene, as it were, the image of full inclusion presumes a "causal logic of place": the detrimental effects of two systems will be removed by forming a single general education; and by extension, enhancing the instructional quality of this single environment will enhance the learning of students with disabilities.

To advocates of full inclusion, the prospect of an increased variation in ability levels, in cultural diversity, and of learning styles is embraced as a welcome instructional challenge. But the causal logic of place leads some to adopt strategies that bear a likeness to utopian schemes that would unlock the riddles of learning itself. Most exemplary is the call to draw on "effective schools" research (see, e.g., Bickel and Bickel, 1986; Lezotte 1989). Findings from this research would guide the reformulation of instructional technologies and interventions. The research appears to fit the image of a unitary system and it fits with the leadership assumed by general education.

Any real test of the "efficacy" of this research to the education of children with disabilities would have to await the actual realization of full inclusion. Nonetheless, some indirect evidence points to unintended consequences: instead of positive effects, flowing from an enhanced general education, there may be negative implications for children with disabilities. The longitudinal research of the School Environment Project (SEP) (Semmel, Gerber and Abernathy 1993) takes the school as the unit of analysis and examines the impact of general education achievement gains on the variation in achievement measures among special education students. Empirical results find no positive relationship between general school achievement and the enhanced performance of special education students. As if mirroring Kauffman's admonishments about place, the findings reveal that schools with gains in general education are not the same schools with gains in special education. More revealing, however, is the finding that gains experienced in a school's general education may be detrimental to special education: "As schools respond to pressures of the most recent school improvement reforms for increasing academic achievement, under conditions of diminishing resources, they may adaptively develop strategies for increasing school means—to the detriment of their nonmodal special education pupils" (Semmel, Gerber and MacMillan 1995, p. 54).

Research such as the School Environments Project retrieves the "noise in available data" and conceives of it as contextual effects. The research conceptualizes the arena of effects above the classroom level and beyond the single school. It is the "nested" or multilevel structure of schooling that forms the environment that bears on special education in ways that may be unique to it. One mechanism may be what Artiles and Trent term the "disability-cultural diversity analogy" (1994, p. 425). While disability is associated with a standard parameter of functioning, cultural diversity is not. Within the education environment, however, the two may be linked "almost unconsciously," activating the negative relation found by the SEP.

The Panel on Selection foreshadowed this final stage of racial overrepresentation. Its reification of *all children* as the ultimate responsibility could hardly be contested. Yet the convergence of its Principles of Responsibility with the movement for full inclusion has fractured professional authority and has abstracted the population of special children. Marx's commentary on Bonaparte's rule is instructive: "Every *common* interest was straightway severed from society, counterposed to it as a higher, *general* interest, snatched from the activity of society's members themselves and made an object of government activity" (1968, p. 122). The imagery of a unitary system, built upon the abolition of special education, denies the categorical meaning of disabilities and handicaps, conceiving of *all* children as composing a continuum of differences. In some likeness, the base of Bonaparte's power was the small-holding peasants, whose social circumstances were the source of the contradictions and absurdities of Bonaparte's power. In Marx's words, the small-holding peasants:

> form a vast mass, the members of which live in similar conditions but without entering into manifold relations with one another . . . In this way, the great mass of the French nation is formed by simple addition of homologous magnitude . . . In so far as there is merely a local interconnection among these small-holding peasants, and the identity of their interests begets no community, no national bond and no political organization among them, they do not form a class. They are consequently incapable of enforcing their class interest in their own name . . . They cannot represent themselves, they must be represented. (pp. 123–124)

The vision of an abolished special education, a system that in Deno's prophetic terms "worked itself out of business," is consistent with an abstract vision of *all children*. A consequence, nonetheless, may be precisely what Marx revealed as the "absurd" or farcical climate of the Second Republic. Like the absurdity of gold as the standard for money, the imagery of *all children* as the ultimate reference for the *evolution* of procedures to eliminate racial disproportion may not only be empirically misguided but conceptually absurd as well.

CONCLUSIONS

Special education has at least three histories: the one that is a stepchild of regular education; the one that is independent of regular education; and the one that sees it as defining regular education itself. Certainly each history is deeply informed by the others. Yet the one that has been given least attention is the third, for this one suggests that regular education is more the stepchild than special education.

Special education indeed has its own, independent history. Like the history of public schooling, special education has been immersed in, and has been a reflection of, the same economic, cultural, and social changes. Yet the divisions and mergers which have created and eliminated categories of exceptional children is a history that has had a defining impact on the pedagogy of regular education. The exclusion of exceptional children is a form of influence; if deaf and blind children are not in regular schools, but are in residential facilities, the public schools face no pedagogical demands to instruct in ASL or Braille. Similarly, if disorderly youth are committed to reformatories, parental schools, or child guidance clinics, public schools face less pedagogical demands to accommodate students from divergent economic levels and contrasting cultural backgrounds.

To view special education as a core, albeit hidden, drama of regular schooling is to reverse the causal relation between the two. From its creation, the special class has been the scene wherein the organizational dilemmas prompted by compulsory attendance have been dramatized. To these classes were sent pupils whose deviance reflected not so much on themselves, as on the incapacity of schools to accommodate difference. Regular instruction could not proceed, much less develop, without the special class. Indeed, normal children became the residual population, once the deviancies of character and health were excluded.

The scene/act of the special class has long been the conscience of a public education. Impairments of vision and hearing, the disabilities of speech and physical mobility, and the slowness of academic learning are acts more than they are conditions. A growing body of research confirms all too well that "handicapping conditions" can result from the contingencies of referral, the accidents of timing, and the conflicting discourse of teachers, school staff, and parents.

In the most intensive ethnographic study of special education, Mehan, Hertweck, and Meihls revealed a stunning finding: "[Furthermore], no correlation existed between deviation from classroom norms and the disposition of referral cases" (1986, p. 74). If referral for special education is not sufficiently explained by deviation from classroom norms, the acts that suggest a "learning disability" are not properties of individual students, but of the scenes in which they are perceived. Special education becomes, in short, a theater of scenes; and the history of theory and treatment moves across the major genres of comedy, tragedy, romance, and satire.

NOTES

1. Groszmann came to the study of exceptional children by way of his involvement with the Ethical Culture Society of New York. The Ethical Culture Societies were a quasi-religious movement begun in 1876 under the intellectual and personal leadership of Alfred Adler. At the close of the century, Groszmann was Superintendent of the Workingman's School in New York.

2. It is noteworthy that Healy allots only one paragraph to "racial characteristics," coming under the subtitle of "Other Peculiarities" (1915b, p. 765). While he makes reference to such characteristics, in stereotypic terms, he does not give them any direct causal status. In his words, "Thus in occasional cases one does feel justified in diagnosing the mental characteristics of the individual as those peculiar to his race. It may be possible to analyze the general character into its constituent parts, but for the purposes of direct expression and understanding, the use of the term racial characteristics is often valuable in explanation of the peculiarities which lead to social offense." At this point the issue is dropped. Elsewhere, in *Mental Conflicts and Misconduct* (1923), he is equally brief, but more direct: "The question of whether different 'races' and 'nationalities' possibly present specific characteristics that have bearing upon the development of conflicts and reactions thereto may be answered in a word. Our cases are drawn from many different nationalities which seem, respectively, to give no intimation of special susceptibilities to conflicts being correlated with national characteristics" (p. 316). This one mention of race is inserted in the Conclusion, and just nine pages before the end of the book.

3. This loose coupling feature of the LD field parallels the very structure of LD theory, which permits, in Burke's terms, "synecdochic reversals" (1969, p. 509). Such reversals are where "representation stresses a relationship or connectedness between two sides of an equation, a connectedness that, like a road, extends in either direction." For LD theory, either minimal brain dysfunction or its behavioral symptoms may be taken as representative of the whole. In contrast, the metonymic reduction of earlier behavioral explanations led in only one direction, reducing delinquent misconduct back (through) the causal intricacy of previous experiences.

In actuality, Strauss proposed a causal logic that posited brain-damage as the determining root of neurological and behavioral symptoms. Yet, in her meticulous review of the staying power of "organicity" in psychological diagnosis, Goodman (1983) dissects the "arbitrariness of Strauss' one-way causality" (p. 114). In so doing, Goodman reveals how LD theory comes to rest on a mere "inference" of brain-damage; in the absence of demonstrated evidence, either neurological or behavioral symptoms can imply the organic presence of brain-damage. Yet, as Goodman details, this is neither logically nor empirically supported.

4. We use the term "extended" purposefully. The four periods in Marx's *Eighteenth Brumaire* correspond to his four forms of human labor value (see White 1973, pp. 320-330). The "agonic" phase of racial overrepresentation is not only metonymic in form, but corresponds to his "general" or "extended" form of human value, where "commodities are conceived on the basis of the apprehension of their placement in a *series* that is infinitely extendable" (White, 1973, p. 295). Similarly, the class action suits against special education placement appear as a series that extends from the early 1970s.

5. In a similar vein, Skrtic states the idea well by uncovering the fundamental compatibility of the restructuring and inclusion debates (1995):

> As we have seen, the inclusion debate is less naïve than the mainstreaming debate because it implicates school organization in the problem of school failure. The mirror image of this in the restructuring debate is that, by pointing to the emergence and persistence of homogeneous grouping practices programs—as an indication of deep structural flaws in traditional school organization, the participants in the restructuring debate implicate school failure in the problem of school organization . . . The mirror image in the restructuring debate is that, although it rejects the assumptions about the rationality of school organization and change, it questions but ultimately retains those about the objectivity of school failure and diagnosis. (p. 246)

In short, the restructuring debate "fails to recognize special education as a form of tracking."

Skrtic's comment here is reminiscent of Judge Wright's summary comment in Hobson v. Hansen (1967). In spite of the declaration to abolish the tracking system, the response of school systems have sustained the very outcome that this court challenge sought to alter. As Judge Write foresaw, a "name change" from Basic track to "special Academic" was largely a euphemistic change, altering nothing in real organizational terms.

CHAPTER 6

The Institutional Shaping of Educational Rights

INTRODUCTION

Special education has come to occupy the high ground of many contemporary educational debates. In many respects, questions of efficient and quality instruction, alternative learning modes, cultural differences impacting student performance, and definitions of ability arise from practical necessity from within special education. The diverse and challenging composition of special education often contrasts with the more homogeneous and routinized classes of general education (Ferguson 1989, pp. 50–51). Such evidence describes an historical irony: From positions of exclusion and exemption, the incorporation of exceptional children leads progressively to an inversion of common schooling, elevating special education to the forefront of pedagogical innovation and judicial reform. Much like the contemporary reforms of deinstitutionalization and diversion that "are the juvenile court and the reformatory turned inside out" (Sutton 1988, p. 207), the maturation of special education has assumed the historic charge of common schooling (Hurt 1988, pp. 189–193). Special education is strategically situated to conceptualize a single system of instruction and to assume much of the innovative leadership to effect its implementation.

Contemporary tests of social and cultural change invert 19th century beginnings. The institutions that encompass delinquency and exceptionality most certainly existed in a different environment during the decades after their 19th century origins. In this century, the environment is especially different on sociolegal and organizational grounds. In a sociolegal context, the prevailing ethos runs against their historical origins, because expanded rights of participation and opportunity conflict with strategies to commit youth as wayward and dependent or to segregate children as handicapped. And, with the enlarged role of the modern polity as protagonist for these rights, mandates to reduce or erase the constraints against participation and opportunity now originate at the national, and increasingly, at the global level. But expanded rights to educational participation and opportunity have been extended as the boundary changes of public education reflect the progressive inclusion of delinquency and exceptionality. A consequence is the proliferation of educational statuses that are seen as evidence for an expanded legal universalism of American common schooling.

Yet the elaboration of these statuses exposes a paradox: Reforms that seek to incorporate groups that have been historically excluded or exempted reinforce cultural and socioeconomic differences. This paradox is most exemplified by the intransigence of racial overrepresentation. As an attribute assigned by law for purposes of jurisdiction, legal status carries with it a "fixed quota of capacities and incapacities" (Graveson 1953, p. 55) to act within the limits imposed by the classification. The capacities and incapacities of statuses are incidents that are imposed on incumbents. While the sources of incapacity may stem from real differences in social and economic circumstances, an added source comes from the legal classification structure itself, which imposes a legal personality on incumbents. The expansion and maturation of special education has both benefited from and contributed to the elaboration of the rights that compose this legal classification.

This chapter offers an institutional view of the elaboration of educational rights. No attempt is made to cover the range of cases that have built the framework of educational rights for exceptional children. The theoretical perspective that has guided this volume, that American education is a trinary structure composed of the common school population and the worlds of delinquent and special school-age children, is the necessary background to these rights. That is, the extension of rights in special education has not occurred without influence from delinquency and from debates and challenges relating to residential populations.

Framing these mutual, institutional influences is the continuum between *in loco parentis* and *parens patriae*, from the delegation of authority to schools as an extension of traditional, parental authority, to the investment of authority in states to intervene against parental authority. I argue in this chapter that the long-term direction has been away from parental authority and toward an elaboration of state powers to define and enforce educational rights. But this cannot be seen as a simple evolutionary movement. Rather, the movement "within" this continuum has been shaped by the contrast between "legal justice" and "substantive justice," the antinomy between procedural rules and substantive principles. In the same manner that compulsory attendance laws embodied the antinomy between democracy and efficiency (see chapter 3), contemporary legislation of educational rights embodies the antinomy between rules pertaining to social categories, and the more abstract principles such rules seek to promote.

Much of the *substantive* content of due process rights extended to exceptional children derives from major court decisions within delinquency and public schooling. The specific element that has been crucial to the formulation of these educational rights is the constitutional claim that involuntary commitment entails a "right to treatment." It is this right that preceded and informed the right to a "free appropriate public education," from which substantive educational rights have evolved.

FROM COVENANT TO STATUS: THE RATIONALIZATION OF BINDING OUT

The criteria governing admission to common schooling emerged as a center point regulating both the formation of institutions and the shifting content of instructional pedagogies. Alongside universal references to a free education, another intent of these criteria was to be exclusionary, specifying groups and conditions subject to expulsion/suspension, segregation or exemption. The evolutionary fate of these criteria has been legislative repeal, and an ever-expanding inclusion of groups historically kept out of common schooling. Challenges were first directed against the authority of schools to control student behavior. These challenges forged a procedural and constitutional affinity between delinquency and common schooling. In turn, these precedents strengthened the legal foundation for the inclusion of exceptional children.

The statute language of expulsion drew its rationale from the Blackstone doctrine of *in loco parentis*. The state's interest in the education of the young is complemented by the delegation of authority to school boards to protect the environment wherein this expectation is fulfilled. In the course of fulfilling this state interest schools may exceed traditional parental authority in the setting of rules covering routine conduct. Yet the terms of the Blackstone formulation did not grant to schools the right to displace parental authority (Goldstein 1969, p. 380; Buss 1971, pp. 559–562), but to continue the educational and vocational function traditionally conferred on families. As parents may bind their children out to a merchant or craftsman, they likewise may bind their children to the care and instruction of teachers. The relevance of *in loco parentis* to school authority is properly interpreted within these limits of a voluntary exchange between families and schools. Once this exchange turned compulsory and states formally expanded upon the right to a free education, *in loco parentis* began to lose its reach as a legal defense for school authority.

Where the principle of *in loco parentis* intends the protection of parental authority, and preserves the voluntary side of binding out, the doctrine of *parens patriae* expresses the interests of the state to authoritatively intervene on behalf of the child. The doctrine presumes the obligation to intervene against conditions that are deemed harmful to the common welfare. To this end, *parens patriae* conceives of "anticipatory outcomes," and exercises an instrumental authority to prevent them before they occur.

Yet despite its deep historical roots, the legal meaning of *parens patriae* has been reinterpreted to fit changing circumstances. As noted earlier (chapter 2), the doctrine was introduced into American law by *ex part Crouse* in 1838, the case that justified the involuntary commitment of juveniles in the Pennsylvania House of Refuge by declaring it a "school" and not a prison. From its feudal origins on matters of property and guardianship, its incorporation into 17th century poor laws, to its application to problems of juvenile misconduct, the doctrine "became a helpful synonym for various state interests that the [chancellor] desired to further" (Cogan 1970, p. 147). The synonymic character of *parens patriae* is greatest from poor relief to juvenile justice, for this legal justification for state authority over juveniles was not inevitable (see Curtis 1976, pp. 895–901).

To be sure, there was a plenitude of circumstances that called on states to anticipate outcomes, and to sever the authority of parents. Yet, when courts turned to state legislatures for alternatives to poverty and conditions of dependency, the latter could offer none. The vacuum between chancery and legislative authority was filled by residential institutions, for they stood alone as the only legally established alternative. Importantly, reliance on institutional commitments withstood reforms "because the *institutions were schools* and not prisons, [and] no more liberty than necessary was taken when the children were placed there" (Rendleman 1971, p. 240, my emphasis). Yet the legitimacy of *parens patriae* was not gained simply by default. It did not secure its legal credentials by invoking a vague claim to protect society. Rather, the claim was itself credible only in light of the formalization of common schooling. *Parens patriae* secured its relevance to the misconduct of juveniles because of the institutional links between reformatories and common schools; and it secured its legitimacy as part of the criteria that regulated admission to the latter.

The contrast between *in loco parentis* and *parens patriae* outlines a continuum from voluntary exchange to the preeminence of state interests and frames the principle of binding out. Movement along this continuum has been away from the parental authority, exploiting and rationalizing the expansive potential of binding out as welfare and administrative authority are assumed by corporate boards and governmental agencies. This sequential movement favors *parens patriae*, but does not eliminate *in loco parentis* (Katz and Teitelbaum 1977; also Fox 1970). The movement is one of scale; in content it is a story of balancing and reconfiguring inherently opposing interests.

Movement along this continuum from traditional to state authority is a record of conflict between the rules of procedure and the values of justice. In Roberto Unger's terms, the conflict is an antinomy of "legal justice" and "substantive justice" (Unger 1975, pp. 88–103; also Katz and Teitelbaum 1977, p. 203, passim). Legal justice delineates rules "to govern general categories of acts and persons." Dispositions for infraction or deviation are *deduced* from these pre-established rules. In contrast, substantive justice delineates goals that are independent of rules. Specific infractions or deviations are *judged* in light of their potential for harm or contribution to the goal. Unger's distinction is especially evident in the original formulation of compulsory school attendance. The formalization of common schooling intertwined the two. Compulsory attendance simultaneously affirmed the goal of a common schooling "for all children of school age," while specifying rules for the exemption of disability categories and the expulsion of delinquent acts. From this original confluence, the changing relation between legal and substantive justice has been dialectical, where rules of exclusion are successively disengaged from their prior substantive foundation. But with the due process revolution of the 1960s, substantive justice gained a momentum that elevated it above and distinct from the procedural rules that relied so long on categories and classifications of people. Yet substantive justice did not replace legal justice; rather, the functional relation between the two widened over time.

SCHOOL DISCIPLINE, DELINQUENCY AND PROCEDURAL DUE PROCESS

Although inherent in the formulation of common schooling, this antinomy between rules and values remained obscure at the turn of the century, and the boundary protecting the common school was enforced. The rationale that schools serve a "host function" and must fulfill their "education per se" charge, continued to invoke in loco parentis, reflecting the functional links between family autonomy in socialization and local school authority (Goldstein 1969, pp. 389–422). In the face of challenge, behaviors that historically constituted grounds for expulsion, or reason for reform school commitment, lose their definitional firmness. Teenage pregnancy, smoking on school grounds, and violations of dress codes force out the rationale of "moral pollution." The case of unwed motherhood is exemplary. Here, precocious female sexuality was dislodged as a criterion for industrial school commitment and became an element relevant to vocational guidance and special class placement (Schlossman and Wallach 1978; also Brenzel 1983, p. 81, passim). The expectation that a proper educational purpose was to instill and shape character further blunted challenges to school authority. The prevailing pedagogy of character led back to reinforce the legality of suspension. This mutual reciprocity confirmed a "morality of duty" matching the prominence of legal justice, and benefiting a social climate that "lays down the basic rules . . . without which an ordered society directed toward certain specific goals must fail of its mark" (Fuller 1964, pp. 5–6).

Yet arguments of "moral pollution" are second-hand; they are borrowed from the original authority to protect against contagious diseases. To invoke the values of patriotism in order to compel rules to salute the flag, or to proclaim the virtues of moral conduct and demeanor so to exclude unwed mothers and violators of dress codes, *relates an unchanged rule to a transitional context.* As a consequence, this differentiation of current legal from earlier substantive justice generates a conflict of jurisdiction. Invoking arguments of moral pollution against teenage pregnancy punishes behavior that took place outside the school; expulsion of students for long hair unduly extends school jurisdiction, for "hair cannot be long outside of school and short in school" (Goldstein 1969, pp. 398–400). The antinomy of rules and values has long been caught in a sequential evolution: *the exercise and defense of legal justice is necessarily reliant on prior conceptions of substantive justice* (see Reschly 1988d, p. 532).

The impact of school discipline cases within public schooling inserted an important wedge into this evolution. With *Dixon v. Alabama State Board of Education* in 1961, the outcome was to entitle a student subject to expulsion a notice and a hearing wherein he must be presented with the evidence against him, and extended the right to produce witnesses in his own defense. By extending fundamental due process rights "normally given to prisoners," *Dixon* signaled a new national standard of protection for the behavioral activities of students. This signal became definitive with the Supreme Court decision in *Goss v. Lopez* (1975). With *Goss*, the court ruled that Ohio must "recognize a student's legitimate entitlement to a public education as a property interest." The procedural rights that safeguard this "property interest" are required to protect against damage to a student's "reputation" that may interfere later with educational and employment opportunities. With *Dixon* and *Goss,* the rhythm of legal and substantive justice was altered, for a new set of rules was the foundation on which more substantive claims could be asserted.

The contemplation of procedural due process rights for students shifted much of the burden of proof onto schools, and yet redefined the jurisdiction of its constitutional authority to shape and control student behavior. With *Tinker v. Des Moines Independent Community School District* (1969), the wearing of armbands in protest of the Vietnam War combined political activity with challenges to dress codes. *Tinker* upheld the right of freedom of expression. What is significant here is the affirmation that the schoolhouse gate does not imply a different juridical boundary.

Cases such as *Dixon, Goss* and *Tinker* (and others) drew the worlds of delinquency and common schooling closer by the substantive claim of "stigmatization." Practices that confer a potentially harmful label on a youth are subject to due process scrutinies whether the site is a public school or a juvenile justice institution. The stigma of delinquent is judicially similar to the stigma of expelled or suspended student. For both, the fundamental standard of fairness emerges as a constitutional right bridging institutionally separated worlds. The claim of stigmatization was abstracted from the particular contexts of the common school and the juvenile proceeding, and framed as an interest warranting constitutional scrutiny. Of larger consequence, this abstraction defined *an outcome harmful to educational opportunity* and joined it to a *legal classification* at the societal level.

This linkage marked the onset of the due process revolution in juvenile justice. With *In re Gault* in 1967, the Supreme Court gave juveniles the right to contest the allegations against them, principally by securing legal counsel. In addition, *Gault* mandated the right to proper notification, the right to cross-examine witnesses and the privilege of impelled self-incrimination. Later decisions expanded upon these rights, requiring prosecutors to prove allegations of delinquency beyond a reasonable doubt with *In re Winship* (1970) and the prohibition against later retrial in adult court under the double jeopardy clause with *Breed v. Jones* (1975). The extension of procedural due process rights to juveniles charged with delinquent acts represents a break in the long history of the juvenile court and its therapeutic mission to intervene into the lives of juveniles considered less than fully responsible for their acts. The juvenile court's long history founded on *parens patriae* was ruptured, and "a court with a clinic replaced the clinic with a court" (Rubin 1996, p. 50).

The mandate of procedural rights begun with the *Gault* decision signaled a qualitative change in the adjudication of cases. Yet, of equal or greater significance to these changes in "legal justice" was the nascent substantive "right to treatment." In *Creek v. Stone* (1967), the District of Columbia recognized that juveniles had a right to effective treatment "promised" by juvenile law. In the case of *Creek*, the federal district court stopped short of requiring that the juvenile court determine the adequacy of treatment, declaring only that the court should determine its jurisdiction over such an issue. Nonetheless, *Creek* signaled a shift away from the historical reliance on *parens patriae* as the rationale for the absence of due process rights.

With *In re Harris* (1967), the right to treatment reached beyond the juvenile court by explicitly identifying *educational* provisions as the necessary and effective treatment. Harris, a deaf-mute, was found to be a neglected minor and held as a ward of the state (Illinois) in a facility that had no provisions for the profoundly deaf and mute. In the judgment of *Harris*, the juvenile court judge affirmed that authorities were constitutionally obliged to provide appropriate treatment for Harris' physical handicap, specifically "to arrange forthwith for the daily transportation . . . to the . . . High school . . . in order that he may *attend the special classes* offered in said school for the deaf and mute" (Criminal Law Reporter 1968, p. 2412, my emphasis). Beyond the importance of basing the right to treatment on constitutional grounds, *Harris* exemplified how special education could be defined as appropriate treatment for the adjudication of delinquency.

The combination of procedural due process rights and the affirmation of the right to treatment led to the passage of the Juvenile Justice and Delinquency Prevention Act of 1974. The federal statute in 1974 signified a new direction within delinquency, that the status offenses of truancy, running away from home, and incorrigibility, must be distinguished procedurally and protected substantively from criminal offenses. As noted earlier (chapter 4), passage of the JJDP Act may have widened the net of delinquency, and indeed this has been the case. Between 1989 and 1993, there was a 37% increase in the number of status offenses petitioned to juvenile courts, and the majority of these were for truancy (Steinhart 1996, p. 88). The empirical assessment of status offenses *within delinquency* has raised doubts about the actual implementation of due process rights (Ainsworth 1996).[1] Yet, viewed *institutionally,* a consequence of distinguishing status offenses has been to embrace special education as an appropriate and effective mode of treatment. As the finding in chapter 4 suggests, the specific nexus linking delinquency and special education is through juvenile diversion and the category of Learning Disability. The contemporary due process protection of truancy as a status offense within delinquency becomes integrally relevant to the elaboration of educational rights for handicapped students in public schools. As due process reforms bring an increased formality (Feld 1984; also Hellum 1979), procedural rules accompany therapeutic goals. Legal and substantive justice are once again intertwined. Sequentially, this strengthens the legal mandates for the education and protection of disobedience ("status offenses") *within* the common school.

FREE APPROPRIATE PUBLIC EDUCATION, EXCEPTIONALITY, AND PROCEDURAL DUE PROCESS

A consequence of formalizing common schooling as compulsory attendance was to more clearly define the *legal capacity* of groups to benefit from education. Paradoxically, this restriction on participation follows upon the assumption by states to finance and administer common schooling and to further extend rights to children of school-age. While authority to exempt was built into compulsory attendance, the correlation reflects a legal evolution as much as it does a means to control deviance. In broad terms, this evolution is akin to Henry Maine's thesis of a master trend from status to contrast (see ftn. 2, Chapter 1). Out of ancient law and through the medieval era, status implied variations of full legal capacity, in contrast to slave status that possessed none. With English common law usage, status comes to mean deviation from full legal capacity, variations of partial statuses that fit the requirements of civil society. Coincident with the development of individual rights distinct from group membership, "the concept that all men are equal with respect to these rights, restrictions in legal capacity—that is, the capacity to bear rights—were converted into limitations on the capacity to act or deal in a particular legal manner" (Rehbinder 1971, pp. 943–4). That reduced legal capacity should arise with the extension of individual rights suggests that Maine's thesis operates in reverse sequence, from contract to status.

For American education there is much to uphold this. The erosion of covenants of apprenticeship anticipated the construction of the "special classes" around which the institutional state was erected. In turn, the erosion of exemption policies reflects the long-term transformation of these 19th century *stigma categories* into 20th century educational *statuses*. As the gradient of school authority ascended upward, the school-age population was organized into pupil classifications. The classifications of Backward, EMR and LD ostensibly denote levels of ability, but organizationally they mark the degree of inclusion into full-time, general education. The post-War expansion of these non-normative statuses complements the pedagogy of health, now displacing a "morality of duty" with a "morality of aspiration." In contrast to the pedagogy of character, the moralism of aspiration elevates the pursuit of excellence and the realization of individual potential over behavioral conformity. The etiology of academic performance shifts accordingly, for a morality of aspiration "condemns for shortcoming, not for wrongdoing" (Fuller 1964, p. 5).

The educational statuses of special education are the beneficiaries of *Dixon, Goss, Tinker* and *Gault*. These cases established a fertile ground for the extension of due process rights to handicapped children, and for the broadening of their incorporation into common schooling. Yet, like delinquency, a critical element was the affirmation of the right to treatment. Theoretical and legal consideration of the right to treatment arose first in matters of involuntary commitment, including cases of tuberculosis, alcoholism and mental illness. From here it may have "traveled" to delinquency.

The decisive case for residential commitments was *Rouse v. Cameron* (1966). Filed in Washington, DC, the claim was made that the hospital in which Charles Rouse had been involuntarily committed had been transformed into a penitentiary because it lacked the appropriate treatment for Rouse. Most important, the court declared that mere availability did not fulfill the legal responsibility. Rather, the standard was "adequacy in light of present knowledge." That is, the state must demonstrate that it sought to find and make available adequate treatment. Failing to do so is a violation of procedural due process rights, for confinement without treatment is punishment, thereby requiring criminal procedural safeguards (Renn 1973, p. 480).

The relevance of *Rouse* to the educational rights of handicapped children is seen in cases that set the stage for *The Education for All Handicapped Children Act*. In *Mills* (1972), the right to a publicly supported education was extended to children excluded as "uneducable;" and with *PARC* (1972), the right to a free and publicly supported education to all retarded school children was mandated, as well as a host of procedural due process rights. In addition to the procedural importance of both cases, it was their substantive content that influenced the language and intent of the *EAHC*. Similar to delinquency, the "right to treatment" emerged in the language of "free appropriate public education."

The right to treatment has been invoked in claims seeking the fulfillment of procedural rights intended by statutory and legislative acts. In *Frederick L. v. Thomas* (1977), the argument was made that failure to conduct comprehensive assessment resulted in the de facto exclusion of a significant number of students from special provisions for learning disabilities. As a class action suit, *Frederick L.* generated an estimated figure of 6,600 students excluded, based on an incidence rate of 3% of the enrolled population in Philadelphia schools. Reversing the arguments in minority overrepresentation claims, *Frederick L.* sought expanded testing, contending that without such assessments it could not be known if in fact placement in regular classes was "appropriate." The absence of referrals, by teachers or parents, did not by itself mean that statutory intent was fulfilled.

A decision that more, not less, assessment was required to meet statutory intent could result from claims of racially discriminatory referral and test bias. In *Lora v. Board of Education* (1978), black and Hispanic students claimed that inadequate evaluations led to their placement in special day schools, removing them inappropriately from regular classroom settings. Although the court found for the plaintiffs, it analyzed the claims using a right to treatment theory, minimizing plaintiff arguments about test bias. In doing so, the court focused more on how assessment practices fall short of treatment goals. While different in details from *Frederick L.*, the result of both cases "was to mandate, rather than restrict, further testing" (Bersoff 1979, p. 107).

The connection between right to treatment and appropriate education was most visibly evident in the first special education case decided by the Supreme Court. In *Board of Education v. Rowley* (1982), the Court reversed the court of appeals by arguing that a school district did *not* have to provide a sign language interpreter as a "related service" to comply with the intent of the *EAHC*. The Court held that the intent of "free appropriate public education" (FAPE) was met to the extent a school district made available an educational opportunity that was *comparable* to that received by non-handicapped children, and to the extent the district engaged a professional team in the construction of an *individualized education program,* or IEP. In essence, *Rowley* stopped at the question of how a meaningful education would be achieved, addressing only the right to pursue it. As such, its impact was limited "by its facts as precedent for other cases" (Turnbull 1986, p.

349). In this respect, *Rowley* symbolized the fine line between procedural and substantive due process rights.

STATE POWER AND SUBSTANTIVE DUE PROCESS: THE *SYNCHRONICITY* OF EDUCATIONAL RIGHTS

With the link made between the right to treatment and access to appropriate education, the sequential evolution of legal and substantive justice is reversed: *the articulation and implementation of substantive justice becomes reliant on prior definitions of legal justice.* Up to the due process decisions of the 1960s, the exercise of legal justice drew its rationale from earlier conceptions of substantive justice, and it did so *within* the jurisdictional boundaries of delinquency or common schooling. With the extension of substantive due process rights, the rules that governed general categories and acts become the necessary content for the delineation of goals that are independent of earlier procedural rules. This reversal reflects a change in the relations *across* the three worlds of American education: across the worlds of common schooling, delinquency, and the residential population of special children.

Up to the 1960s, educational rights evolved "diachronically," that is, within each sector. A significant determinant of this diachronic evolution was the *institutional age* of state school systems. As explored in Chapters 3 and 4, the timing of enacting compulsory attendance explains much of the variation in the levels of non-normative categories across states. The institutionally older state school systems led the way in building the categorical structure of special education. Beginning with classes for Backward children, these states moved sequentially to Mentally Deficient and EMR classes and more recently to LD classes. Insofar as the *institutional age* of state school systems has shaped the growth of this categorical structure, it influenced both the extension and incorporation of the procedural rights that have accompanied these provisions.

This tie between the *institutional age* of state school systems and the evolution of procedural rights has been resilient up to the 1960s. Yet, the "age" of a state school system is affected by more than its internal, systemic growth. A state may be institutionally "young" by virtue of a comparatively late enactment of compulsory attendance. Yet, by virtue of certain conditions and circumstances it may be "thrust forward" into a more rapid pace of educational change. A chronologically young state school system may age quickly by economic and political circumstances that link it to national educational issues. In addition to *institutional age,* a state school system is affected by its *national status* (Richardson 1984, p. 489), its position in a national hierarchy of economic and political power.

In contrast to the close tie between *institutional age* and geographic region, the *national status* of state school systems transcends this traditional definition of region. Large and diverse cities will link states across considerable geographic space and across long-standing historical differences as well. Economic and political similarities link Dallas, Denver, Miami, and Atlanta to New York, Boston, Los Angeles, and Chicago. These ties, in turn, form a common membership in the judicial arena of substantive due process rights for exceptional children. The elaboration of these rights draws its content from mutually similar circumstances and consequences *across* the jurisdictions of public schools, reformatories, and residential special schools.

Texas and Florida are exemplary. Texas enacted its compulsory attendance law in 1915, defining it as an institutionally young state school system. Yet because of the economic and political power exerted by its urban centers, the cultural diversity of its school population acquires an educational significance that "overrides" its institutional youthfulness. As a result of demographic forces, Texas is linked to states that have defined the content of educational issues and the direction of policy change. Most of these states have been institutionally older school systems. Thus Texas has been in the forefront of major court cases, from school finance (*Rodriquez v. San Antonio Independent School District* 1973) to the educational rights of children of alien status (*Plyler v. Doe* 1982).

The role of Texas in expanding substantive due process rights for handicapped children is most conspicuous in the Supreme Court's decision in *Tatro (Irving Independent School District v. Tatro* 1984). First filed against the Irving Independent School District in 1979, the case involved Amber Tatro, then 3 1/2 years old, whose spina bifida required a catheterization procedure every three to four hours to prevent a kidney infection. The school district argued that Clean Intermittent Catheterization (CIC) did not need to be a part of Amber's IEP, for it was not a "related service" as specified by *EAHA.* The U.S. District

Court agreed; the CIC was essential for life support, but was not related to Amber's "ability to learn."

In its review of the lower court's decision, the Supreme Court reversed its interpretation. Although in *Rowley* the Court decided against the requirement that an interpreter was a necessary related service for which a school district must pay, in *Tatro* the court affirmed that a CIC was not simply a medical service the cost of which had to borne by parents, but was indeed a related service required to fulfill the intent of a free appropriate public education. Without the CIC, Amber Tatro could not attend school and would therefore be deprived of access to a comparable education. Significantly, *Tatro* "affirms judicial review of the appropriateness of a handicapped child's IEP, *not merely review of adherence to procedural safeguards*" (Vitello 1986, p. 355, my emphasis). Thus, all handicapped children have a procedural right of access to an appropriate education. Yet, from *Tatro* (see Katsiyannis and Maag 1997), against this standard of comparable access, the nature of a child's disability will determine the extent of related services. These services, however, reach beyond merely opening the classroom doors procedurally. They reflect the substantive content and intent of "right to treatment."

Similar to Texas, the influence of court challenges and decisions stemming from Florida has been considerable. Like Texas, Florida is an institutionally young school system, enacting its compulsory attendance law in 1915. Yet, as a reflection of its major cities, its school population is large and culturally diverse. Its comparatively strong *national status* links it to major issues involving the educational rights of handicapped children. This involvement was especially evident in *S-1 v. Turlington* (1980–1981), a case that linked the procedural safeguards surrounding school discipline to the substantive rights of maintaining an appropriate educational placement. Of particular significance was the "nexus issue": the question of how a school district determines that a student's misconduct is related to his or her handicapping condition.

In the case of *S-1*, eight students were expelled for conduct ranging from sexual acts to vandalism. All students were classified as EMR and were expelled for nearly two years. In the court's decision, it was held that the expulsion of the students constituted a change in educational placement. Moreover, the court held that even if a district determined that misconduct was not related to a student's handicap, the intent of federal law to ensure an appropriate educational environment could take priority.

By posing the challenge to school disciplinary procedures as a nexus issue, the court's finding in *S-1* drew the substantive rights given to exceptional children closer to the procedural rights gained by students in general education. *S-1* made note that the expelled plaintiffs were accorded the procedural protections required by *Goss*. Nonetheless, with the determination that, related or not to a handicapping condition, by changing a student's educational placement expulsion was a violation of a substantive right, a sensitive distinction was implied between the school discipline of disabled and nondisabled students.

This distinction was largely affirmed, but not fully clarified, in *Honig v. Doe* (1988), the leading Supreme Court case on special education discipline. In *Honig*, the Court upheld the "stay-put" provision of the *EAHA* requiring that states ensure that disabled students *remain* in their current educational placement pending the completion of the steps of procedural due process rights. In fact, the Court found this provision to be "unequivocal," underscoring that "Congress very much meant to strip schools of the unilateral authority they had traditionally employed to exclude disabled students" (Tucker, Goldstein, and Sorenson 1993, p. 5:25). In addition, the Court rejected the (San Francisco) school district's wish that "dangerousness" be grounds to override the stay-put provision of the EAHC. The Court, nonetheless, did acknowledge that school officials "are entitled to seek injunctive relief" if a student's current placement was likely to result in injury to himself or herself or to others. By not wanting to overly restrict the discretion of school officials, the Court attempted to balance the interests of parents, student, and school, but it placed the burden of proof on the latter.

SUBSTANTIVE DUE PROCESS RIGHTS AND DIVERGENT EDUCATIONAL PATHS: A CONCLUDING NOTE

At face value, there is a romantic character to the extension of due process rights, both procedural and substantive. The achievement of these rights appears as a triumph over practices that restrict and/or harm, through indifference, inattention, or deliberate discrimination. The language of "safeguards" and "protections" portray this image. At an abstract level, the close affinity between cases involving school suspension and special education placement can be seen. It is alluring to believe that an outcome will be a greater consistency of experience in settings that have an "educational" function. Whether it is treatment, rehabilitation, or academic instruction, the extension of due process rights has drawn the common, delinquent, and special worlds closer.

Yet, there is evidence that points to the contrary. There is evidence that suggests the emergence of divergent educational paths, resulting quite unintentionally from the extension of due process rights. For the world of nonhandicapped students in common schools, one such path seeks to undo the practice of grouping according to ability differences, to "detrack" curricular placements that prejudge learning potential and harm educational opportunities. For the world of handicapped students in special education, there are pressures to ensure the retention of different educational environments, to "stay- put" in placements appropriate to a student's disability. Both paths are grounded in due process arguments that comprise the essential content of lawsuits against local and state school systems.

The conceptual and empirical critique of school tracking has matured to the level of active litigation aimed at eliminating tracking practices. The focus of critiques is akin to the challenges against racial overrepresentation in special education: there is, in many city school systems, a disproportionate concentration of African-American and Hispanic students in lower tracks and a greater concentration of white students in higher tracks. This pattern of disproportionate placement can arise from current practices that are found to be highly subjective and inconsistent (Oakes 1992; 1995; Welner and Oakes 1996) and/or traceable to the perpetuation of historical patterns of segregation (Wells and Crain 1994). Such evidence of racial (and class) disproportion negatively impacts the learning and the "life chances" of students placed in lower tracks.

The efforts aimed at "detracking" have invoked due process claims that are strikingly similar to challenges to ensure the educational opportunities of handicapped students. In exemplary cases such as *People Who Care v. Rockford Board of Education* (1994), and *Vasquez v. San Jose Unified School District* (1994), a variety of evidence, including moral arguments, historical background evidence, and statistical analyses, demonstrated the ongoing and "active" pattern of discrimination that perpetuates harmful effects on minority students. In both cases, the courts declared that the practice of tracking should be disallowed and the districts were ordered to engage immediately in detracking.

The success of these and other cases has not been achieved without local resistance (Wells and Serna 1996). Nonetheless, there is a considerable and growing recognition of the harmful effects of tracking. What is noteworthy here is that such recognition, both lay and professional, can be formulated from the stated educational rights found in state constitutions and reinforced with reference to the Due Process Clause of the Fourteenth Amendment. Independent of moral, historical, or statistical evidence, constitutional and legal theory has supported much of the call for detracking. At minimum, the curricular structures of general education, the hierarchy of tracks that grew up upon the foundation of special education classes (see Chapter 4), is highly susceptible to immediate and fundamental reform. A "stay-put" provision is antithetical to detracking.

In contrast to detracking efforts in general education, the focus of many due process challenges in special education has been on protecting educational placements, not on seeking their dissolution. The stability of an educational environment is more consistent with the goal of a free appropriate public education than is a challenge that may threaten this by enlarging the placement options for handicapped students. Nonetheless, the extension of due process rights to handicapped children runs through its own gauntlet, between the mandate that placement be in the *least restrictive environment* (LRE), and the goal that placement be in the *mainstream* of regular classes.

Although both share the same essential motivation, their difference has led to quite divergent judicial interpretations, which in turn led to divergent placements. LRE is a legal principle, asserting that "students with disabilities are to be educated *as close as possible* to the general education environment"; mainstreaming is the educational term that "refers to the practice of placing students with disabilities in general education classes *with appropriate instructional support*" (Osborne and DiMattia 1994, pp. 6–7, my emphases). The importance of this distinction is that mainstreaming is but one mode of satisfying the LRE mandate. Possibly more important is that the very term "least restrictive environment" is not to be found in the Individuals with Disabilities Education Act *(IDEA),* but has emerged as a principle that "creates a presumption in favor of the integration of children with disabilities" (Tucker, Goldstein and Sorenson 1993, p. 4:20).

In large measure, the goal of mainstreaming has been reached for mildly handicapped students. But for the more severely handicapped, the evidence is quite different: most have remained in segregated settings (Danielson and Bellamy 1989). Such evidence as this does not necessarily run against the legal intent of LRE. Indeed, circuit courts have approved of segregated placements insofar as they are best able to provide the related services appropriate to a student's disability (*Daniel R. R. v. State Board of Education* 1989; *Briggs v. Board of Education of Connecticut* 1989). In these judgments, the courts have relied heavily on the professional expertise of school officials and special educators, at times overriding the wishes of parents. In other decisions, however, courts have weighed in favor of mainstreaming (see *Oberti v. Board of Education of the Borough of Clementon School District* 1992). The contrast between these two kinds of decisions reflects the paradox that special education reform faces, especially as substantive rights are sought: attempts to implement educational rights for handicapped children can reinforce the very conditions that sustained their exclusion from general education. This, in turn, can reinforce their placement in segregated educational settings.

CONCLUSIONS

The expansion of the legal and statutory responsibility charged to general education threatens the institutional boundaries that confine delinquent and special children in places separate from common schools. The reform school becomes the training school, which is later supplemented by diversion and the detention home. The residential institution gives way to home and day schools, and in turn to special education classes. These twentieth-century changes of "deinstitutionalization" (Lerman 1982) are not ones specific to the delinquent and special worlds, but are comprehensible only as a continued expansion of education broadly conceived as a trinary system in place by the late nineteenth-century. The changes by no means spell the elimination of institutions and rationales that pervade the worlds of delinquency and exceptionality. Rather, they are changes in the geometry of a single unit whose three parts remain interlinked, albeit under changing terms.

The terms that have mattered have largely been legal. For American education, in the most recent decades they have been the constitutionally enforceable rights to due process. The appearance of procedural due process rights in the 1960s began a legally induced interchange between delinquency and common schooling. This mutuality is best exemplified by the similarities in content between the *Gault* decision in juvenile justice and the significant school discipline cases in general education. The content that was mutual was the rights to procedural due process. The implication that was significant was the achievement of these rights *across* quite different institutional settings.

The achievement of procedural rights, to proper notification and a hearing at minimum, drew the worlds of delinquency and common schooling closer in a way that had never been achieved earlier. As I have argued, a crucial bridge between the two was the claim to a "right to treatment," then a nascent concept that nonetheless held potential for a broad application.

Indeed, this right was first aroused in the institutional settings of state hospitals and asylums. Once it "traveled" to delinquency, it would certainly travel to common schooling. By the mid 1970s, the mutuality signaled by *Gault* and school discipline was given more concrete form in federal legislation, by the strikingly similar statutory language of the *Education for All Handicapped Children Act* and the *Juvenile Justice and Delinquency Prevention Act*. The temporal coincidence of these two acts could be seen as fortuitous. From an institutional perspective, however, their coincidence makes sense: delinquency and exceptionality have historically been linked to common schooling by way of similar statutory language, albeit a language of exclusion and exemption.

With the *EAHC* Act, exceptional children secured a right to a free appropriate public education. This achievement of this right was momentous, yet its implementation rested largely on the fulfillment of procedural requirements. It was, as I have argued here, the embodiment of *legal justice*, for the rules it articulated were founded on general categories of persons, specifically by the designating handicapping conditions deemed "educationally disabled." Like the "right to treatment," the substantive rationale for these procedural rules was more nascent: a right to a hearing could be specified more concretely than appropriate education could be objectively defined. Yet *substantive justice*, the articulation of goals that are relatively free of specific procedures, was more than nascent. It was critical to the implementation of this first wave of due process rights. Actual fulfillment of procedural rights may in fact vary, but the substantive intention of EAHC is more invariant (see Walker 1987). As Justice Brennan declared in *Honig v. Doe*, Congress meant to "strip schools" of their traditional authority to exclude disabled students.

Affirming that handicapped children have a right to a free appropriate public education exposed all the more how strictly procedural compulsory attendance laws were. Not until the latter part of this century did the right of access to public education gain an adjective that implied substantive rights of due process. Yet appropriate implies more than access; it concerns passage, through the graded curriculum of general education, to an occupation and participatory citizenship.

The reciprocal or "dialectical" relationship between procedural and substantive due process rights has been shaped by the *institutional age* of state school systems. Institutionally older systems led the way in the formulation of the EAHC Act. By the time educational rights for handicapped children had been affirmed as a national priority, older state school systems had moved beyond their procedural foundation. Massachusetts was already "ahead" of the EAHC by its passage of chapter 766 in 1972, a legislation that sought to weaken the dependency of educational provisioning on categories that defined handicapped conditions. Massachusetts had begun to "reverse" the relationship between procedural and substantive rights, or between legal and substantive justice. The expansion of substantive rights needed to be freed from their prior procedural framework.

This freeing of substantive justice coincided with the decline of *institutional age* as a determinant of the growth of special education. The extension of substantive rights was increasingly promoted by contextual similarities that linked diverse groups by way of legally defined "educational fates." Thus, states with large and multicultural school populations are the participants in legal claims for substantive educational rights. Claims that reach beyond procedural safeguards reach beyond jurisdictional boundaries as well; that is, beyond the organizational lines that have separated delinquency and exceptionality from general education. Substantive rights draw the three worlds of American education even closer.

There are, nonetheless, reasons to be cautious. Much like the "antinomy" between democracy and efficiency that has contributed to the rise of tracking in general education, the antinomy between mainstreaming and LRE suggests important limits to special education reform. It underscores real conditions that not only restrain the goal of inclusion, but also may unintentionally effect a return to historical patterns of separation.

What I have called the *paradox* of special education is an attempt to capture the link between judicial or legislative intent and unanticipated, and largely undesired, outcomes. The extension of due process rights, intended to expand the educational participation and the quality of "life chances" for handicapped children, has stripped much of the bad from the unilateral practice to exclude. Yet, the extension of these rights has been across the organizationally distinct but institutionally linked worlds of American education. There is, as such, an important caveat when speaking of the extension of rights "within" special education: educational rights are not so much "within" special education as they are conferred from "without."

Special education reflects a jurisdictional space, much of which is defined by the overlap between general education and the worlds of delinquency and exceptionality. But special education has not simply been the residual of these two. Nor, as I have argued earlier, has special education been the stepchild of general education. On the contrary, much of the "due process revolution" in educational rights has taken place within the jurisdictional space of special education and, indeed, has been defined and led by special education. Although challenged and attacked, special education has emerged with an expanded jurisdiction and enhanced autonomy. I turn to this "unanticipated" outcome in the Epilogue.

NOTES

1. The range of behaviors that define status offenses overlaps with school sanctions of expulsion and suspension. This, in turn, reactivates historical grounds for commitment to reform or industrial schools. This contemporary interdependence was vividly demonstrated in *Gesicki v. Oswald* (1971). Here, a nineteen year old girl whose father had died and whose mother was confined in a mental hospital, was expelled from school for "sexual promiscuity." This, in turn, led to her adjudication as a wayward minor and to placement in a foster home. Upon running away, she was subsequently confined in the state reformatory. In the challenge to this confinement, *Gesicki* found PINS (Persons in Need of Supervision) statutes void-for-vagueness. But its larger significance

was its challenge to the very legitimacy of *parens patriae*. The challenge successfully distinguished a presumed *condition* of waywardness or moral depravity, from specific *acts* that were argued to be its cause. The distinction outlined grounds for judicial restraint, for without knowledge of alleged acts that constitute the conditions, punishment supercedes treatment.

Epilogue

To study special education is to learn about public schooling, juvenile delinquency, and the history and treatment of the "special classes." If I have succeeded in demonstrating that compulsory attendance laws were documents that formalized the jurisdiction of special education, then support is given to the central thesis of this volume, that American education must be conceived broadly to encompass the three worlds of common, delinquent and special youth. What arose with the passage of these laws was indeed what Michel Foucault called a *discursive formation*, a new way of looking at and speaking about education. This new discourse arose to accommodate the new institutional arrangements for whole categories of youth, the "tutelary complex" that was so feared and resisted before compulsory attendance laws were enacted. The nineteenth-century roots of special education are the origins of this new discourse.

The construction of the special class for atypical and laggard children was a critical gear for the institutional relations that joined delinquency and exceptionality to common schooling. As this common schooling expanded and became more stratified, special education became even more important. But its strategic importance still remained veiled.

Condemned and assaulted for practices routinely exercised by regular education, special education was suddenly thrust onto the legal stage in the 1960s and became a driving force for major educational reforms (Gliedman and Roth 1980). This is indeed the irony. For so many court challenges, special education was the defendant, charged with discriminatory referrals, inaccurate diagnoses, disproportionate placement, or even insufficient assessment. Yet the cumulative consequence of this legal assault has not been to delimit the professional jurisdiction of special education and to narrow its client population. On the contrary, the outcome has been an enlarged jurisdiction and a broadened client population. Special education has emerged from the shadows of its historical origins to assume a legally enforced presence in the conduct of public education. It has moved from the portable to the regular classroom, from defendant to plaintiff.

However dramatic this organizational and legal ascendancy of special education has been, it reflects a much broader change. To draw again from Foucault, it is one reflection of the institutionalization of *disciplinary* power. The maturation of special education, and of school psychology as well, has brought with it an expanded surveillance of children, whether they are in public schools, reformatories, or residential institutions. The professional debates and court challenges over *rules of passage* testify to the prominence of disciplinary power in defining the issues of public education and in determining their resolutions as well.

The emergence of this disciplinary power was at the heart of Foucault's historical studies of the rise of the clinic and the prison. In contrast to earlier (Marx, Durkheim) and contemporary theorists (Habermas), Foucault presents a "genealogical account" of modernization, an account of what he saw as the significant transformation beginning in the eighteenth-century and accelerating throughout the nineteenth: the emergence of the "whole series of institutions which, well beyond the frontiers of criminal law, constituted what one might call the carceral archipelago" (Foucault 1979, p. 297). The rise of this carceral society was founded on the construction of the prison, lunatic asylum, and other forms of incarceration. With these new arrangements of confinement, forms of disciplinary power could now "gaze" at these populations. Penology and psychiatry could grow in both theory and practice, for the prison and clinic stabilized the material basis of their disciplinary power.

Foucault by no means limits his attention to the prison and asylum. This carceral archipelago arising throughout the nineteenth-century included the school and reformatory, and the orphanage and almshouse as well. But what linked this range of institutions was not so much a common property of "confinement," but a new framework for the interpretation of deviance, a new "normalizing principle." From its ideological beginnings in the eighteenth-century to its material, institutional foundation in the nineteenth, this principle increasingly wove through a considerable diversity of confinements, subtly but effectively transforming the very definition of power. What "haunted" the prison and clinic diffused outward to haunt the school. Theories of pedagogy would join the theories of crime and lunacy.

Foucault's account of modernization is really an account of the rise of "civil society" (see Cohen and Arato 1992, p. 272, passim). At the center of Foucault's image of civil society is the uneasy co-existence of disciplinary power with its historical predecessor, the *juridical model* of power rooted in the old regime and absolutism. The juridical model is the most widely understood view of power, conceiving of it as arising freely from contractual exchange and checked by the rules and mechanisms of law. The juridical model facilitated the emergence of the modern democratic state, and its social sphere of public life. With the erection of large state institutions during the nineteenth-century, disciplinary power spread as a normalizing principle, a form of coercive regulation conceived not as a possession that is exchanged and recoverable, but "as a relation of forces" (Cohen and Arato 1992, p. 266) that *circulates* through a *net-like organization*. Although these two forms of power contrast sharply, it is their mutual interrelationship that is most important. It is useful to quote Foucault's full words (1979):

> Historically the process by which the bourgeoisie became in the course of the eighteenth century the politically dominant class *was masked by the establishment of an explicit, coded, and formally egalitarian juridical framework* . . . But the development and generalization of disciplinary mechanisms constituted the other, *dark side of these processes*. The general juridical form that guaranteed a system of rights that were egalitarian in principle was supported by these tiny, everyday, physical mechanisms, by all those systems of micropower that are essentially nonegalitarian, and asymmetric that we call the disciplines. (p. 222, my emphases).

Whereas the "formally egalitarian juridical framework" is associated with state powers, the "dark side of these processes" is diffused throughout society.

The contrast between these two models of power offers one way to summarize both the historical "origins" of special education, and its "modernization" as well. Enactment of compulsory attendance laws was a defining example of juridical power. These laws expressed the interests and scope of state powers, specifying the exchange of responsibility between parental authority and the jurisdictional authority of school officers. Like the rise of the modern nation-state, compulsory attendance laws defined the corporate boundary of a state or territory likely more than any other legislation. The fact that these laws did not have as their juridical purpose the compelling of school attendance illustrates their "masking" of hidden, nonegalitarian, and asymmetric processes. Behind this explicit and formally egalitarian juridical framework was the "dark side" of a universal education, the menace of the feebleminded and the threat of delinquency. The juridical definition of the powers to exempt and expel gave formal credence to Samuel Gridley Howe's "chain of common schools." It also defined the juridical inequalities across this "carceral archipelago."

The juridical powers embodied in compulsory attendance laws were, as Chapter 2 explored, complicated by the antinomy of democracy and efficiency. The very need to define powers of exemption and expulsion reflects how state school systems were inescapably implicated in the organizational dilemma of common schooling. Once the school-age population was juridically divided into the common, delinquent, and special worlds, however unequal their relations, the direction of change was set: toward the long-term incorporation into common schooling of groups historically exempted and excluded. Or in Foucault's term, toward the "deinstitutionalization" of disciplinary techniques that emerged originally in separate institutions and progressively diffused outward (1979, p. 211).

It is this long-term process of deinstitutionalization that I call the *inversion* of common schooling by the maturation of special education. Special education has certainly matured in organizational size, administrative stature, and instructional relevance. These aspects of its maturation are juridical, and reflect powers invested in state school systems with enactment of compulsory attendance. But the maturation of special education over the past few decades has also occurred as a form of disciplinary power.

One outcome of the legal challenges over racial overrepresentation has been to enlarge the *ethical scope* of special education and of school psychology. The legal attacks on overrepresentation stimulated critical debate about student rights and the categorical structure of special education (NASP/NCAS 1985). What began as reform within special education led to a revolution in school psychology (Reschly 1988d). Special education and school psychology have engaged in their own self-reflection, prompted in part by the erosion of professional control. Among the lessons learned was the awareness that [school psychology] had an "unfortunate tradition of high levels of inference whereby fairly simple behaviors are attributed to highly complex underlying dynamics" (Reschly 1988d, p. 469). Acknowledged as a "paradigmatic shift" (Reschly and Ysseldyke 1995), the focus of special education is turning to "system reform," the core of which is an emphasis on *outcomes* rather than interventions. With the anticipated decline in the categorical structure for mild handicaps, the knowledge base and assessment technology of special education and school psychology will be assessment of outcomes reached in *natural settings,* not measured against categorical labels. In ways most likely unforeseen by Deno in 1970, special education has reformed itself out of business, but out of the old business that relied too much on its legacy of non-normative categories.

The contemporary focus on "system reform" is consistent with the institutional view of American education as a trinary structure. The "institutional shape" of special education has emphasized the essential integration of this *single unit* from the late nineteenth-century forward. Special education is not a separate field or discipline removed from the shifting structure of general education, nor is it removed from the shifts in delinquency. What is key is the historical behavior of this single unit. Composed of three interrelated worlds, this single unit has exhibited features that remind one of medieval structures. The social order of feudal society distinguished *oratores* (the power of prayer), *bellatores* (the power of fighting), and *laboratores* (the power of toil) so to constitute a tripartite or trinary system whose hierarchy symbolized a just and proper universe. When the medieval order was breached, as when "rustics were included in the deliberations of the peace assemblies," strain was placed on this (necessary) scheme of inequality (Duby 1980, p. 59). As groups historically excluded, exempted, or segregated "were included in the deliberations" of general education, strain was indeed placed on prevailing explanations and theories of "educability." As the history of special education tells, much of the content of these explanations and theories has changed to accommodate, and indeed to control the integration of these groups.

We may again draw on medieval scholarship. In his brilliant account of the "fiction theory" of dynamic continuity, Ernst Kantorowicz underscores the significance of a "vertical" principle denoting those "living successively." This principle allowed the realization of the fictitious person or *corpus mysticum*. As Kantorowicz put it: "that is, one constructed a body corporate whose members were echeloned longitudinally so that its cross-section at any given moment revealed one instead of many members—a mystical person by perpetual devolution; whose mortal and temporary incumbent was of relatively minor importance as compared to the immortal body corporate by succession which he represented" (1957, pp. 312–313). Indeed, much of what has constituted educability has been "fictional," constructed to ensure the perpetuity of common schooling. And thus, the study of special education may offer the best explanation for how common schooling has been able to remain protected by elements of mystery, ensuring its perpetuation as an "immortal body corporate."

References

Abbott, Andrew. "Sequences of Social Events: Concepts and Methods for the Analysis of Order in Social Processes." *Historical Methods* 16 (1983): 129–147.

Abbott, Andrew. *The System of Professions*. Chicago: University of Chicago Press, 1988.

Abbott, Edith, and Sophonisba P. Breckinridge. *Truancy and Nonattendance in the Chicago Schools*. Chicago: University of Chicago Press, 1917.

Ainsworth, Janet E. "The Court's Effectiveness in Protecting the Rights of Juveniles in Delinquency Cases." *The Future of Children* 6 (Winter, 1996): 64–74.

Algozzine, B., and J. E. Ysseldyke. "Learning Disability as a Subset of School Failure: The Over-Sophistication of a Concept." *Exceptional Children* 50 (1983): 242–246.

Algozzine, B., J. E. Ysseldyke, and S. Christenson. "An Analysis of the Incidence of Special Class Placement." *The Journal of Special Education* 17 (1983): 141–147.

Allen, Nicholas Murray. "Education of Defectives." In *Monographs on Education in the United States*, edited by Nicholas Murray Allen. New York: J. B. Lyon Co., 1899.

Angus, David L., and Jeffrey E. Mirel. "Equality, Curriculum, and the Decline of the Academic Ideal: Detroit, 1930–1968." *History of Education Quarterly* 33 (Summer, 1993): 107–207.

Angus, David L., Jeffrey E. Mirel, and Maris A. Vinovskis. "Historical Development of Age Stratification in Schooling." *Teachers College Record* 90 (1988): 211–235.

Argulewicz, Ed. N. "Effects of Ethnic Membership, Socioeconomic Status, and Home Language on LD, EMR, and EH Placements." *Learning Disabilities Quarterly* 6 (1983): 195–200.

Artiles, Alfredo J., and Stanley C. Trent. "Overrepresentation of Minority Students in Special Education: A Continuing Debate." *Journal of Special Education* 27 (1994): 410–437.

Association of Masters [of the Boston Public Schools]. "Remarks on the Seventh Annual Report of the Hon. Horace Mann." Boston: Charles C. Little and James Brown, 1844.

Ayers, Leonard. *Laggards in Our Schools, A Study of Retardation and Elimination in City School Systems.* New York: Charities Publication Committee, Russell Sage Foundation, 1909.

Bailyn, Bernard. *Education in the Forming of American Society.* Chapel Hill: University of North Carolina Press, 1960.

Bartlett, Larry. "Disciplining Handicapped Students: Legal Issues in Light of *Honig v. Doe.*" *Exceptional Children* 55 (1989): 357–366.

Bellingham, Bruce. "Institution and Family: An Alternative View of Nineteenth Century Child Saving." *Social Problems* 33 (1986): 533–557.

Bender, Thomas. *Toward an Urban Vision, Ideas and Institutions in Nineteenth Century America.* Lexington: University Press of Kentucky, 1975.

Bender, Thomas. *Community and Social Change in America.* Baltimore: The Johns Hopkins University Press, 1978.

Bennett, Charles A. *History of Manual and Industrial Education, 1870–1917.* Peoria, Ill.: Manual Arts, 1937.

Berman, Harold. *Law and Revolution, The Formation of the Western Legal Tradition.* Cambridge, Mass.: Harvard University Press, 1983.

Bersoff, Donald N. "Regarding Psychologists Testily: Legal Regulation of Psychological Assessment in the Public Schools." *Maryland Law Review* 39 (1979): 27–120.

Best, Harry. *The Deaf, Their Position in Society and the Provision For Their Education in the United States.* New York: Thomas Y. Crowell Company, 1914.

Bestor, Arthur. *Educational Wastelands.* Urbana & Chicago: University of Illinois Press, 1985.

Bickel, William E., and Donna D. Bickel. "Effective Schools, Classrooms, and Instruction: Implications for Special Education." *Exceptional Children* 52 (1986): 489–500.

Bina, Michael. "Mainstreaming, Schools for the Blind, and Full Inclusion: What Shall the Future of Education for Blind Children Be?" In *The Illusion of Full Inclusion,* edited by James M. Kauffman and Daniel P. Hallahan. Austin, TEX: pro-ed, 1995.

Board of Education of Hendrick Hudson Central School District v. Rowley, 458, U.S. 176, 102 S.Ct. 3034, 73 L.Ed.2d 690, 5 Ed. Law Rep. 34 (1982).

Booth, Tony. "Policies Towards the Integration of Mentally Handicapped Children in Education." *Oxford Review of Education* 9 (1983): 255–268.

Brace, Charles L. *Address Upon the Industrial School Movement.* New York: Wynkoop, Hallenbeck & Thomas, 1857.

Brace, Charles L. *The Best Method of Disposing of Our Pauper and Vagrant Children.* New York: Wynkoop, Hallenbeck & Thomas, 1859.

Breed v. Jones, 421 U.S. 519 (1975).

Brenzel, Barbara. *Daughters of the State: A Social Portrait of the First Reform School for Girls in North America, 1856–1905.* Cambridge, Mass. MIT Press, 1983.

Briggs v. Board of Education of Connecticut, 882 F.2d 156, 688, 55 Ed. Law Rep. 423 (3nd Cir. 1989).

Bronner, Augusta. *The Psychology of Special Abilities and Disabilities.* Boston: Little, Brown & Co., 1917.

Brown v. Board of Education 347 U.S. 483 (1954).

Brown, F. "The SOMPA: A System of Measuring Potential Abilities?" *School Psychology Digest* 8 (1979): 37–46.

Burke, Kenneth. *Language As Symbolic Action, Essays on Life, Literature, and Method.* Berkeley: University of California Press, 1966.

Burke, Kenneth. *A Grammar of Motives.* Berkeley: University of California Press, 1969.

Buss, William G. "Procedural Due Process for School Discipline: Probing the Constitutional Outline." *University of Pennsylvania Law Review* 119 (1971): 545–641.

Callahan, Raymond E. *Education and the Cult of Efficiency.* Chicago: University of Chicago Press, 1962.

Canguilhem, Georges. *The Normal and the Pathological.* New York: Zone Books, 1991.

Carrier, James. "Knowledge, Meaning, and Social Inequality in Kenneth Burke." *American Journal of Sociology* 88 (1982): 43–61.

Carrier, James. "Masking the Social in Educational Knowledge: The Case of Learning Disability Theory." *American Journal of Sociology* 88 (1983): 948–974.

Carrier, James. *Learning Disability, Social Class and the Construction of Inequality in American Education.* New York: Greenwood, 1986a.

Carrier, James. "Sociology and Special Education: Differentiation ,and Allocation in Mass Education." *American Journal of Education* 94 (1986b):281–312.

Carrier, James. "The Politics of Early Learning Disability Theory." In *Learning Disability: Dissenting Essays*, edited by Barry M. Franklin. London: The Falmer Press, 1987.

Castel, Robert. *The Regulation of Madness, The Origins of Incarceration in France.* Berkeley & Los Angeles: University of California Press, 1988.

Chapman, Paul Davis. *Schools as Sorters, Lewis M. Terman, Applied Psychology, and the Intelligence Testing Movement, 1890–1930.* New York & London: New York University Press, 1988.

Christoplos, F., and P. Renz . "A Critical Examination of Special Education Programs." *Journal of Special Education* 3 (1969): 371–380.

Cicourel, Aaron V., and John I. Kitsuse. *The Educational Decision-Makers.* Indianapolis: Bobbs-Merrill, 1963.

Clement, Priscilla F. "Families and Foster Care: Philadelphia in the Late Nineteenth Century." In *Growing Up in America, Children in Historical Perspective*, edited by N. Ray Hiner and Joseph M. Hawes. Urbana & Chicago: University of Illinois Press, 1985a.

Clement, Priscilla F. "The City and the Child, 1860–1885." In *American Childhood, A Research Guide and Historical Handbook*, edited by Joseph M. Hawes and N. Ray Hiner. Westport, Conn.: Greenwood, 1985b.

Clews, Elsie. *Educational Legislation and Administration of the Colonial Governments.* New York: The Macmillan, Company. Columbia University Contributions to Philosophy, Psychology and Education, 1899.

Cogan, Neil Howard. "Juvenile Law, Before and After the Entrance of 'Parens Patriae.'" *South Carolina Law Review* 22 (1970): 147–181.

Cohen, Jean L., and Andrew Arato. *Civil Society and Political Theory.* Cambridge, Mass. MIT Press, 1992.

Cohen, Sol. *Progressives and Urban School Reform: The Public Education Association of New York City, 1895–1954.* New York: Teachers College Press, 1964.

Cohen, Sol. "The Industrial Education Movement, 1906–1917." *American Quarterly* 20 (1968): 95–110.

Coles, G. S. "The Learning-Disabilities Test Battery: Empirical and Social Issues." *Harvard Educational Review* 48 (1978): 313–340.

Coles, Gerald. *The Learning Mystique, A Critical Look at "Learning Disabilities".* New York: Pantheon Books, 1987.

Conant, James B. *The Identification and Education of the Academically Talented Student in the American Secondary School: The Conference Report.* NEA, 1958.

Conant, James Bryant. *The American High School Today.* New York: McGraw-Hill, 1959a.

Conant, James Bryant. *The Child, The Parent, and The State.* Cambridge, Mass. Harvard University Press, 1959b.

Conant, James Bryant. *Slums and Suburbs.* New York: McGraw-Hill, 1961.

Coulanges, Fustel de. *The Ancient City.* Garden City, New York: Doubleday & Company, Inc., 1956

Counts, George S. *The Selective Character of American Secondary Education.* Chicago: University of Chicago Press, 1922.

Counts, George S. *Secondary Education and Industrialism.* Cambridge, Mass. Harvard University Press, 1929.

Covarrubias v. San Diego Unified School District, 70–394. February, 1971.

Creek v. Stone, 379 F.2d 106 (D.C. Cir. 1967).

Cremin, Lawrence A. (Ed.). *The Republic and the School, Horace Mann on The Education of Free Men.* New York: Teachers College Press, 1957.

Cremin, Lawrence, A. *American Education, The Colonial Experience.* New York: Harper & Row, 1970.

Criminal Law Reporter. "Juvenile Court Orders Treatment for Deaf-Mute." 2 (1968): 2412.

Curtis, George B. "The Checkered Career of Parens Patriae?" *De Paul Law Review* 25 (1976): 895–915.

Daniel R. R. v. State Board of Education, 874 F.2d 1036, 53 E. Law Rep. 824 (5 Cir. 1989).

Danielson, L. C., and G. T. Bellamy. "State Variation in Placement of Children with Handicaps in Segregated Environments." *Exceptional Children* 55 (1989): 448–455.

Darrah, Joan. "Diagnostic Practices and Special Classes for the Educable Mentally Retarded–A Layman's Critical View." *Exceptional Children* 33 (1967): 523–527.

Davies, Margaret Gay. *The Enforcement of English Apprenticeship.* Cambridge, Mass. Harvard University Press, 1956.

Demos, John. *A Little Commonwealth, Family Life in Plymouth Colony.* New York: Oxford University Press, 1970.

Deno, E. "Special Education as Developmental Capital." *Exceptional Children* 37 (1970): 229–237.

Department of the Interior. "Cities Reporting the Use of Homogeneous Grouping and of the Winnetka Technique and the Dalton Plan." Bureau of Education. City School Leaflet no. 22. Washington D.C.: Government Printing Office, 1923.

Dewey, John. "An Undemocratic Proposal." *Vocational Education* 2 (1913): 374–77.

Dewey, John. *Democracy and Education, An Introduction to the Philosophy of Education.* New York: The MacMillan Company, 1916/1929.

Dewson, Mary W., and Hastings H. Hart. "Schools for Delinquent Girls." In *Preventive Treatment of Neglected Children,* edited by Hastings Hart. New York: Russell Sage, 1910.

Diana v. California State Board of Education, Civil No. 70–37 RFP (N.D. California 1970).

DiMaggio, Paul J., and Walter W. Powell. "The Iron Cage Revisited: Institutional Isomorphism and Collective Rationality in Organizational Fields." In *The New Institutionalism in Organizational Analysis,* edited by Walter W. Powell and Paul J. DiMaggio. Chicago: University of Chicago Press, 1991.

Dixon v. Alabama State Board of Education, 294 F.2d 150 (5th Cir.), cert. Denied, 368 U.S. 930 (1961).

Doll, Edgar. *Clinical Studies in Feeble-mindedness.* Boston: Richard G. Badger, 1917.

Donzelot, Jacques. 1979. *The Policing of Families.* New York: Pantheon Books, 1991.

Douglas, Paul. *American Apprenticeship and Industrial Education.* New York: Columbia University Studies in History, Economics and Public Law, Vol. 95, no. 2. 1921.

Duby, Georges. *The Three Orders, Feudal Society Imagined.* Chicago: University of Chicago Press, 1980.

Dunlop, O. Jocelyn. *English Apprenticeship and Child Labour, A History.* New York: The Macmillan Company, 1912.

Dunn, L. M. "Special Education for the Mildly Retarded: Is Much of It Justified?" *Exceptional Children* 45 (1968): 5–22.

Educational Policies Commission, *Education for All American Youth.* Washington, D.C.: National Education Association of the United States, 1944.

Eliot, Charles W. "Industrial Education as an Essential Factor in Our National Prosperity." Bulletin, National Society for the Promotion of Industrial Education No. 5, 1908.

Eliot, Thomas D. "Welfare Agencies, Special Education, and the Courts." *American Journal of Sociology* 31 (1925): 58–78.

Elliott, R. (1987). *Litigating Intelligence, IQ Tests, Special Education, and Social Science in the Courtroom.* Dover, Mass.: Auburn House.

Emerson, R. W. "Truant Absences from the Schools and Upon the Best Means of Treating such Offenders." *Report to the Boston School Committee,* 1831.

Epps, S., J. E. Ysseldyke, and M. McGue. "Differentiating LD and non-LD Students: I Know One When I See One." *Learning Disability Quarterly* 7 (1984): 89–101.

Fass, Paula S. "The IQ: A Cultural and Historical Framework." *American Journal of Education* 88 (1980): 431–58.

Feld, Barry C. "Criminalizing Juvenile Justice: Rules of Procedure for Juvenile Court." *Minnesota Law Review* 69 (1984): 141–276.

Fenton, Norman. *Mental Hygiene in School Practice.* Stanford: Stanford University Press, 1943.

Ferguson, Dianne L. "Severity of Need and Educational Excellence: Public School Reform and Students with Disabilities." In *Schooling and Disability,* edited by Douglas Biklen, Dianne Ferguson, and Alison Ford. Eighty-eighth Yearbook of the

National Society for the Study of Education, Part 2. Chicago: University of Chicago Press, 1989.

Finkelstein, Barbara. "Casting Networks of Good Influence: The Reconstruction of Childhood in the United States, 1790–1870." In *American Childhood, A Research Guide and Historical Handbook*, edited by Joseph M. Hawes and N. Ray Hiner. Westport, Conn. & London: Greenwood, 1985.

Finn, Jeremy D. "Patterns in Special Education Placement as Revealed by the OCR Surveys." In *Placing Children in Special Education: A Strategy for Equity*, edited by Kirby A. Heller, Wayne H. Holtzman, and Samuel Messick. Washington, D.C.: National Academy Press, 1982.

Fisher, Berenice M. *Industrial Education: American Ideals and Institutions*. Madison: University of Wisconsin Press, 1967.

Foucault, Michel. *The Archaeology of Knowledge, and The Discourse on Language*. New York: Pantheon, 1972.

Foucault, Michel. *The Birth of the Clinic: An Archaeology of Medical Perception*. New York: Random House, 1975.

Foucault, Michel. *Discipline and Punish*. New York: Pantheon, 1979.

Fox, Sanford J. "Juvenile Justice Reform: An Historical Perspective." *Stanford Law Review* (June, 1970): 1187–1239.

Franklin, Barry M. "From Backwardness to LD: Behaviorism, Systems Theory, and the Learning Disabilities Field Historically Reconsidered." *Journal of Education* 162 (1980): 5–22.

Franklin, Barry M. (ed.). *Learning Disability: Dissenting Essays*. London: The Falmer Press, 1987.

Frederick L. v. Thomas, 419 F. Supp. 960 (E.D. Pa. 1976), *aff'd*, 557 F. 2d 373 (ed Cir. 1977).

Fritschner, Linda Marie. "Women's Work and Women's Education." *Sociology of Work and Occupations* 4 (1977): 209–234.

Fulcher, Gillian. "Integrate and Mainstream? Comparative Issues in the Politics of These Policies." In *Integration: Myth or Reality?* edited by Len Barton. London: The Falmer Press, 1989.

Fuller, Lon L. *The Morality of Law*. New Haven & London: Yale University Press, 1964.

Gardner, Phil. *The Lost Elementary Schools of Victorian England*. London: Croom Helm, 1984.

Garlock, Peter D. " 'Wayward' Children and the Law, 1820–1900: The Genesis of the Status Offense Jurisdiction of the Juvenile Court." *Georgia Law Review* 13 (Winter 1979): 341–447.

Garrison, Mortimer, Jr., and Donald D. Hammill. "Who Are the Retarded?" *Exceptional Children* 38 (1971): 13–20.

Gartner, Alan, and Dorothy Kerzner Lipsky. "Beyond Special Education: Toward a Quality System for All Students." *Harvard Educational Review* 57 (1987): 367–395.

Gelb, Steven A., and Donald T. Mizokawa. "Special Education and Social Structure: The Commonality of 'Exceptionality.'" *American Educational Research Journal* 23 (1986): 543–557.

Gerber, M. M., and M. I. Semmel. "Teacher as Imperfect Test: Reconceptualizing the Referral Process." *Educational Psychologist* 19 (1984): 137–148.

Gerber M. M., and M. I. Semmel. "Microeconomics of Referral and Reintegration: A Paradigm for Evaluation of Special Education." *Studies in Educational Evaluation* 11 (1985): 13–29.

Gesicki v. Oswald. 336 F. Supp. 371 (S.D.N.Y. 1971), aff'd mem., 406 U.S. 913 (1972).

Gilhool, Thomas K. "The Right to an Effective Education, From *Brown* to PL 94–142 and Beyond." In *Beyond Separate Education, Quality Education for All,* edited by Dorothy K. Lipsky and Alan Gartner. Baltimore: Paul H. Brookes Publishing Co., 1989.

Gliedman, William, and William Roth. *The Unexpected Minority: Handicapped Children in American.* New York: Harcourt Brace Jovanovich.m, 1980.

Goddard, Henry. *School Training of Defective Children.* New York: World Book Company, 1915.

Goddard, Henry H.. *Juvenile Delinquency.* New York: Dodd, Mead & Company, 1921.

Goldstein, Stephen. "The Scope and Sources of School Board Authority to Regulate Student Conduct and Status: A Nonconstitutional Analysis." *University of Pennsylvania Law Review* 117(3) (1969): 373–430.

Goodman, Joan F. "The Diagnostic Fallacy: A Critique of Jane Mercer's Concept of Mental Retardation." *Journal of School Psychology* 15 (1977): 197–205.

Goodman, Joan F. "Organicity as a Construct in Psychological Diagnosis." In *Advances in School Psychology,* vol. 3, edited by

Thomas R. Kratochwill. Hillsdale, N.J.: Lawrence Erlbaum Associates, Publishers, 1983.

Gordon, Robert. "Examining Labeling Theory: The Case of Mental Retardation." In *The Labeling of Deviance,* edited by Walter Gove. Beverly Hills, CA: Sage, 1980.

Goss v. Lopez, 419 U.S. 565 (1975).

Gough, Aidan R. "Beyond-Control Youth in the Juvenile Court—The Climate for Change." Pp. 271–296 in *Beyond Control, Status Offenders in the Juvenile Court,* edited by Lee E. Teitelbaum and Aidan R. Gough. Cambridge, Mass.: Ballinger, 1977.

Graveson, R. H. *Status in the Common Law.* London: The Athlone Press. 1953.

Grossberg, Michael. "Children's Legal Rights? A Historical Look at a Legal Paradox." In *Children at Risk in America, History, Concepts, and Public Policy,* edited by Roberta Wollons. New York: SUNY, 1993.

Groszmann, Maximilian. *The Exceptional Child.* New York: Charles Scribner's Sons, 1917.

Grubb, W. Norton, and Marvin Lazerson. "Rally 'Round the Workplace: Continuities and Fallacies in Career Education." *Harvard Educational Review* 45 (1975): 451–74.

Grubb, W. Norton, and Marvin Lazerson. *Broken Promises, How Americans Fail Their Children.* New York: Basic Books, 1982.

Guadalupe Organization, Inc., v. Tempe Elementary School District No. 3. Civil Action No. 71–435, Phoenix District, Arizona, January 24, 1972.

Gusfield, Joseph R. (Ed). *Kenneth Burke On Symbols and Society. Chicago*: University of Chicago Press, 1989.

Gutkin, T. B., and C. R. Reynolds. "Factorial Similarity of the WISC-R for Anglos and Chicanos Referred for Psychological Services." *Journal of School Psychology* 18 (1980): 34–39.

Gutkin, T. B., and C. R. Reynolds. "Factorial Similarity of the WISC-R for White and Black Children from the Standardization Sample." *Journal of Educational Psychology* 73 (1981): 227–231.

Hallahan, D. P., C. E Keller, J. D. McKinney, J. W. Lloyd, and T. Bryan. "Examining the Research Base of the Regular Education Initiative: Efficacy Studies and the Adaptive Learning Environments Model." *Journal of Learning Disabilities* 21 (1988): 29–35, 55.

Haller, Mark H. *Eugenics: Hereditarian Attitudes in American Thought.* New Brunswick, N. J.: Rutgers University Press, 1963.

Hamilton, Gary G., and John R. Sutton. "The Problem of Control in the Weak State, Domination in the United States, 1880–1920." *Theory and Society* 18 (1989): 1–46.

Handlin, Oscar. *Race and Nationality in American Life.* New York: Doubleday, 1957.

Hannon, Joan Underhill. "Poor Relief Policy in Antebellum New York State: The Rise and Decline of the Poorhouse." *Explorations in Economic History* 22 (1985): 233–256.

Hansot, Elisabeth, and David B. Tyack. *Learning Together, A History of Coeducation in American Schools.* New Haven & London: Yale University Press, 1990.

Hanus, Paul, H. *School Efficiency, A Constructive Study Applied to New York City.* New York: World Book Company, 1913.

Harry, B. *Cultural Diversity, Families, and the Special Education System: Communication for Empowerment.* New York: Teachers College Press, 1992.

Hartshorne, Hugh. *Character in Human Relations.* New York: Charles Scribner's Sons, 1933.

Hartshorne, Hugh, and Mark A. May. *Studies in the Nature of Character, I. Studies in Deceit.* New York: The MacMillan Company, 1928.

Hartshorne, Hugh, Mark A. May, and F. K. Shuttleworth. *Studies in the Nature of Character, III, Studies in the Organization of Character.* New York: The MacMillan Company, 1930.

Hartwell, C. S. "The Grading and Promotion of Pupils." *Addresses and Proceedings of the National Education Association* 48 (1910): 294–306.

Harvard University. Committee on the Objectives of a General Education in a Free Society. *General Education in a Free Society.* Cambridge, Mass.: Harvard University Press, 1945.

Hawes, Joseph M. *Children in Urban Society, Juvenile. Delinquency in Nineteenth Century America.* New York: Oxford University Press, 1971.

Healy, William. *Honesty.* Indianapolis: The Bobbs-Merrill Company, 1915a.

Healy, William. *The Individual Delinquent.* Boston, Little Brown, and Company, 1915b.

Healy, William. *Pathological Lying, Accusation, and Swindling.* Boston, Little, Brown and Company, 1915c.

Healy, William. *Mental Conflicts and Misconduct.* Boston: Little, Brown and Company, 1923.

Healy, William, and Augusta F. Bronner. *New Light on Delinquency and Its Treatment.* New Haven: Yale University Press, 1936.

Hehir, Thomas, and Thomas Latus. *Special Education at the Century's End, Evolution of Theory and Practice Since 1970.* Cambridge, Mass.: Harvard University Press, 1992.

Heller, K., W. Holtzman, and S. Messick (Eds.). *Placing Children in Special Education: A Strategy for Equity.* Washington, D.C: National Academy Press, 1982.

Hellum, Frank. "Juvenile Justice: The Second Revolution." *Crime and Delinquency* 25 (1979): 299–401.

Heywood, Colin. *Childhood in Nineteenth Century France: Work, Health and Education Among the "Classes Populaires."* Cambridge: Cambridge University Press, 1988.

Hiatt, James S. 1915. "The Truant Problem and the Parental School." U.S. Bureau of Education Bulletin 29:7–32.

Hinsdale, B. A. *Horace Mann and the Common School Revival in the United States.* New York: Charles Scribner's Sons, 1900.

Hobbs, Nicholas (ed.). *Issues in the Classification of Children.* San Francisco: Jossey-Bass, 1975

Hobson v. Hansen, 269 F. Supp. 401 (D.D.C. 1967).

Hogan, David. *Class and Reform: School and Society in Chicago, 1880–1930.* Philadelphia: University of Pennsylvania Press. 1985.

Holmes, Arthur. *Backward Children.* Indianapolis: Bobbs-Merrill, 1915.

Honig v. Doe. 484 U.S. 305, 108 S. Ct. 592 (1988).

Horn, John Louis. *The Education of Exceptional Children.* New York: The Century Co., 1924.

Horwitz, Morton. "The Emergence of An Instrumental Conception of American Law, 1780–1820." *Perspectives in American History* 5 (1971): 287–326.

Houston, Susan E. "The 'Waifs and Strays' of a Late Victorian City: Juvenile Delinquents in Toronto." In *Childhood and Family in Canadian Society,* edited by Joy Parr. Toronto: McClelland & Stewart, 1982.

Howe, Samuel Gridley. "An Essay on Separate and Congregate Systems of Prison Discipline; Being A Report Made to The Boston Prison Discipline Society." Boston: William D. Ticknor and Company, 1846.

Howe, Samuel Gridley. *On the Causes of Idiocy.* New York: Arno Press & The New York Times, [1848] 1972.

Howe, Samuel Gridley. "Remarks Upon the Education of Deaf Mutes." Boston: Walker, Fuller & Co., Publishers, 1866.

Hurd, Henry M. *The Institutional Care of the Insane in the United States and Canada.* Volumes 2 and 3, New York: Arno Press, 1973.

Hurst, James W. *Law and Social Order in the United States.* Ithaca & London: Cornell University Press, 1977.

Hurt, J.S. *Outside the Mainstream, A History of Special Education.* London: B. T. Batsford, Ltd., 1988.

In re Gault, 387 US. 1 (1967).

In re Harris, 2 Criminal Law Reporter 2412 (Cook County Circuit Court, Illinois Court, Juvenile Division (1967).

In re Winship, 397 U.S. 358 (1970).

Irving Independent School District v. Tatro, 104 S. Ct. 3371, 82 L.Ed. 2d 664 (1984).

Jepperson, R. "Institutions, Institutional Effects, and Institutionalism." In *The New Institutionalism in Organizational Analysis,* edited by Walter W. Powell and Paul J. DiMaggio. Chicago: University of Chicago Press, 1991.

Jepperson, Ronald L., and John W. Meyer. "The Public Order and the Construction of Formal Organizations." In *The New Institutionalism in Organizational Analysis,* edited by Walter W. Powell and Paul J. DiMaggio. Chicago: University of Chicago Press, 1991.

Jernegan, Marcus S. *Laboring and Dependent Classes in Colonial America 1607–1783.* New York: Frederick Ungar Publishing Company, 1931.

Jirsa, James E. "The SOMPA: A Brief Examination of Technical Considerations, Philosophical Rationale, and Implications for Practice." *Journal of School Psychology* 21 (1983): 13–21.

Johnson, G. O. "Special Education for the Mentally Handicapped: A Paradox." *Exceptional Children,* 19 (1962): 62–69.

Johnson, J. L.. "Special Education for the Inner City: A Challenge for the Future or Another Means for Cooling the Mark Out?" *The Journal of Special Education* 3 (1969): 241–251.

Johnson, Richard. "Educational Policy and Social Control in Early Victorian England." *Past and Present* 49 (1970): 96–119.

Johnson, V. M. "Analysis of Factors Influencing Special Educational Placement." *Journal of School Psychology* 18 (1980): 191–202.

Juvenile Justice and Delinquency Prevention Act. 1974. Public Law 93–415 (September 7): 1109–1143.

Kaestle, Carl F. *The Evolution of an Urban School System: New York City, 1750–1860.* Cambridge, Mass.: Harvard University Press, 1973.

Kaestle, Carl F. *Pillars of the Republic, Common Schools and American Society, 1780–1860.* New York: Hill and Wang, 1983.

Kantor, Harvey A. *Learning to Earn, School, Work, and Vocational Reform in California, 1880–1930.* Madison: University of Wisconsin Press, 1988.

Kantor, Harvey, and David B. Tyack (Eds.). *Work, Youth, and Schooling, Historical Perspectives on Vocationalism in American Education.* Stanford: Stanford University Press, 1982.

Kantorowicz, Ernst H. *The King's Two Bodies, A Study of Mediaeval Political Theology.* Princeton University Press, 1957.

Katsiyannis, Antonis, and John W. Maag. "Ensuring Appropriate Education: Emerging Remedies, Litigation, Compensation, and Other Legal Considerations." *Exceptional Children* 63 (1997): 451–462.

Katz, Al, and Lee E. Teitelbaum. "PINS Jurisdiction, the Vagueness Doctrine, and the Rule of the Law." In *Beyond Control, Status Offenders in the Juvenile Court,* edited by Lee E. Teitelbaum and Aidan R. Gough. Cambridge, Mass.: Ballinger, 1977.

Katz, Michael. *The Irony of Early School Reform.* Boston: Beacon Press, 1968.

Katz, Michael. "The Institutional State." *Marxist Perspectives* 1 (1978): 6–22.

Kauffman, James J. "How We Might Achieve the Radical Reform of Special Education." In *The Illusion of Full Inclusion,* edited by James Kauffman and Daniel Hallahan. Austin, Tex.: pro-ed, 1995.

Kauffman, James M., Michael M. Gerber, and Melvyn I. Semmel. "Arguable Assumptions Underlying the Regular Education Initiative." *Journal of Learning Disabilities* 21 (1988): 6–11.

Kauffman, James M., and Daniel P. Hallahan. *The Illusion of Full Inclusion.* Austin, Tex.: pro-ed, 1995.

Kavale, Kenneth A., and Steven R. Forness. "The Historical Foundation of Learning Disabilities." *Remedial and Special Education* 6 (1984): 18–24.

Kavale, Kenneth A., and Steven R. Forness. "Learning Disability and the History of Science: Paradigm or Paradox?" *Remedial and Special Education* 6 (1985): 12–23.

Kephart, Newell C. *The Slow Learner in the Classroom.* Columbus, Ohio: Charles E. Merrill, [1960] 1971.

Kephart, Newell C. *Learning Disability: An Educational Adventure.* West Lafayett, IN: Kappa Delta Pi Press, 1968.

Kett, Joseph F. *Rites of Passage.* New York: Basic, 1977.

Kirp, David. "Schools as Sorters: The Constitutional and Policy Implications of Student Classification." *University of Pennsylvania Law Review* 121 (1973): 705–797.

Kirp, David. "Proceduralism and Bureaucracy: Due Process in the School Setting. *Stanford Law Review* 24 (1976): 841–876.

Kirp, David L., and Donald Jensen. "What Does Due Process Do?" *Public Interest* 73 (1983): 75–90.

Kirp, David L., Peter J. Kuriloff, and William G. Buss. "Legal Mandates and Organizational Change." In *Issues in the Classification of Children,* vol 2, edited by Nicholas Hobbs. San Francisco: Jossey-Bass Publishers, 1975.

Kirst, Michael W. and Kay A. Bertken. "Due Process Hearing in Special Education: Some Early Findings from California." In *Special Education Policies: The History, Implementation, and Finance,* edited by Jay G. Chambers and William T. Hartman. Philadelphia: Temple University Press, 1983.

Kliebard, Herbert M. *The Struggle for the American Curriculum, 1893– 1958.* New York: Routledge & Kegan Paul, 1987.

Klein, Malcom. "Deinstitutionalization and Diversion of Juvenile Offenders: A Litany of Impediments." In *Crime and Justice: An Annual Review of Research,* vol. 1, edited by Norval Morris and Richard Tonry. Chicago: University of Chicago Press, 1979.

Krug, Edward A. *The Shaping of the American High School.* New York: Harper & Row, 1964.

Kubler, George. *The Shape of Time.* New Haven & London: Yale University Press, 1962.

Landes, William W., and Lewis G. Solmon. "Compulsory Schooling Legislation: An Economic Analysis of Law and Social Change in the Nineteenth Century." *Journal of Economic History* 23 (March 1972): 54–91.

Lane, Harlan. "The Education of Deaf Children: Drowning in the Mainstream." In *The Illusion of Full Inclusion,* edited by J.M. Kauffman and D.P. Hallahan. Austin, Tex.: pro-ed, 1995.

Langston, Daniel. *History and Background of County Level Guidance in California.* Unpublished dissertation, Department of Education, Stanford University, 1950.

Larry P. v. Riles, 343 F. Supp. 1306 (1972).

Lasch, Christopher. *The Worlds of Nations.* New York: Alfred A. Knopf, 1973.

Laws of Wisconsin. 1885. "An Act to Establish A State Public School for Dependent and Neglected Children." Ch. 377. Madison: Democrat Printing Company.

Lazerson, Marvin. *Origins of the Urban School, Public Education in Massachusetts, 1870–1915.* Cambridge: Mass.: Harvard University Press, 1971.

Lazerson, Marvin. "The Origins of Special Education." In *Special Education Policies: Their History, Implementation, and Finance,* edited by J. G. Chambers and W. T. Hartman. Philadelphia: Temple University Press, 1983.

Lazerson, Marvin, and W. Norton Grubb. "Reports of the Committee on Industrial Education (1910) and Commission on Industrial Relations (1915)." In *American Education and Vocationalism: A Documentary History, 1870–1970,* edited by Marvin Lazerson and W. Norton Grubb. New York: Teachers College Press, 1974.

Lekkerkerker, Eugenia Cornelia. *Reformatories for Women in the United States.* Batavia, Holland: Bij J. B. Wolters' Uitgevers-Maatschappif, 1931.

Lemert, Charles C., and Garth Gillan. *Michel Foucault, Social Theory and Transgression.* New York: Columbia University Press, 1982.

Lerman, Paul. *Deinstitutionalization and the Welfare State.* New Brunswick, N. J. Rutgers University Press, 1982.

Lewis, Richard G., Strauss, Alfred, and Laura E. Lehtinen. *The Other Child.* New York: Grune & Stratton, 1951.

Lezotte, L. W. "School Improvement Based on the Effective Schools Research." In *Beyond Separate Education: Quality Education For All,* edited by D. K. Lipsky and A. Garter. Baltimore: Paul H. Brookes, 1989.

Lilly, M. S.. "Special Education: A Teapot in a Tempest." *Exceptional Children* 37 (1970): 43–49.

Lilly, M. S. "The Relationship Between General and Special Education: A New Face on an Old Issue." *Counterpoint* (1986): 10.

Lipset, Seymour Martin. *The First New Nation, The United States in Historical and Comparative Perspective.* New York: Basic Books, Inc., 1963.

Lipset, Seymour Martin. *American Exceptionalism, A Double-Edged Sword.* New York: W. W. Norton & company, 1996.

Lipsky, Dorothy K., and Alan Gartner. "Building the Future." In *Beyond Separate Education, Quality Education for All,* edited by Dorothy K. Lipsky and Alan Gartner. Baltimore: Paul H. Brookes Publishing Co., 1989.

Lora v. Board of Education, 456 F. Supp. 1211 (E.D.N.Y. 1978).

Ludmerer, Kenneth M. *Genetics and American Society, A Historical Appraisal.* Baltimore & London: Johns Hopkins University Press, 1972.

MacMillan, Donald, L., Reginald L. Jones, and C. Edward Meyers. "Mainstreaming the Mildly Retarded: 0Some Questions, Cautions, and Guidelines." *Mental Retardation* 14 (1976): 3–10.

MacMillan, Donald L., Semmel, Melvyn I., and Michael M. Gerber. "The Social Context of Dunn: Then and Now." *The Journal of Special Education* 27 (1994): 466–480.

MacQuery, T. Hill, "Schools for Dependent, Delinquent and Truant Children in Illinois." *American Journal of Sociology* 16 (1903): 1–23.

Maguin, Eugene, and Rolf Loeber. "Academic Performance and Delinquency." In *Crime and Justice, A Review of Research,* Vol. 20, edited by Michael Tonry. Chicago and London: The University of Chicago Press, 1996.

Maheady, L., B. Algozzine, and J. E. Ysseldyke. "Minority Overrepresentation in Special Education: A Functional Assessment Perspective." *Special Services in Schools* 1 (1984): 5–19.

Maheady, Larry, Richard Towne, Bob Algozzine, Jane Mercer, and James Ysseldyke. "Minority Overrepresentation: A Case for Alternative Practices Prior to Referral." In *Critical Voices on Special Education*, edited by Scott B. Sigmon. New York: SUNY, 1990.

Maine, Henry S. *Ancient Law.* New York: Dutton & Co., 1954.

Mann, Horace. *Lectures on Education.* New York: Arno, 1969.

Mann, Horace, Bezaleel, Taft, and W. B. Calhoun. *Report of Commissioners to Superintend the Erection of a Lunatic Hospital at Worcester.* Boston: Dutton & Wentworth, 1832.

Marks, Russell. "Lewis M. Terman: Individual Differences and the Construction of Social Reality." *Educational Theory* 24 (1974): 336–355.

Marshall et al. v. Georgia. U.S. District court for the Southern District of Georgia, CV482–233, June 28, 1984; Aff'd (11th cir. No 84–8771, Oct. 29, 1985).

Martens, Elise H. *Clinical Organization for Child Guidance Within the Schools.* Washington, D.C.: Government Printing Office, 1939.

Marx, Karl. *The Eighteenth Brumaire of Louis Bonaparte.* New York: International Publishers, 1968.

Mayer, John A. "Notes Towards a Working Definition of Social Control in Historical Analysis." In *Social Control and the State,* edited by Stanley Cohen and Andrew Scull. New York: St. Martin's Press, 1983.

McDonald, Robert A. F. *Adjustment of School Organization to Various Population Groups.* New York: Teachers College Press, 1915.

Mehan, Hugh, Alma Hertweck, and J. Lee Meihls. *Handicapping the Handicapped, Decision Making in Students' Educational Careers.* Stanford: Stanford University Press, 1986.

Meier, K. J., Stewart, J., and R. E. England. *Race, Class, and Education: The Politics of Second-Generation Discrimination.* Madison: University of Wisconsin Press, 1989.

Mendez v. Westminister School District of Orange County, 161 F. 2d 774 (9th Cir. 1947), aff'd 64 F. Supp. 544 (San Diego, California) 1946.

Mercer, Jane R. "Institutionalized Anglocentricism: Labeling Mental Retardates in Public Schools." In *Race, Change and Urban Policy,* edited by P. Orleans and W. Russell. New York: Sage Publications, 1971.

Mercer, Jane R. *Labeling the Mentally Retarded.* Berkeley: University of California Press, 1973.

Mercer, Jane R. *System of Multicultural Pluralistic Assessment, Technical Manual.* New York: Psychological Association, 1979.

Meyer, John W., Francisco O. Ramirez, and Yasemin Nuhoglu Soysal. "World Expansion of Mass Education, 1870–1980." *Sociology of Education* 65 (1992): 128–149.

Meyer, John W., and Brian Rowan. "The Structure of Educational Institutions." In *Environments and Organizations,* edited by Marshall Meyer. San Francisco: Jossey-Bass, 1978.

Meyer, John W., and Brian Rowan. "Institutionalized Organizations: Formal Structure as Myth and Ceremony." In *The New Institutionalism in Organizational Analysis,* edited by Walter W. Powell and Paul J. DiMaggio. Chicago & London: University of Chicago Press, 1991.

Meyer, John, David Tyack, Joane Nagel, and Audri Gordon. "Public Education and Nation-Building in America: Enrollments and Bureaucratization in the American States, 1870–1930." *American Journal of Sociology* 85 (1979): 591–613.

Miller, Jerome G. "The Revolution in Juvenile Justice: From Rhetoric to Rhetoric." In *The Future of Childhood and Juvenile Justice,* edited by LaMar T. Empey. Charlottesville: University of Virginia Press, 1979.

Mills v. Board of Education, 348 F. Supp. 866 (D.D.C. 1972).

Milofsky, Carl. 1986. "Is the Growth of Special Education Evolutionary or Cyclic? A Response to Carrier." *American Journal of Education* 94 (May, no. 3): 313–21.

Mirel, Jeffrey E. *The Rise and Fall of an Urban School System.* Ann Arbor: University of Michigan Press, 1993.

Mirel, Jeffrey E., and David L. Angus, "The Rising Tide of Custodialism: Enrollment Increases and Curriculum Reform in Detroit, 1928–1940." *Issues in Education,* 4 (1986):101–20.

Morgan, *The Puritan Family.* New York: Harper & Row, 1966.

National Association of School Psychologists/National Coalition of Advocates for Students (NASP/NCAS). *Advocacy for Appropriate Educational Services for All Children.* Washington, D.C.: Author, 1985.

National Advisory Committee on Criminal Justice Standards and Goals-Task Force on Juvenile Justice and Delinquency Prevention.

Juvenile Justice and Delinquency Prevention. U.S. Department of Justice, Law Enforcement Assistance Administration, Washington D.C., 1976.

National Education Association. "Report of the Committee on the Place of Industries in Public Education." *Addresses and Proceedings of the National Education Association* 48 (1910): 552–773.

Neal, David, and David L. Kirp. "The Allure of Legalization Reconsidered: The Case of Special Education." In *School Days, Rule Days,* edited by David L. Kirp and Donald N. Jensen. London: The Falmer Press, 1986.

Nejelski, Paul. "Diversion of Juvenile Offenders in the Criminal Justice System." In *New Approaches to Diversion and Treatment of Juvenile Offenders.* LEAA, Washington, D.C.: U.S. Department of Justice, 1973.

Oakes, J. "Can Tracking Research Inform Practice? Technical, Normative, and Political Considerations." *Educational Researcher* 21 (1992): 12–21.

Oakes, J. "Two Cities' Tracking and Within-School Segregation." *Teachers College Record* 96 (1995): 681–690.

Oakland, T. "Research with the Adaptive Behavior Inventory for Children and the ELP." *The School Psychology Digest* 8 (1979): 63–70.

Oakland, T. "Nonbiased Assessment of Minority Group Children." *Exceptional Education Quarterly* 1 (1980): 31–46.

Oberti v. Board of Education of the Borough of Clementon School District, 789 F. Supp. 1322, 75 Ed. Law Rep. 258, (D.J.J. 1992); 801 F. Supp. 1393(D.J.J. 1992), affirmed 995 F.2d 1204, 83 Ed. Law Rep. 1009 (3d Cir. 1993).

Osborne, Allan G., Jr. "Legal Standards for an Appropriate Education in the Post-Rowley Era." *Exceptional Children* 58 (1992): 488–494.

Osborne, Allan G., Jr., and Philip DiMattia. "The IDEA's Least Restrictive Environment Mandate: Legal Implications." *Exceptional Children* 61 (1994): 6–14.

Palmer, Phyllis. *Domesticity and Dirt: Housewives and Domestic Servants in the United States, 1920–1945.* Philadelphia: Temple University Press, 1989.

Panel on Selection and Placement of Students in Programs for the Mentally Retarded. "Introduction: Disproportion in Special

Education." In *Placing Children in Special Education: A Strategy for Equity*, edited by Kirby A. Heller, Wayne H. Holtzman, and Samuel Messick. Washington, D.C.: National Academy Press, 1982.

Pennsylvania Association for Retarded Children (PARC) v. Commonwealth of Pennsylvania, 343 F. Supp. 279 (E. D. PA. 1972).

PASE v. Hannon, 506 F. Supp. 831 (N.D. Ill. 1980).

Patrick, J., and D. Reschly. "Relationship of State Educational Criteria and Demographic Variables to School-System Prevalence of Mental Retardation." *American Journal of Mental Deficiency* 86 (1982): 351–360.

Pennsylvania Association for Retarded Children v. Commonwealth of Pennsylvania, 343 F. Supp. 279 (Ed.D.Pa. 1972).

People ex rel. O'Connell v. Turner. 55 Ill. 280 (1870).

People Who Care v. Rockford Board of Education School District No. 205, 851 F. Supp. 905 (N.D. Ill. 1994).

Perrin, John, W. 1904–1905. "The Truancy Problem in Massachusetts 1845–1890." *Journal of Pedagogy* 17: 214–224.

Peterson, L. J., Rossmiller, R. A., and M. M. Volz. *The Law and Public School Operation*. New York: Harper & Row, 1969.

Philbrick, John D. "Supplementary Report on Truancy and Compulsory Education." Annual Report of the School Committee of the City of Boston. Boston: J. E. Farwell & Company, 1861.

Pisciotta, Alexander W. "Saving the Children: The Promise and Practice of Parens Patriae, 1838–98." *Crime and Delinquency*, (1982) 28: 410–425.

Plyler v. J. and R. Doe et al. 80–1538 (1982).

Poggi, Gianfranco. *Calvinism and the Capitalist Spirit, Max Weber's Protestant Ethic*. London: The MacMillan Press Ltd., 1983.

Prasse, David P., and Daniel J. Reschly. "*Larry P.:* A Case of Segregation, Testing, or Program Efficacy?" *Exceptional Children* 52 (1986): 333–346.

Presser, Stephen B. "The Historical Background of the American Law of Adoption." *Journal of Family Law* 11 (1972): 443–516.

Prosser, Charles A., and Charles R. Allen. *Vocational Education in a Democracy*. New York & London: The Century Co., 1925.

Rafter, Nicole Hahn. *Partial Justice, Women in State Prisons, 1800–1935*. Boston: Northeastern University Press, 1985.

Ravitch, Diane. *The Troubled Crusade, American Education, 1945–1980.* New York: Basic Books, Inc., 1983.

Rehbinder, Manfred. "Status, Contract, and the Welfare State." *Stanford Law Review* 23 (1971): 941–955.

Rendleman, Douglas R. "Parens Patriae: From Chancery to the Juvenile Court." *South Carolina Law Review* 23 (1971): 205–259.

Renn, Donna E. "The Right to Treatment and the Juvenile." *Crime and Delinquency* 19 (October, 1973): 477–484.

Report of the Commissioner of Education. "Truant Schools," Vol. 1, pp. 85–219. Washington, D. C.: Government Printing Office, 1901.

Report of Senate Fact Finding Committee on Education: Subcommittee on Special Education. 1963. "Divergent Youth," Sacramento: California.

Reschly, D. J. "Psychological Evidence in the *Larry P.* Opinion: A Case of Right Problem—Wrong Solution." *School Psychology Review* 9 (1980): 123–135.

Reschly, D. J. "Beyond IQ Test Bias: The National Academy Panel's Analysis of Minority Overrepresentation." *Educational Researcher* 13 (1984): 15–19.

Reschly, D. J. "Learning Characteristics of Mildly Handicapped Students and Implications for Classification, Placement, and Programming." In *The Handbook of Special Education: Research and Practice,* edited by M. C. Wang, M. C. Reynolds, and H. J. Walberg. Oxford: Pergamon Press, 1987.

Reschly, D. J. "Alternative Delivery Systems: Legal and Ethical Influences." In *Alternative Educational Delivery Systems, Enhancing Instructional Options for All Students,* edited by Janet L. Graden, Joseph E. Zins, and Michael J. Curtis. Washington, D.C.: NASP, 1988a.

Reschly, Daniel J. "Minority Mild Mental Retardation: Legal Issues, Research Findings, and Reform Trends." In *Handbook of Special Education: Research and Practice: Vol. 2. Mildly Handicapped Conditions,* edited by M. C. Wang, M. C. Reynolds, and H. J. Walberg. Oxford: Pergamon Press, 1988b.

Reschly, D. J. "Minority MMR Overrepresentation and Special Education Reform." *Exceptional Children* 54 (1988c): 316–323.

Reschly, D. J. "Special Education Reform: School Psychology Revolution." *School Psychology Review* 17(3), (1988d): 459–475.

Reschly, D. J., Kicklighter, R., and P. McKee. "Recent Placement Litigation, Part I: Regular Education Grouping: Comparison of *Marshall* (1984, 1985) and *Hobson* (1967, 1969)." *School Psychology Review* 17 (1988a): 9–21.

Reschly, D. J., Kicklighter, R, and P. McKee. "Recent Placement Litigation, Part II: Minority EMR Overrepresentation Comparison of *Larry P.* (1979, 1984, 1986) with *Marshall* (1984, 1985)." *School Psychology Review* 17 (1988b): 22–38.

Reschly, D. J., Kicklighter, R., and P. McKee. "Recent Placement Litigation, Part III: Analysis of Differences in *Larry P., Marshall* and *S-1* and Implications for Future Practices." *School Psychology Review* 17 (1988c): 39–50.

Reschly, D. J., and J. E. Ysseldyke. "School Psychology Paradigm Shift." In *Best Practices in School Psychology—III,* edited by Alex Thomas and Jeff Grimes. Washington, D.C.: National Association of School Psychologists, 1995.

Reynolds, M. C. "The Surge in Special Education." *National Education Association Journal* 56 (November, 1967): 46–48.

Richardson, John G. "The Case of Special Education and Minority Misclassification in California Public Education." *Educational Research Quarterly* 4 (1979): 25–40.

Richardson, John G. "Variation in Date of Enactment of Compulsory Attendance Laws: An Empirical Inquiry." *Sociology of Education* 53 (1980): 153–63.

Richardson, John G. "The American States and the Age of State School Systems." *American Journal of Education* 92 (1984): 473–502.

Richardson, John G. "Historical Sequences and the Origins of Common Schooling in the American States." In *Handbook of Theory and Research for the Sociology of Education,* edited by John G. Richardson. Westport, Conn.: Greenwood, 1986.

Richardson, John G. "Historical Expansion of Special Education." In *The Political Construction of Education,* edited by Bruce Fuller and Richard Rubinson. Westport, Conn.: Praeger, 1992.

Richardson, Theresa R. *The Century of the Child.* New York: SUNY Press, 1989.

Rodriguez v. San Antonio Independent School District, 36 L. E. 2d 16, 93 S. Ct. 1278 (1973).

Rosenberg, Irene Merker, and Yale L. Rosenberg. "The Legacy of the Stubborn and Rebellious Son." *Michigan Law Review* 74 (1976): 1097–1165.

Rothman, David J. *The Discovery of the Asylum, Social Order and Disorder in the New Republic.* Boston: Little Brown, 1971.

Rouse v. Cameron, 373 F.2d 451 (D.C. Cir. 1966).

Rubin, Ted H. "The Nature of the Court Today." *The Future of Children* 6 (Winter, 1996): 40–52.

Rubinson, Richard. "Class Formation, Politics, and Institutions: Schooling in the United States." *American Journal of Sociology* 92 (1986): 519–548.

Rury, John L. *Education and Women's Work: Female Schooling and the Division of Labor in Urban America, 1870–1930.* New York: SUNY Press, 1991.

S-1 v. Turlington. 635 F.2d 342 (5th Cir. 1981); *cert. Denied* 454 U.S. 1030, 102 S. Ct. 566, 70 L. Ed. 2d 473 (1981).

Sacks, Oliver. "The Revolution of the Deaf," pp. 23–27, *New York Review of Books,* 1988.

Sarason, Seymour B., and John Doris. *Educational Handicap, Public Policy and Social History, A Broadened Perspective on Mental Retardation.* New York: The Free Press, 1979.

Sattler, J. M. "Intelligence Tests on Trial: An 'Interview' with Judges Robert F. Peckham and John F. Grady." *Journal of School Psychology* 19 (1981): 359–369.

Schlossman, Steven L. *Love and the American Delinquent.* Chicago: University of Chicago Press, 1977.

Schlossman, Steven, and Stephanie Wallach. "The Crime of Precocious Sexuality: Female Juvenile Delinquency in the Progressive Era." *Harvard Educational Review* 48 (1978): 65–94.

Schwartz, Harold. *Samuel Gridley Howe, Social Reformer, 1801–1876.* Cambridge, Mass.: Harvard University Press, 1956.

Scott, W. Richard, and John W. Meyer. "The Organization of Societal Sectors: Propositions and Early Evidence." In *The New Institutionalism in Organizational Analysis,* edited by Walter W. Powell and Paul J. DiMaggio. Chicago: University of Chicago Press, 1991.

Scull, Andrew T. "Madness and Segregative Control: The Rise of the Insane Asylum." *Social Problems* 24 (1977): 337–351.

Scull, Andrew T. *Madhouses, Mad-Doctors and Madness: The Social History of Psychiatry in the Victorian Era.* Philadelphia: University of Pennsylvania Press, 1981.

Sears, Jesse B., *The School Survey.* Boston: Houghton Mifflin, 1925.

Seguin, Edward. "Origin of the Treatment and Training of Idiots." *American Journal of Education* 2 (1856): 145–152.

Seguin, Edward. *Idiocy: And Its Treatment By The Physiological Method.* New York: Teachers College, 1907.

Semmel, M. I., M. Gerber, and T. Abernathy. "The Relationships Between School Environment Variables and Educational Outcomes for Students with Mild Disabilities (SERL/SEP Research Report)." Santa Barbara: University of California, Special Education Research Laboratory, 1993.

Semmel, Melvyn, I., Michael M. Gerber, and Donald L. MacMillan. "A Legacy of Policy Analysis Research in Special Education." In *The Illusion of Full Inclusion,* edited by James M. Kauffman and Daniel P. Hallahan. Austin, Tex.: pro-ed, 1995.

Semmel, Melvyn I., Jay Gottlieb, and Nancy M. Robinson. "Mainstreaming: Perspectives on Educating Handicapped Children in the Public School." In *Review of Educational Research,* edited by David C. Berliner. vol 7. Washington, D.C.: American Educational Research Association, 1979.

Sexton, Patricia Cayo. *Education and Income, Inequalities in Our Public Schools.* New York: Viking Press, 1961.

Seybolt, Robert Francis. *Apprenticeship and Apprentice Education in Colonial New England and New York.* New York: Arno Press, 1969.

Shepard, L. A. "The New Push for Excellence: Widening the Schism Between Regular and Special Education." *Exceptional Children* 53 (1987): 327–329.

Sigmon, Scott B. (Ed). *Critical Voices on Special Education, Problems and Progress Concerning the Mildly Handicapped.* New York: SUNY, 1990.

Signorile, Vito. "Ratios and Causes, The Pentad As an Etiological Scheme in Sociological Explanation." In *The Legacy of Kenneth Burke,* edited by Herbert W. Simons and Trevor Melia. Madison: University of Wisconsin Press, 1989.

Silver, Harold. *Education as History, Interpreting Nineteenth- and Twentieth-Century Education.* London & New York: Methuen, 1983.

Simmons, Allan, James. *A History of Special Education in California.* Unpublished dissertation, School of Education, University of Southern California, 1972.

Skowronek, Stephen. *Building a New American State, The Expansion of National Administrative Capacities, 1877–1920.* Cambridge: Cambridge University Press, 1988.

Skrtic, Thomas M. "The Crisis in Special Education Knowledge: A Perspective on Perspective." *Focus on Exceptional Children* 18 (1986): 1–16.

Skrtic, Thomas M. *Behind Special Education: A Critical Analysis of Professional Culture and School Organization.* Denver: Love Publishing, 1991a.

Skrtic, Thomas M. "The Special Education Paradox: Equity As the Way to Excellence." *Harvard Educational Review* 61(2) (1991b): 148–206.

Skrtic, Thomas M. (Ed.). *Disability & Democracy, Reconstructing (Special) Education for Postmodernity.* New York: Teachers College Press, 1995.

Sleeter, Catherine. "Learning Disabilities: The Social Construction of a Special Education Category." *Exceptional Children* 53 (1986): 46–54.

Sleeter, Catherine. "Literacy, Definitions of Learning Disabilities, and Social Control." In *Learning Disabilities: Dissenting Essays*, edited by Barry M. Franklin. London: The Falmer Press, 1987a.

Sleeter, Catherine. "Why Is There Learning Disabilities? A Critical Analysis of the Birth of the Field in Its Social Context." In *The Formation of School Subjects, The Struggle for Creating an American Institution*, edited by Thomas S. Popkewitz. New York: The Falmer Press, 1987b.

Smith, Barry C. "The Commonwealth Fund Program for the Prevention of Delinquency." *Proceedings of the National Conference of Social Work*, Chicago, 1922.

Smith, G. R. "Desegregation and Assignment of Children to Classes for the Mildly Retarded and Learning Disabled." *Integrated Education* 21 (1983): 208–211.

Snedden, David. *The Administrative and Educational Characteristics of American Juvenile Reform Schools*. Ph.D. Dissertation, Columbia University, 1907.

Snedden, David. *Vocational Education*. New York: The MacMillan Company, 1920.

Spring, Joel H. *The Sorting Machine, National Educational Policy Since 1945*. New York: David McKay Company, 1976.

Spring, Joel. *The American School, 1642–1985*. New York & London: Longman, 1986.

Stapleton, V., David P., Aday, and Jeanne A. Ito. "An Empirical Typology of American Metropolitan Juvenile Courts." *American Journal of Sociology* 88 (1982): 549–564.

Steinhart, David J. "Status Offenses." *The Future of Children* 6 (Winter, 1996): 86–99.

Stephens, W. Richard. *Social Reform and the Origins of Vocational Guidance*. Monograph of the National Vocational Guidance Association. Washington, D.C., 1970.

Strauss, Alfred A., and Newell C. Kephart. *Psychopathology and Education of the Brain-Injured Child, vol. 2, Progress in Theory and Clinic*. New York: Grune & Stratton, 1955.

Strauss, Alfred A., and Laura E. Lehtinen. *Psychopathology and Education of the Brain-Injured Child*, vol. 1. New York: Grune & Stratton, 1947.

Strauss, Alfred A., and Heinz Werner. "Disorders of Conceptual Thinking in the Brain-Injured Child." *Journal of Nervous and Mental Diseases* 96 (1942): 153–172.

Strayer, George D. "Age and Grade Census of Schools and Colleges." Bureau of Education Bulletin, No. 5, Department of the Interior, Washington, D.C: Government Printing Office, 1911.

Strayer, Joseph. *On the Medieval Origins of the Modern State*. Princeton: Princeton University Press, 1970.

Sutherland, Gillian. "The Origins of Special Education." In *The Practice of Special Education*, edited by Will Swann. London: Basil Blackwell, 1981.

Sutton, John R. "The Juvenile Court and Social Welfare: Dynamics of Progressive Reform." *Law & Society Review* 19 (1985): 107–145.

Sutton, John R. *Stubborn Children, Controlling Delinquency in the United States, 1640–1981*. Berkeley: University of California Press, 1988.

Terman, Lewis. "Survey of Mentally Defective Children in the Schools of San Luis Obispo." *Psychological Clinic* 6 (1912): 131–39.

Terman, Lewis. "Feeble-Minded Children in the Public Schools of California." *School and Society* V (1917): 161–165.

Terman, Lewis. *Intelligence; Tests and School Reorganization.* New York: World Book Company, 1922.

Thomas, William I., and Dorothy Swaine Thomas. *The Child in America, Behavior Problems and Programs.* New York: Alfred A. Knopf, 1928.

Thorndike, Edward L. "The Elimination of Pupils from School." Bureau of Education Bulletin, No. 4, (1907), Department of the Interior, Washington: Government Printing Office, 1908.

Tinker v. Des Moines Independent Community School District, 393 U.S. (1969).

Tocqueville, de, Alexis. *Democracy in America.* New York: Vintage Books, 1945.

Tomlinson, Sally. *A Sociology of Special Education.* London: Routeledge & Kegan Paul, 1982.

Tomlinson, Sally. "The Expansion of Special Education." *Oxford Review of Education* 11 (1985): 157–165.

Trent, James W., Jr. *Inventing the Feeble Mind, A History of Mental Retardation in the United States.* Berkeley: University of California Press, 1994.

Tropea, Joseph L. "Bureaucratic Order and Special Children: Urban Schools, 1890s-1940s." *History of Education Quarterly* 27 (1987): 29–53.

Tropea, Joseph L. "Structuring Risks: The Making of Urban School Order." In *Children at Risk in America, History, Concepts, and Public Policy,* edited by Roberta Wollons. New York: SUNY. 1993.

Trow, Martin. "The Second Transformation of American Secondary Education." In *The School in Society, Studies in the Sociology of Education,* edited by Sam D. Sieber and David E. Wilder. New York: The Free Press, 1973.

Tucker, Bonnie P., Bruce A. Goldstein, and Gail Sorenson. *The Educational Rights of Children with Disabilities, Analysis, Decisions and Commentary.* Horsham, Penn.: LRP Publications, 1993.

Tucker, J. "Ethnic Proportions in Classes for the Learning Disabled: Issues in Nonbiased Assessment." *Journal of Special Education* 14 (1980): 93–105.

Turnbull, Rutherford H. III. "Appropriate Education and *Rowley*." *Exceptional Children* 52 (1986): 347–352.

Tyack, David. *The One Best System*. Cambridge, Mass.: Harvard University Press, 1974.

Tyack, David. "Ways of Seeing: An Essay on the History of Compulsory Schooling." *Harvard Educational Review* 46 (August,1976): 355–389.

Tyack, David, and Thomas James. "State Government and American Public Education: Exploring the 'Primeval Forest.' "*History of Education Quarterly* 26 (1986): 39–69.

Tyack, David, and William Tobin. "The 'Grammar' of Schooling: Why Has it Been so Hard to Change?" *American Educational Research Journal* 31 (1994): 453–479.

Unger, Roberto M. *Knowledge and Politics*. New York & London: The Free Press, 1975.

Unwin, George. "Medieval Guilds and Education." In *Studies in Economic History*, edited by R. H. Tawney. New York: Augustus M. Kelly, Publishers 1966.

U.S. Office of Juvenile Justice and Delinquency Prevention. *Comprehensive Strategy for Serious, Violent, and Chronic Juvenile Offenders*. Washington, D.C.: Author, 1993.

U.S. Office of Juvenile Justice and Delinquency Prevention. Guide for Implementing the Comprehensive Strategy for Serious, Violent, and Chronic Juvenile Offenders. Washington, D.C.: Author, 1995.

Van Cleve, John Vickrey, and Barry A. Crouch. *A Place of Their Own*. Washington, D.C.: Gallaudet University Press, 1989.

Van Sickle, J. H., L. Witmer, and L. P. Ayres. "Provision for Exceptional Children in Public Schools." U.S. Bureau of Education Bulletin, No. 14, Washington, D. C.: Government Printing Office, 1911.

Vasquez v. San Jose Unified School District (N.D. Cal. 1994), case no. C-71–2130.

Vitello, Stanley J. "The *Tatro* Case: Who Gets What and Why." *Exceptional Children* 52 (1986): 353–356.

Walker, Lisa J. "Procedural Rights in the Wrong System: Special Education Is Not Enough." In *Images of the Disabled, Disabling*

Images, edited by Alan Gartner and Tom Joe. New York: Praeger 1987.

Wallin, Wallace J. E. *The Mental Health of the School Child.* New Haven, Conn.: Yale University Press, 1914.

Wallin, Wallace J. E. *The Education of Handicapped Children.* Boston & New York: Houghton Mifflin, 1924.

Wang, M. C., and H. J. Walberg. "Four Fallacies of Segregationism." *Exceptional Children* 55 (1988): 128–137.

Wang, Margaret C., Maynard C. Reynolds, and Herbert J. Walberg. *Special Education: Research and Practice: Synthesis of Findings.* Oxford & New York: Pergamon, 1987.

Weatherley, Richard A. *Reforming Special Education: Policy Implementation from State Level to Street Level.* Cambridge, Mass.: MIT Press, 1979.

Weiss, Janice. "Educating for Clerical Work: The Nineteenth-Century Private Commercial School." *Journal of Social History* 14 (1981):407–423.

Wells, A. S., and R. L. Crain. "Perpetuation Theory and the Long-Term Effects of School Desegregation." *Review of Educational Research* 64 (1994): 531.

Wells, A. S., and I. Serna. "The Politics of Culture: Understanding Local Political Resistance to Detracking in Racially Mixed Schools." *Harvard Educational Review* 66 (1996); 93–118.

Welner, Kevin G., and Jeannie Oakes. "(Li)Ability Grouping: The New Susceptibility of School Tracking Systems to Legal Challenges." *Harvard Educational Review* 66 (1996): 451–470.

White, Hayden. *Metahistory, The Historical Imagination in Nineteenth-Century Europe.* Baltimore & London: Johns Hopkins University Press, 1973.

Wiebe, Robert H. *The Opening of American Society.* New York: Alfred A. Knopf, 1984.

Will, M. C. "Educating Children with Learning Problems: A Shared Responsibility." *Exceptional Children* 52 (1986): 411–415.

Wirth, Arthur G. *Education in the Technological Society: The Vocational-Liberal Studies Controversy in the Early Twentieth Century.* Scranton, Penn.: Intext Educational Publishers, 1972.

Wolfensberger, Wolf. "The Origin and Nature of Our Institutional Models." In *Changing Patterns in Residential Services for the*

Mentally Retarded. President's Committee on Mental Retardation, Washington, D.C.: U.S. Government Printing Office, 1976.

Wollons, Roberta. "Introduction." In *Children at Risk in America, History, Concepts, and Public Policy*, edited by Roberta Wollons. New York: SUNY, 1993.

Woodward, C. Vann. *The Old World's New World.* New York: The New York Public Library and Oxford University Press, 1991.

Wright, P., and R. Santa Criz. "Ethnic Composition of Special Education Programs in California." *Learning Disability Quarterly* 6 (1983): 387–394.

Yell, Mitchell L. "*Honig v. Doe:* The Suspension and Expulsion of Handicapped Students." *Exceptional Children* 56 (1989): 60–69.

Ysseldyke, J. E. "Classification of Handicapped Students." In *Handbook of Special Education: Research and Practice,* edited by M. C. Wang, M. C. Reynolds, and H. J. Walberg. Vol. 1, New York: Pergamon Press, 1987.

Ysseldyke, James, Bob Algozzine, and Susan Epps. "A Logical and Empirical Analysis of Current Practice in Classifying Students as Handicapped." *Exceptional Children* 50 (1983): 160–166.

Ysseldyke, J. E., B. Algozzine, L. Ridley, and J. Graden. "Declaring Students Eligible for Learning Disability Service: Why Bother with the Data?" *Learning Disability Quarterly* 5 (1982): 37–44.

Ysseldyke, J. E., B. Algozzine, M. R. Shinn, and M. McGue. "Similarities and Differences Between Low Achievers and Students Classified Learning Disabled." *The Journal of Special Education* 16 (1982): 73–85.

Zatz, Julie. "Problems and Issues in Institutionalization: Laws, Concepts, and Goals." In *Neither Angels Nor Thieves: Studies in Deinstitutionalization of Status Offenders,* edited by Joel F. Handler and Julie Zatz. Washington, D.C.: National Academy Press, 1982.

Zenderland, Leila. "The Debate over Diagnosis: Henry Herbert Goddard and the Medical Acceptance of Intelligence Testing." In *Psychological Testing and American Society, 1890–1930*, edited by Michael M. Sokal. New Brunswick & London: Rutgers University Press, 1987.

Subject Index

209

American secondary
education), 76
Segregationism, 138
Smith Hughes Act (1917), 59, 68
n.5
SOMPA, 131, 132
Status offenses, 97
Stay-put, 162-163
Synchronicity (of educational
rights), 159

Tinker v. Des Moines
Independent Community

School District (1969),
153
Tracking (school), 76
Truancy, 38, 51
Tutelary complex, 26

Ungraded class, 63

Vasquez v. San Jose Unified
School District (1994),
163
Vocational education, 57-60

"Wild Boy" of Aveyron, 12

Name Index